'Neal Dreamson provides a profound exploration of culture and its potential to embody, support and shape the educative process and in doing so moves beyond the positioning of cultures as palettes from which to take isolated experiences. Dreamson's model promotes the transmogrification of cultural knowing and being as intrinsic to education as human endeavour.'

Gary Thomas, Associate Professor, the Queensland University of Technology, Australia

Reinventing Intercultural Education

Most existing books in the fields of multicultural or intercultural education have been written based on anthropologists' cultural dimensions, which presume culture is a fixed entity. *Reinventing Intercultural Education* is the first book to review multiple cultures and religions from a metaphysical understanding. It argues that intercultural value-interactions can be managed and taught in a way that facilitates individuals to reveal how they are metaphysically positioned within intercultural value networks.

This book proposes a metaphysical understanding of interculturality, by reviewing popular cultural and religious narratives found in multicultural society. By doing so, it develops an alternative pedagogy for multicultural education founded on the concept of intercultural hermeneutics. Beginning with a critical review of multicultural policies and existing models of multicultural education, Dreamson advocates the necessity of an intercultural approach to multicultural education. He then moves on to argue for the methodological aspects of interculturality by reviewing and adopting philosophical hermeneutics theories. Throughout the book, it is argued that values incarnated as a cultural framework are networked and interact via our minds to sustain our intercultural realities. Furthermore, when intercultural interactions transpire, which is the goal of multicultural education, we can see a larger part of the world that, in turn, helps us cultivate ourselves for further intercultural interactions.

The book should be of great interest to academics, researchers, and postgraduate students engaged in the study of multicultural education, the philosophy of education, religious pluralism, religious education, cultural studies, theology, and indigenous education.

Neal Dreamson is a senior lecturer in the School of Curriculum, Faculty of Education, Queensland University of Technology, Australia. Through his interdisciplinary research and engagement in cultural/religious studies, indigenous education, philosophy, design and technology education, and ICT in education he has articulated transcultural/disciplinary methodologies to multicultural/religious interactions and technological integration. Recently, he has extensively researched in metaphysical aspects of cross-cultures/religions and the digital divide in Learning Management Systems and developed philosophical understandings of and pedagogical approaches to value-interactions.

Routledge International Studies in the Philosophy of Education

For a full list of titles in this series, please visit www.routledge.com

32 Systems of Reason and the Politics of Schooling
School Reform and Sciences of Education in the Tradition of Thomas S. Popkewitz
Edited by Miguel A. Pereyra & Barry M. Franklin

33 Education, Justice and the Human Good
Fairness and equality in the education system
Kirsten Meyer

34 Education Reform and the Concept of Good Teaching
Derek Gottlieb

35 Posthumanism and Educational Research
Edited by Nathan Snaza and John A. Weaver

36 Parallels and Responses to Curricular Innovation
The Possibilities of Posthumanistic Education
Brad Petitfils

37 The Educational Prophecies of Aldous Huxley:
The Visionary Legacy of Brave New World, Ape and Essence, and Island
Ronald Lee Zigler

38 Popper's Approach to Education
A Cornerstone of Teaching and Learning
Stephanie Chitpin

39 Neuroscience and Education
A Philosophical Appraisal
Edited by Clarence W. Joldersma

40 Teachability and Learnability
Can Thinking Be Taught?
Paul Fairfield

41 Reinventing Intercultural Education
A metaphysical manifest for rethinking cultural diversity
Neal Dreamson

Reinventing Intercultural Education
A metaphysical manifest for rethinking cultural diversity

Neal Dreamson

LONDON AND NEW YORK

First published 2017 by Routledge

2 Park Square, Milton Park, Abingdon, Oxfordshire OX14 4RN

711 Third Avenue, New York, NY 10017

Routledge is an imprint of the Taylor & Francis Group, an informa business

First issued in paperback 2018

Copyright © 2017 Neal Dreamson

The right of Neal Dreamson to be identified as author of this work
has been asserted by him in accordance with sections 77 and 78 of the
Copyright, Designs and Patents Act 1988.

All rights reserved. No part of this book may be reprinted or reproduced
or utilised in any form or by any electronic, mechanical, or other means,
now known or hereafter invented, including photocopying and recording,
or in any information storage or retrieval system, without permission in
writing from the publishers.

Notice:
Product or corporate names may be trademarks or registered trademarks,
and are used only for identification and explanation without intent to
infringe.

British Library Cataloguing in Publication Data
A catalogue record for this book is available from the British Library

Library of Congress Cataloging-in-Publication Data
Names: Dreamson, Neal.
Title: Reinventing intercultural education : a metaphysical manifest
    for rethinking cultural diversity / Neal Dreamson.
Description: New York : Routledge, 2016. | Includes bibliographical
    references.
Identifiers: LCCN 2016028558 | ISBN 9781138217768 (hardcover) |
    ISBN 9781315439365 (electronic)
Subjects: LCSH: Multicultural education.
Classification: LCC LC1099 .D73 2016 | DDC 370.117—dc23

ISBN: 978-1-138-21776-8 (hbk)
ISBN: 978-1-138-61380-5 (pbk)

Typeset in Galliard
by Apex CoVantage, LLC

Acknowledgements

I would like to acknowledge the Traditional Owners of this land and pay my respects to the Elders past, present, and future, for they hold the memories, the traditions, the culture, and the hopes of Indigenous Australia. Aboriginal and Torres Strait Islander people's cultural values, practices, and knowledges have significantly contributed to this research. I also pay my respects to great cultural/religious and humane teachers, including Buddhist *bodhisattvas*, Confucian and Taoist *masters/sages*, Hindu *gurus*, and Muslim *prophets and teachers*. I am most indebted to their teachings, wisdom, and insights that have broadened my horizons of research and teaching practice.

I would like to express my deep sense of gratitude to Associate Professor Grace Sarra and Associate Professor Gary Thomas for their valuable guidance, interest, collegiality, mentorship, and encouragement at various stages of this book writing. I would like to extend my thanks to Alison Quinn, who provided her help on proofreading and editing. I am also indebted to the School of Curriculum, Faculty of Education, Queensland University of Technology for its rich and supportive academic environments, especially Professor Kar-Tin, Head of School, for her mentorship, encouragement, and support over the years.

I also thank Routledge for support and encouragement in writing this book. Heidi Lowther, an editor in Education, Psychology, and Mental Health Research, Routledge, provided helpful assistance and much appreciated advice. In particular, she was very gentle and offered me options while I completed this book. It has been a pleasure to work with her and her team at Routledge. I also thank seven anonymous reviewers for their careful reading and for providing constructive feedback, which was certainly helpful to improve the quality of this book.

Lastly, I dedicate this book to my loving wife, Grace Dreamson, who supported me on this long journey with her intellectual, thoughtful, and insightful questions about my research by reflecting *our* life and her professional experiences as a nurse in aged care. Without her faith and confidence in me, this work would not have been completed.

Contents

Acknowledgements	vii
List of figures and tables	xiii
List of abbreviations	xv

Introduction   1
Overview of chapters 5

PART I
Metaphysical understanding of culture for education   13

Part I Introduction: Non-ontological culturally inclusive education   15
References 18

**1 Beyond cultural identity: Postcolonial approaches
to cultural diversity**   21

    *1.1 The position of culture in understandings of cultural diversity
and cultural identity 22*
    1.2 Ethnicity as cultural identity: Anti-dualism 26
    1.3 A methodological approach to super-diversity 29
    1.4 Conclusion: Metaphysical tensions between cultures 33
    References 35

2 Metaphysical aspects of culture   37

    2.1 Ontological justification 38
    2.2 Epistemological assumptions 40
    2.3 Axiological interaction 46
    *2.4 Conclusion: A holistic approach to multicultural
education 52*
    References 53

x *Contents*

3 Underlying assumptions of multicultural education   57

3.1 White privilege and multiculturalism 57
3.2 Contemporary multicultural education for intercultural interaction 59
3.3 Multicultural education as a new mode of being and thinking 61
3.4 Multicultural education models and their underlying values 65
3.5 Conclusion: Metaphysical issues and challenges of multicultural education models 71
References 74

Part I Conclusion: Multicultural education towards intercultural interaction   77

PART II
Interculturality and its methodology   81

Part II Introduction: Intercultural interaction   83

4 Interculturality: Values, minds, and realities   87

4.1 Values: Primordial unity 87
4.2 The multilayered self 91
4.3 Multiple realities 94
4.4 Conclusion: A methodological value 98
References 99

5 Interactive methodology for intercultural interaction   101

5.1 Metaphysical assumptions of methodological individualism, holism, and relationism 102
5.2 Nodes of connectiviism 104
5.3 Conclusion: Interactive methodology 105
References 108

6 Philosophical hermeneutics for intercultural interaction   109

6.1 Values: Fore-structure of understanding 111
6.2 Intersubjectivity: A fusion of horizons and paradigm shifts 113
6.3 Interobjectivity: Effective-historical consciousness and plurality of audience 116
6.4 Emergent values: Linguisticality and universality 119
6.5 Axiological mapping: Rhizome and situatedness 122
6.6 Conclusion: Value networks 125
References 126

Contents xi

Part II Conclusion: New individuality | 129

PART III
Intercultural valuism as emergent pedagogy | 133

Part III Introduction: Intercultural instruction | 135

7 Intercultural self-reflection | 139

7.1 Intercultural valuism circle 140
7.2 Analysis and discussion 144
7.3 Conclusion: Towards whole individuality 153
References 156

8 Interculturality of non-Western cultures | 158

8.1 Non-Western cultures/religions 159
8.2 Interculturality of value networks 168
8.3 Conclusion: Metaphysics of interculturality 172
References 173

9 Pedagogical interculturality | 176

9.1 Western pedagogies and interculturality 176
9.2 Monistic pedagogies and interculturality 184
9.3 Holistic pedagogies and interculturality 188
9.4 Conclusion: Towards an intercultural pedagogy 193
References 195

Part III Conclusion: Intercultural valuism | 200

Conclusion: Intercultural valuism pedagogy | 202

Index | 209

Figures and tables

Figures

1	A value is valueless unless it works with other values	204
2	Value relational ontology	205
3	A holistic culture in value networks	205
4	A monistic culture in value networks	206
5	A dualistic culture in value networks	206
6	Intercultural value networks	207

Tables

7.1	An example of the intercultural valuism circle	145
7.2	The intercultural valuism circle versus the 5Rs framework for self-reflection	148
7.3	Common mistakes of and recommendations for the intercultural valuism circle	154

Abbreviations

CHI: Confucian Heritage Cultures
IHC: Islam Heritage Cultures
IM: Interactive Methodology
UNESCO: The United Nations Educational, Scientific and Cultural Organization
ZPD: Zone of Proximal Development

Introduction

The concept of *culture* is commonly used to define a collective characteristic of a certain group of people, including ethnicity, religion, gender, and race (Hall, 1981; Schein, 1985; Selfridge & Sokolik, 1975). It is also believed that culture is learned and transmitted, is shared, involves perception and interpretation, is subject to change, is expressed as behaviour, and affects one's identity (Hall, 1981; Schein, 1985; Selfridge & Sokolik, 1975). This implies that cultural characteristics are deep-rooted and complex and, therefore, difficult to change, but historically play an important function in giving meaning to the world and passing such meaning as knowledge through rituals and education. In a philosophical understanding, the concept of culture is a form of human beings and a system of human activity, which is generalised into certain frameworks through social historical apparatuses (Kagan, 1996/2009). As a result of human nature and activities, culture upholds human agency and social creativity (Kagan, 1996/2009). Inversely, the processes of man-made constructs determine one's consciousness. This means that culture as a mode of being is metaphysically positioned at the same ontological layer of other systems such as nature and society. Also, culture develops and establishes itself with its own metaphysical mechanism, thus culture enables human beings to understand the world (Gadamer, 1960/2004; Hall, 1981). As terms such as *cultural conflict, cultural diversity, cultural identity, cultural formation, intercultural communication, intercultural competences*, and *cross-cultural awareness* also imply, the existence of a variety of cultural values and beliefs and a form of collective thinking and behaviour has its own distinct value system (Hall, 1981; Kagan, 1996/2009). In practice, a culture or cultures is used in different fields of work, including postcolonial studies (e.g., Ang, 2001; Bhabha, 1994; Nieto & Bode, 2010), cultural studies (e.g., Manathunga, 2014), philosophy (e.g., Moghaddam, 2003), multicultural education (e.g., Banks, 1997), psychology (e.g., Gardner, Gabriel & Lee, 1999), religious studies (e.g., Orr, 2002), non-profit intergovernmental activities (e.g., UNESCO, 2013), critical theory (e.g., Freire, 1970/2000), and so on. This indicates that the concept of *a culture* should be viewed as a distinct metaphysical framework, while the concept of *culture* refers to a manifestation of human beings. However, our perceived binary dichotomy between nature and culture blocks off the path to philosophical speculation about culture and cultures and divides culture into various sub-disciplines such as ethnography,

2 Introduction

anthropology, and aesthetics. Thus its structure and mechanism, particularly intercultural interaction, is not considered for pedagogical approaches, and its methodological concerns are also marginalised by the mainstream. An example can be seen in Dewey.

In education, Dewey (1922/1983) is known as a philosopher who developed "a philosophy based on cultural exchange of ideas and pluralistic interaction among different communities" (p. 32) and suggested issue-based curriculum. Yet he depicts "non-Western European groups as socially deficient" (p. 33). This is because his vision for a democratic curriculum is based on the *civilised* versus *uncivilised* framework (Fallace, 2010). Dewey insists that citizens in an under-developed state or "inferior races" must "develop traits and dispositions of character intellectual and moral, which fit men and women for self-government, economic self-support and industrial progress" (Dewey, 1922/1983, p. 276). His central focus is more on justifying culture-free individuality for democratic community than on exploring value structures embedded in minds. As a result, he neither accepts ontological challenges of intercultural interaction nor explores axiological meaning of intercultural interaction. In other words, he may be unable to respond to the questions, how does his curriculum for democracy work in different cultural systems and what are the impacts of cultural values on education? Such an *unintentional* dualism exerts ideological power and contributes to political control over interculturality through advocating atomistic individualism and Western values embedded in the concept of universal humanity. This deprivation of ontology and axiology and his unreflective epistemological assumptions compel minority groups or other cultures to accept namely (Western) universal values.

In the last decade, international public and political debates on multiculturalism have been mostly concerned with "the global threat of terrorism and the challenges of ensuring social cohesion in societies characterised by ethno-cultural diversity" (Koleth, 2010, para. 1; Meer & Modood, 2012). Such debates bring into question epistemological limitations and socio-cultural-political boundaries of multiculturalism and raise its socio-moral-political issues, including social isolation of immigrants (residential ghettoisation), prejudice and discrimination between ethnic groups (increased stereotyping), anti-human-right practices (e.g., restricting the rights and liberties of girls and women), and political radicalism (e.g., Muslim youth) (Koleth, 2010; Meer & Modood, 2012). In educational settings, as Antonette (2003), Auster (2004), and Goodin (2006) identify, such debates rationalise the conservation of the existing structure and infuse its legitimacy into students. In multicultural education, the debates promote cultural differences as relative preferences and support the belief that our conscious constructions are not or are only limitedly influenced by cultures. In practice, without instantiating authentic intercultural interaction in the learning environment, teachers unintentionally and easily become advocates for the supremacy of a dominant culture and facilitating agents of the *othering* process. In this context, furthermore, teachers perceive cultural diversity as a provisional and temporal phenomenon that conceals a superordinate-subordinate relationship between cultures (Giroux, 1988; O'Grady, 2000; Sugiharto, 2013). Such a hierarchical distance becomes wider when they perceive that *other cultures* are only valid for the protection and promotion of a dominant culture. Consequently, such an approach to intercultural interaction can prevent teachers and students from pondering their authentic experiences of cultural diversity and intercultural interaction. This implies that critical self-reflection has to be discussed in a context of cultural diversity and integrated in intercultural interaction, which is a hermeneutic process.

Gadamer (1960/2004) argues for philosophical hermeneutics that deals with the meaning of human life and a matter of universal significance. Drenthen (2011, p. 124) describes a hermeneutic process as "find[ing] ourselves . . . in meaningful places", and Hainic (2012, p. 230) defines it as "draw[ing] the meaning of [our] lives from the objects and experiences". Our mistaken point of departure is that we believe we can have no prejudice against other cultures and be free from our own cultural framework. As Gadamer (1960/2004) argues, we understand the world based only on our own cultural assumptions, and our habitual dualistic thinking separates reality from being and excludes us from understanding. This means that we tend unconsciously to resist being aware that our prejudice is a fore-structure or pre-understanding of understanding. This is consistent with a Western understanding of *the self* that is closer to Husserl's transcendental consciousness and Cartesians' prioritisation of epistemological ego on immediate and transparent consciousness (Ricoeur, 1973/1981). As Ricoeur (1973/1981, p. 312) contends, "the objectification of the other is premised on the forgetting of oneself; and absolute knowledge", and indeed, we cannot understand others as well as ourselves by removing our cultural assumptions, beliefs, and values. I have also observed such a habitual dualistic thinking in Indigenous education for teacher education. Pre-service teachers are hardly given opportunities to interact with Indigenous* perspectives and values such as *interrelatedness* and *interconnectedness* because assessment and tutorial activities are driven by how *I* (ego) cognitively understand *their* cultural assumptions and values. One of the reasons is that self-reflection models used in the teacher education program require teachers to demonstrate their intellectual capacity to make use of given knowledge and skills. Indeed, the self is restricted to expressions of teachers' personal feelings and experiences. Such a reflection is not a *self-awareness* sense of self-reflection, but an *egocentrism* sense of self-reflection. A similar case can also be seen in multicultural education. Intercultural competences in education tend to be used to develop individual students' communication skills and improve their capacity to tolerate ambiguity in culturally diverse situations (UNESCO, 2013). This means that intercultural competences tend to exclude the self and ignore epistemological distances between cultures in social circumstances and ontological relations between cultures in the world (UNESCO, 2013). As a result, intercultural interaction is confined to individual students' sets of skills and knowledge. Therefore, the absence of the self and the loss of relationship need to be addressed to realise intercultural interaction.

Although our personality affects *what* we think, it does not dictate *how* and *why* we think, but cultures do. The concept of cultural identity refers to how culture incorporates one's worldview, beliefs, or values about a certain aspect of reality, which is a matter of metaphysical and methodological commitments. According

---

*Spell with a capital when referring to Australia's Indigenous population, but use lowercase when referring to indigenous populations in general.

4 *Introduction*

to Pai and Adler (1997), the concept of cultural identity is used in two different ways: (a) "a reference to the collective self-awareness" and (b) "the identity of the individual in relation to his or her culture" – that is, "a fundamental symbol of a person's existence" (p. 364). For Pai and Adler, cultures represent various value systems, attitudes, and beliefs of groups, as cultural identity is a symbolic structure of one's innately, essentially given experience. In a metaphysical understanding of a culture, then, we can infer that one's culture determines forms of values; values form one's cultural mind or self (*i.e.*, personal, relational, and collective minds); and one's cultural mind reproduces values unless one attempts to disclose its metaphysical structure. In this sense, intercultural interaction is really metaphysical. Educational metaphysics includes ontology, epistemology, and axiology, which are also associated with methodology and rhetoric. In education, ontology reflects cultural conventions and its resulting educational models and systems intensify values embedded in those conventions (Breuker, Muntjewerff, & Bredeweg, 1999); epistemology refers to the practices and beliefs that reflect cultural attitudes towards knowledge and its justification (Knorr-Cetina, 1999); and axiology is the study of the nature of values such as *right* and *good* in the two realms of individual and social conduct and value judgement such as *beauty* and *harmony* in nature and art (Freimuth, 2009). Researchers argue that educational models and pedagogical strategies are greatly associated with these three dimensions (e.g., Breuker *et al.*, 1999; Freimuth, 2009; Knorr-Cetina, 1999). In this sense, the three dimensions of educational metaphysics can be useful to reconceive multicultural education and pedagogy in ways which redefine us (ontology), expand our epistemic horizons (epistemology), and reveal (new) values (axiology) in and for intercultural interaction. Furthermore, such metaphysical approaches to interculturality can be used as a pedagogical foundation for individuals' active participation in intercultural interaction. Consequently, intercultural interaction needs to be approached through our hermeneutic understanding of interculturality in terms of how our minds engage with cultural values and reproduce them. In this sense, philosophical hermeneutics is becoming a methodological basis for intercultural interaction. Its meta-questions on our own culture raise an assumption that other cultures also have fundamentally different questions on interculturality. Such mutual understanding can entail a dramatic shift from a subject-object relationship to the subject-subject relationship and legitimise that cultural diversity cannot be transcultural.

In essence, cultural diversity is considered either a new cultural paradigm or a cultural phenomenon of metropolis (Gilroy, 2004; Moore-Gilbert, Stanton, & Maley, 1997). The former has its own value system that is distinguished from other cultures, whereas the latter refers to an outcome of communication and interaction between people of different cultures and societies. Consequently, both are not oppositional, but supplement each other and form a concept, intercultural-*ity*, denoting the quality or condition of interaction between different cultures. Thus interculturality can be metaphysically explored and its structure and mechanism of intercultural interaction can be studied. The study should commence with an investigation of how cultures respond to interculturality. To do so, metaphysical structures of both interculturality and relevant cultures need to be explored concurrently, as they are constantly interacting with one another. Although this process cannot fully represent a culture or may even misrepresent it, it is pedagogically meaningful in which metaphysical understanding of interculturality can be a preliminary reference to authentic intercultural interaction as it extends our cognitive horizons.

Overview of chapters

This study is composed of three parts and each part contains three chapters. As the title of each part indicates, this study is aimed at arguing for why we need metaphysical approaches to interculturality (Part I), what methodological aspects we should consider in designing intercultural interaction (Part II), and what pedagogical approaches to intercultural interaction we need to consider (Part III).

Part I Metaphysical understanding of culture for education
Part II Interculturality and its methodology
Part III Intercultural valuism as emergent pedagogy

Each part contains three chapters. Although each part can be read on its own, together they complement each other by providing different perspectives on different layers of interculturality and intercultural interaction in education as well as complementary dimensions of each other's claims. In Part I, postcolonial approaches to cultural identity and cultural diversity (Chapter 1) help frame metaphysical questions for interculturality (Chapter 2). Metaphysical dimensions applied in the questions help disclose underlying assumptions of various multicultural education models (Chapter 3). In this way, the role of Part I is to justify metaphysical questions of intercultural interaction. The questions recur in the chapters in Part II, particularly in relation to methodological understandings of intercultural interaction. The essential forms of culture, including values, minds, and realities (Chapter 4), support an integration of methodologies towards intercultural interaction (Chapter 5). As a result, the forms become foundational concepts within discussion of philosophical hermeneutics for interculturality (Chapter 6). The philosophical and methodological discussion of Part II and the metaphysical questions of Part I enable pedagogical and instructional access to interculturality (Part III). Equal participation of other cultures in intercultural interaction (Chapter 9) is supported by metaphysical characteristics of each culture (Chapter 8) and implemented through an instructional model of intercultural introspection (Chapter 7).

Part I Metaphysical understanding of culture for education

Chapter 1: I will review various postcolonialists' theories in terms of their understandings of cultural diversity and cultural identity, including ethnicity, and argue their metaphysical and methodological implications on and approaches to intercultural interaction. First, I will argue for their criticism on binary oppositions of cultural representation and clarify the ontology of cultural diversity through

6 Introduction

a critical review of Said's *Orientalism*, Bhabha's *cultural hybridity*, and Spivak's *othering*. These postcolonialists attempt to deconstruct dualistic approaches to cultures and reconstruct authentic cultural identity or propose conceptual links to intercultural interaction. Second, I will argue for ethnicity as cultural identity by critically applying Bhabha's *Third Space*, Hall's *emergent ethnicity*, and Ang's *togetherness-in-difference*, as these offer transcultural concepts based on the ambivalence of cultural diversity. Third, I will extend my argument to a methodological concern: *how we can break down binary oppositions of cultural representation*. The extension will be done based on three concepts: Gilroy's *double consciousness – diasporic cultural exchange and continuity*, Vertovec's *super-diversity*, and Amin's *conviviality*. Consequently, I will articulate the existence of metaphysical tensions between cultures and advocate a metaphysical approach to intercultural interaction, which is concealed by ontological reductionism and epistemic violence.

Chapter 2: I will discuss three dimensions of educational metaphysics for interculturality: ontological justification, epistemological assumptions, and axiological interaction. These three dimensions undermine binary structures of cultural representation and uphold the subject-subject relationship of all cultures in intercultural interaction. Ontological justification can be used to equally position and empower each culture to engage in intercultural interaction; epistemological assumptions indicate that participants need to understand their own thinking framework or belief system on a matter by resolving three concerns: epistemic justification, knowledge acquisition, and knowing frameworks. Axiological interaction in the context of interculturality is justified by epistemological assumptions, and the subject position of participants is supported from ontological justification. With these understandings, I will argue for the three dimensions of metaphysics that are supportive of a methodological approach to intercultural interaction, which helps avoid ontological reductionism and minimises epistemic violence.

Chapter 3: I will investigate underlying assumptions of white multiculturalism and multicultural education models with the three dimensions of metaphysics. I will also criticise ideological aspects of white supremacy by accepting Hage's *concept of ecological fantasy* in that ontological reductionism and epistemic violence are enhanced by the absence of the self, the loss of relationship, and the non-subject position of others in intercultural interaction. After this, I will review contemporary multicultural education discourses through reviewing Banks and McGee Banks' *four levels of multicultural education* and Nieto's *socio-political context of multicultural education*. Both theorists criticise dualism and stress the importance of practising non-dualistic thinking, yet they do not address its specific mode of being and thinking, which is the concept of *culture*. In this sense, I will further discuss that matter through reviewing Nussbaum's *cultivating humanity* and Rizvi's *cosmopolitan learning*. Both theorists address philosophical and pedagogical justifications for multicultural education in the age of globalisation. For example, Nussbaum promotes rational individuality and Rizvi proposes instructional methods such as collaboration and interrogation. However, their arguments do not fully support intercultural interaction because they set their ideas and methods as culturally unbound. I will criticise such metaphysical

Introduction   7

issues that are also found in various multicultural educational models, including conservative multiculturalism, liberal multiculturalism, pluralist multiculturalism, left-essentialist multiculturalism, critical multiculturalism, and intercultural dialogue.

Part II Interculturality and its methodology

Chapter 4: Part I indicates that intercultural interaction requires the ontologically equal relation between cultures – namely, the absence of the self, the loss of relationship, and the non-subject position of others in intercultural interaction. These methodological concerns mean that interactional interaction requires us to verify correlations and relationships between structures of cultural realities and multiple self-construal. In this chapter, I will argue that our self-perception relies heavily on a particular cultural framework. Specifically, I will focus on why cultures are representations of values and how values are embedded in our minds, relations, and society. This will be done by adopting Nietzsche's argument of *Dionysian and Apollonian worlds* and his concept of *a table of values.* Nietzsche deconstructs our metaphysical myths by articulating that a culture is composed of a set of values, and values are interconnected and form cultural realities. His metaphysical interpretation has the potential to develop a new concept of *intercultural value networks* in that it addresses ontological complexity and diverse cultural realities. For ontological complexity, I will critically incorporate the concept of multi-levelled self-construal (personal, relational, collective, and humane) used in cross-cultural psychology into the concept of *the multilayered self.* To configure multiple realities, on the other hand, I will critically review Popper's theory of *three worlds of knowledge* and Habermas's theory of *communicative action on the Lifeworld* in terms of a critical extension of intersubjectivity for intercultural interaction.

Chapter 5: I will comparatively review three methodologies prevailing in education research – namely, methodological individualism, methodological holism, and methodological relationism, in order to articulate an appropriate methodological approach to intercultural value networks. By adopting *the theory of distributed knowledge* in networked learning environments, I will articulate the notion of *nodes* of networks to synthesise the three methodologies. The articulation indicates that methodological individualism reveals the epistemic relationship between learners and networks, methodological holism lays the ontological foundations for the networked world, and methodological relationism is used to develop new values of interculturality. In the conclusion of this chapter, I will argue that these three methodologies are logically aligned with the three dimensions of metaphysics: ontological justification, epistemological assumptions, and axiological interaction.

Chapter 6: By reviewing philosophical hermeneutic concepts and theories (i.e., Heidegger's *being-in-the-world*, Gadamer's *fusions of horizons* and *historically effective consciousness*, Kuhn's *paradigm shift*, and Deleuze and Guattari's *rhizomatic theory*), I will argue for five key concepts of intercultural hermeneutics that shape intercultural value networks: values, intersubjectivity, interobjectivity, emergent values, and axiological mapping. A brief overview

8 Introduction

of each concept is as follows: First, values embedded in participants' cultural fore-structure on a matter need to be identified to commence intercultural interaction. Second, intersubjectivity is a collective pre-understanding and can be used as *perspective-taking* in intercultural interaction. Third, interobjectivity is a new *whole* emergent from inter-intersubjectivity of different cultural frameworks in which it exercises its own power over multi-levelled self-construal and cultural frameworks. Fourth, emergent values arising from intercultural interaction are evidence of the connectedness between intersubjectivity and interobjectivity that upholds the subject-subject position of participants. The connection reconceives interculturality as well as the multilayered self and cultural frameworks by undermining egocentrism, in a sense, transcendental and transcultural. Last, axiological mapping refers to a topographic change in value networks that participants undertake with emergent values, which reveals larger parts of the networks.

Part III Intercultural valuism as emergent pedagogy

Chapter 7: I will argue why the three metaphysics issues of intercultural interaction – namely the absence of the self (as a result, the absence of relations), the non-subject position of others, and the myth of value-free methods, appear in the teachers' reflection writings. I will propose a new model named *intercultural valuism circle* in comparison with a mostly used self-reflection model (i.e., Bain *et al.*'s (2002) five levels of self-reflection model). It consists of five stages: stage 1 intercultural introspection, stage 2 value-awareness, stage 3 value-interactions, stage 4 value-emergence, and stage 5 a set of value networks. I will present some findings from the results of its use as a weekly activity in a teacher education program. For example, pre-service teachers experience difficulty escaping from their dualistic thinking patterns when using self-reflection models by assuming that values such as *individualism, beneficiary*, and *equity* are culturally unbound.

Chapter 8: I will review non-Western cultural/religious concepts, narratives, and doctrines such as Aboriginal *Dreaming*, Hindu *Atman*, Buddhist *Sunyata*, Taoist *Yin and Yang*, Confucianist *Tao*, and Islamic *Tawhid* with questioning: *What intercultural characteristics do they have when they are understood in value networks*. Each one appears unique and has different metaphysical characteristics that represent its own cultural identity and formation. Each one's interculturality is defined as ontological, epistemological, or axiological interculturality. The ontological interculturality supports holistic individuality, the epistemological interculturality systemises value-interaction, and the axiological interculturality promotes values and ethical engagement of participants in intercultural interaction. These results are consistent with cultural pedagogies in the next chapter.

Chapter 9: I will review cultural/religious pedagogies and compare them with Western pedagogical theories in order to articulate an intercultural pedagogical framework. In Western pedagogies, I will review three major ones: *behaviourism, cognitivism*, and *constructivism*, whereas, in cultural/religious pedagogies, I will include *Confucian virtuological pedagogy, Islamic totalistic pedagogy, Aboriginal holistic pedagogy, Hindu spiritual pedagogy*, and *Buddhist mindful pedagogy*.

In intercultural value networks, Western pedagogies have the potential to reveal values embedded in each culture and emergent values arising from intercultural value-interaction, monistic pedagogies (Confucianism and Islamism) suggest collective moral responsibilities through interobjectivity of interculturality, holistic pedagogies (Aboriginality, Hinduism, and Buddhism) extend the concept of individuality that is transcendental to the frame of interdependence-independence and to the material senses, mind, and intelligence. In value networks, diverse cultural/religious pedagogical frameworks can be used to facilitate intercultural value-interaction and enrich interculturality.

Conclusion: I will conclude this study by further articulating preconditions for *intercultural valuism pedagogy*. The preconditions are *value nodes, multiple realities, the multilayered self, interstice adjustments*, and *whole individuality*. The intercultural valuism pedagogy is aimed at providing a hermeneutic key to intercultural interaction that encompasses ontological, epistemological, and axiological aspects of interculturality for intercultural education. In practice, it is aimed at facilitating individual participants to understand how their cultural values are interconnected and interrelated in the interculturally networked world. In intercultural interaction, participants are not encouraged by what they must learn, but they are encouraged to be aware of where values are and how they affect them. Consequently, participants can reveal a new set of value networks through value reticulating for self-, relational-, and social transformation. In this sense, learning is not *connecting activities*, but *revealing new values* in larger parts of value networks by *readjusting interstices* where they are ontologically anchored surrounding value nodes.

References

Ang, I. (2001). *On not speaking Chinese: Living between Asia and the West*. London: Routledge.

Antonette, L. (2003). Liberal and conservative multiculturalism after September 11. *Multicultural Review, 12*(2), 29–35.

Auster, L. (2004). How the multicultural ideology captured America. *The Social Contract, 14*(3), 197–208.

Bain, J.D., Ballantyne, R., Mills, C., & Lester, N.C. (2002). *Reflecting on practice: Student teachers' perspectives*. Flaxton, QLD, Australia: Post Pressed.

Banks, J.A. (1997). *Educating citizens in a multicultural society*. New York: Teachers College Press.

Bhabha, H.K. (1994). *The location of culture*. London and New York: Routledge.

Breuker, J., Muntjewerff, A., & Bredeweg, B. (1999, July). *Ontological modelling for designing educational systems*. Paper presented at Proceedings of the Workshop on Ontologies for Intelligent Educational Systems at AIE99, Le Mans, France. Retrieved from http://citeseer.ist.psu.edu/viewdoc/download;jsessionid=7326DD61AAFE ABFA52DC3A1D289C431E?doi=10.1.1.331.7057&rep=rep1&type=pdf

Dewey, J. (1983). *Human nature and conduct. In the middle works of John Dewey.* Carbondale: Southern Illinois University Press. (Original work published 1922)

Drenthen, M. (2011). Reading ourselves through the land: Landscape hermeneutics and ethics of place. In F. Clingerman & M. Dixon (Eds.), *Placing Nature on the Borders of Religion, Philosophy, and Ethics* (pp. 123–138). Farnham: Ashgate.

10 Introduction

Fallace, T.D. (2010). Was John Dewey ethnocentric? Reevaluating the philosopher's early views on culture and race. *Educational Researcher, 39*(6), 471–477.

Freimuth, H. (2009). Educational research: An introduction to basic concepts and terminology. *University General Requirements Unit (UGRU) Journal, 8*, 1–9.

Freire, P. (2000). *Pedagogy of the oppressed.* (M.B. Ramos, Trans.). New York: Continuum. (Original work published 1970)

Gadamer, H.G. (2004*). Truth and method* (2nd rev, ed.). (J. Weinsheimer & D.G. Marshall, Trans.). New York: Crossroad. (Original work published 1960)

Gardner, W.L., Gabriel, S., & Lee, A.L. (1999). "I" value freedom, but "we" value relationships: Self-construal priming mirrors cultural differences in judgment. *Psychological Science, 10*(4), 321–326.

Gilroy, P. (2004). *After empire: Melancholia or convivial culture?* Oxon: Routledge.

Giroux, H.A. (1988). *Teachers as intellectuals: Toward a critical pedagogy of learning.* Granby, MA: Bergin and Garvey. Retrieved from http://teacherrenewal.wiki. westga.edu/file/view/Rethinking+the+Language+of+Schooling.html

Goodin, R.E. (2006). Liberal multiculturalism: Protective and polyglot. *Political Theory, 34*(3), 289–303.

Hainic, C. (2012). The Heideggerian roots of everyday aesthetics: A hermeneutical approach to art. In F. Dorsch & D.E. Ratiu (Eds.), *Proceedings of the European Society for Aesthetics* (pp. 230–249). Amsterdam: The European Society for Aesthetics (vol. 4).

Hall, E.T. (1981). *Beyond culture.* New York: Random House.

Kagan, M.S. (2009). *Philosophy of culture.* (Korean version) (H.S. Lee, Trans.). Saint Petersburg: Petropolis LLP TK. (Original work published 1996)

Knorr-Cetina, K. (1999). *Epistemic cultures. How the sciences make knowledge.* Boston, MA: Harvard University Press.

Koleth, E. (2010). *Multiculturalism: A review of Australian policy statements and recent debates in Australia and overseas.* Parliament of Australia. Retrieved from http://www.aph.gov.au/About_Parliament/Parliamentary_Departments/ Parliamentary_Library/pubs/rp/rp1011/11rp06

Manathunga, C. (2014). *Intercultural postgraduate supervision: Reimagining time, place and knowledge.* Milton Park, Abingdon, Oxon; New York: Routledge.

Meer, N., & Modood, T. (2012). How does interculturalism contrast with multiculturalism? *Journal of Intercultural Studies, 33*(2), 175–196.

Moghaddam, F.M. (2003). Interobjectivity and culture. *Culture & Psychology, 9*(3), 221–232.

Moore-Gilbert, B., Stanton, G., & Maley, W. (1997). *Postcolonial criticism.* London: Routledge.

Nieto, S., & Bode, P. (2010). School reform and student learning: Multicultural perspectives. In J.A. Banks & C.A.M. Banks (Eds.), *Multicultural Education: Issues and Perspectives* (7th ed.) (pp. 395–416). Hoboken, NJ: John Wiley & Sons, Inc.

O'Grady, C. (Ed.). (2000). *Integrating service learning and multicultural education in colleges and universities.* Mahwah, NJ: Lawrence Erlbaum Associates.

Orr, D. (2002). The uses of mindfulness in anti-oppressive pedagogies: Philosophy and praxis. *Canadian Journal of Education, 4*, 477–490.

Pai, Y., & Adler, S.A. (1997). *Cultural foundations of education.* Upper Saddle River, NJ: Prentice Hall.

Ricoeur, P. (1981). *Hermeneutics and the human sciences.* (B. Thompson, Trans.). Cambridge: Cambridge University Press. (Original work published 1973)

Schein, E.H. (1985). *Organizational culture and leadership*. San Francisco: Jossey-Bass Publishers.

Selfridge, R., & Sokolik, S. (1975). A comprehensive view of organizational management. *MSU Business Topics, 23*(1), 46–61.

Sugiharto, S. (2013). Critical multiculturalism and the politics of identity in academic writing. *K@ta, 15*(1), 19–24.

UNESCO. (2013). *Intercultural competences: Concept and operational framework*. Retrieved from http://unesdoc.unesco.org/images/0021/002197/219768e.pdf

Part I

Metaphysical understanding of culture for education

Part I Introduction: Non-ontological culturally inclusive education

Culturally inclusive education is difficult to define because it is ascribed various meanings and contexts. It can indicate inclusive education in special education – the term suggesting exclusion rather than equal participation (Cologon, 2013), pedagogical inclusion of cultural diversity and multicultural perspectives in higher education (Quaye & Harper, 2007), culturally responsive classrooms where stakeholders acknowledge cultural diversity and find the relevant pedagogical and curricular needs (Jones-Goods, 2015; Montgomery, 2001), and culturally inclusive pedagogy that responds to students' diverse learning styles caused by cultural background and knowledge is context dependent (Blasco, 2015; McLoughlin, 2001). To sum up, culturally inclusive learning can be defined as a learning philosophy through which stakeholders recognise, appreciate, and capitalise on cultural diversity in order to promote students' equal participation in teaching and learning. However, this understanding raises two questions that have rarely been asked and answered in the context of a culturally diverse learning environment. The first question is how can cultural inclusivity be paralleled with equal participation if the underlying assumptions of equal participation are perceived differently within a culture? The second question is how are teachers and students confident that culturally inclusive learning and teaching appropriately addresses cultural diversity if an agreed or shared concept of cultural inclusivity is exclusive of a particular cultural value or practice? If culturally inclusive learning should be realised for a particular group of students (e.g., Aboriginal and Torres Strait Islander students) in the learning environment, how can we confirm that the concept of cultural inclusivity addresses their cultural values and pedagogies? Furthermore, how can we ensure that the concept of cultural diversity cannot be ideologically subordinate to equal participation that is not inclusive of other cultures?

In the literature, equal participation is deemed a parameter of inclusive learning because cultural exclusivity or enculturated exclusion, such as racism, sustains "structural power relations in society" and reproduces "inequalities located in institutional relations and social processes" (Cologon, 2013, p. 17). In this sense, teachers should make a conscious effort to pay attention to all students and involve them equally in all learning activities (Montgomery, 2001). In practice, teachers are required to become culturally responsive and inclusive by "validating

16 *Metaphysical understanding of culture*

students and promoting equity within the classroom" (Jones-Goods, 2015, p. 7) and students are invited to "bring their unique cultural experiences and perspectives to classroom discourse" (Quaye & Harper, 2007, p. 38). As Blasco (2015) points out, ironically, such strategic approaches to culturally inclusive learning cause a discrepancy with the equal participation defined earlier, do not shift "responsibility for inclusion from the learner to the educational institution" (p. 86), and have little room for consideration of other cultures. This may be because the concept of equal participation has been predicated on responsibilities and roles of individual teachers and students. This assumption requires ontological justification for cultural inclusivity in a culturally diverse learning environment. If cultural inclusivity is subordinate to a predefined cultural diversity, the power relation between dominant and non-dominant cultures determines an acceptable range of cultural inclusivity, thereby enhancing its structure and transforming neither the institution nor the individual stakeholders. In this context, culturally inclusive learning and teaching would remain individual students' acquisition of knowledge of other cultures and have nothing to do with their culture. Such a binary opposition between different cultures is exclusive of cultural diversity and other cultures. Thus the concept of equal participation needs to be reviewed and reframed based on ontological understanding of cultural inclusivity and cultural diversity in the context of interculturality. In practice, as cultural inclusivity is a necessary condition for equal participation, each concept needs to be de- and re-conceptualised and theorised in line with a contextualised inclusivity and engagement of each culture. Otherwise, culturally inclusive learning degenerates into individuals' value-free conduct or becomes an ideological tool for a dominant culture, which causes unintentional exclusion of other cultures.

Banks and McGee Banks (2010) argue that construction of equity in schools should be paired with culturally sensitive teaching methods, which is called *equity pedagogy*. In multicultural education, they insist that equity pedagogy is one of their proposed five dimensions of multicultural education and intersects with the other four dimensions: content integration, the knowledge construction process, prejudice reduction, and an empowering school culture and social structure. They define it as a teaching strategy that helps students from diverse cultural backgrounds to "attain the knowledge, skills, and attitudes [that are] needed to function effectively within, and help create and perpetuate, a just, humane, and democratic society" (p. 152). They use this definition to emphasise the significance that students need to question the "assumptions, paradigms, and hegemonic characteristics" (p. 152), which enable teachers to identify "effective instructional techniques and methods" (p. 153). If contextual issues are not addressed, they assert that pedagogies on multicultural education "reinforce stereotypes and inequality in the classroom" (p. 153). However, Banks and McGee Banks do not address my ontological questions about properties of cultural inclusivity and diversity in their articles. Instead, they argue how equity is intertwined with the other four dimensions. For example, they articulate that the most important ability for teachers in terms of equity pedagogy is "reflective self-analysis" and insist that teachers are required "to identify, examine, and reflect on their attitudes toward different ethnic, racial, gender, and social-class groups" (p. 156). In their earlier work, Banks and McGee Banks (1995) also argue that reflective self-analysis helps teachers examine why people continue to believe the "myths that perpetuate social class, gender, and racial privilege" (p. 156). Such suggestions would have three assumptions in relation to understanding the concepts of culture and cultures: (a) culture is a subcategory of social phenomena such as gender and class, (b) cultural diversity cannot be explained by cultures, and, consequently, (c) cultural identity is part of one's self-perception. These assumptions fundamentally reject my ontological questions about cultural inclusivity in which (a) those individuals who have different cultures are not considered social agents, (b) intercultural interaction is only valid for artefacts that are acceptable in the mainstream curricular, and (c) the self, which knows things, is prioritised over the self, which is a known object of any action. In the learning environment, as a result, equal pedagogy remains normative, and it cannot be methodologically discussed and revised because it is believed that reflective self-analysis is culturally unbound. In this sense, what the teacher can do would be waiting until social inequity is resolved or ignoring that multicultural education continues to reproduce stereotypes and othering. This can be subverted when teachers reinterpret and reconceptualise cultural diversity and pedagogy with other cultural frameworks.

A widely accepted proposition of culturally inclusive learning endorses the existence of cultural diversity, although it is not clearly defined in the literature. Instead, it refers to being *inclusive of all types of diversity* (Germain-Rutherford & Kerr, 2008), *inclusivity and different orientations to learning* (McLoughlin, 2000), *diverse learning styles and cognitive preferences* (McLoughlin & Oliver, 2000), *different cultural and linguistic backgrounds* (Hannon & D'Netto, 2007), and *the variety of participants' cultural backgrounds* (Economides, 2008). Such understandings of cultural diversity in inclusive or multicultural education are based on the belief that instructional design should cater to multiple cultural contexts and accommodate learners who have different cultural backgrounds (Henderson, 1996). In short, it has a hypothesis that there is a truly universal framework applicable to all people, which regards it as an unchangeable, fixed entity. Yet, as Gergen (2015) argues, universalist culturally inclusive learning is not free from "an array of traditional assumptions about knowledge, the person, and culture" (p. 96). It is worthwhile to pay attention to Gergen's insight that such a universalist standpoint has been adopted and extended in constructivist cognitive content without addressing cultural particularity of mental life. This means that instructional design, such as Banks and McGee Banks' reflective self-analysis, should not be understood as a universal, but culturally bound.

Some may argue whether or not my questions are aimed at supporting cultural relativism. My argument is that cultural inclusivity, equal participation, and cultural diversity are cultural artefacts, and different cultures can be justifiably critiqued within a question of how each culture deconstructs and reconstructs those concepts. Thus, to ensure that the concept of cultural inclusivity is inclusive of values and pedagogies of diverse cultures, it needs to be first understood as a sub-concept of a culture and then that sub-concept needs to be used to articulate equal participation in intercultural interaction. This argument supports

18 *Metaphysical understanding of culture*

substantial intercultural interaction through ongoing reflection on different cultures, which requires pedagogical and cultural praxis of the praxis. In this sense, cultural diversity neither refers to a collection of cultures nor simple acknowledgement of others in a sense of cultural relativism, but a cultural phenomenon that is differently observable in different cultural contexts. Consequently, intercultural interaction occurs in a predefined interculturality that is always affected by participants' cultures. This also indicates that metaphysical conflicts and tensions between cultures or cultural artefacts always manifest themselves in diverse contexts of cultural diversity.

Such an inferential conclusion reminds teachers that instructional design is not culturally neutral, but is determined by "particular epistemologies, learning theories and goal orientations of the [instructional] designers themselves" (McLoughlin & Oliver, 2000, p. 58). I am only partly in support of this statement, which tends to understand the concept of culture in a narrow sense and places it as a subordinate concept of a teacher's selective paradigms of instructional design. We need to remember that "instructional design is an intangible aspect of [a] culture, but once it is transformed into a material object, it becomes (part of) that cultural artefact" (Henderson, 1996, p. 86). This means that a comprehensive metaphysical interpretation of relevant concepts on culture and cultures are needed in order to identify the position of multicultural education in intercultural interaction. Such an approach will be helpful to identify underlying assumptions, values, and beliefs entrenched in contemporary multicultural education discourses and educational models.

References

Banks, J.A., & McGee Banks, C.A. (1995). Equity pedagogy: An essential component of multicultural education. *Theory into Practice, 34*(3), 152–158.

Banks, J.A., & McGee Banks, C.A. (2010). *Multicultural education: Issues and perspectives* (7th ed.). Hoboken, NJ: John Wiley & Sons, Inc.

Blasco, M. (2015). Making the tacit explicit: Rethinking culturally inclusive pedagogy in international student academic adaptation. *Pedagogy, Culture & Society, 23*(1), 85–106.

Cologon, K. (2013). *Inclusion in education: Towards equality for students with disability* (Issues paper). Children with Disability Australia.

Economides, A.A. (2008). Culture-aware collaborative learning. *Multicultural Education & Technology Journal, 2*(4), 243–267.

Gergen, K.J. (2015). Culturally inclusive psychology from a constructionist standpoint. *Journal for the Theory of Social Behaviour, 45*(1), 95–107.

Germain-Rutherford, A.G., & Kerr, B. (2008). An inclusive approach to online learning environments: Models and resources. *Turkish Online Journal of Distance Education-TOJDE, 9*(2), 64–85.

Hannon, J., & D'Netto, B. (2007). Cultural diversity online: Student engagement with learning technologies. *International Journal of Educational Management, 21*(5), 418–432.

Henderson, L. (1996). Instructional design of interactive multimedia: A cultural critique. *Educational Technology Research and Development, 44*(4), 85–104.

Jones-Goods, K.M. (2015). The culturally responsive classroom: Why we need to transform instructional strategies. *Reading Today, 32*(5), 6–7.

McLoughlin, C. (2000). Cultural maintenance, ownership, and multiple perspectives: Features of web-based delivery to promote equity. *Journal of Educational Media, 25*(3), 229–241.

McLoughlin, C. (2001). Inclusivity and alignment: Principles of pedagogy, task and assessment design for effective cross-cultural online learning. *Distance Education, 22*(1), 7–29.

McLoughlin, C., & Oliver, R. (2000). Designing learning environments for cultural inclusivity: A case study of Indigenous online learning at tertiary level. *Australian Journal of Educational Technology, 16*(1), 58–72.

Montgomery, W. (2001). Creating culturally responsive, inclusive classrooms. *Teaching Exceptional Children, 33*(4), 4–9.

Quaye, S.J., & Harper, S.R. (2007). Faculty accountability for culturally inclusive pedagogy and curricula. *Liberal Education, 93*(3), 32–39.

1 Beyond cultural identity
Postcolonial approaches to cultural diversity

Some proponents insist that multiculturalism enriches our society economically, socially, culturally, and politically, whereas some opponents claim that it preserves ongoing barriers to equality, participation in and access to services, social inclusion, and multidimensional approaches to disadvantage. The proponents tend to promote social stability and cohesion, whereas the opponents tend to preserve ethnicity and Indigeneity. Regardless of the pros and cons of multiculturalism, there are great campaigns to promote particular values and beliefs as actions (e.g., liberal individualism, communitarian social cohesion, national identity, and ethno-centrism). Such underlying assumptions of cultural diversity and cultural identity are often concealed beneath the rhetoric of political slogans. In this context, this chapter focuses on how cultural diversity and cultural identity are understood in relevant literature and how each is positioned for intercultural interaction.

In multicultural education, intercultural interaction is often regarded as beneficial to learning a skill set of interpersonal communication, but it ignores intrapersonal intelligence – a high level of self-awareness. As a result, multicultural education often becomes a guided tour of other cultures and focuses on developing business communication skills. In this context, other cultures are perceived as *peripheral* in knowledge construction or used to enhance a dominant form of knowledge construction. Postcolonial theorists impute such marginalisation, exclusion, and alienation of other cultures to the binary opposition between Third World and First World that engenders ideological discourses of modernity. On the other hand, some sociologists in multicultural policies claim that different cultures offer an opportunity for us to expand our own horizon of thought and have to be understood to promote morality and humanity. A well-known postcolonial theorist, Bhabha (1994), argues for why we need to examine the culture of Western modernity from a postcolonial perspective. He explains that various forms of cultural identity (thus *cultural identities* and *ethnic identities* as subsets of identity categories) are placed on the boundaries of in-between forms (or intersections) across class, gender, race, nation, generation, and location. He defines this phenomenon as hybridity of colonial identity and claims that cultural diversity and cultural identity need to be understood to intervene in "the colonial testimony of Third World countries and the discourses of minorities" (1994, p. 171). Meanwhile, sociologists, Meer and Modood (2012) who debate cultural hybridity and

22   Metaphysical understanding of culture

consider *interculturalism* as complementary to multiculturalism, argue that different cultures "alert each other to new forms of human fulfilment" and therefore cultural interaction should "encourage [participants] to cultivate their moral and aesthetic insights for humanity as a whole" (p. 186). They view cultural diversity within a frame of pluralistic relativism, which is believed to lead to appreciation and tolerance of others. For Meer and Modood, cultural diversity is a political ideology that represents "a desirable feature of a given society (as well as the different types of ways in which the state could recognize and support it)" (p. 179). For Bhabha, on the other hand, cultural diversity is "the recognition of pre-given cultural contents and customs" (p. 4) that conceals the problem of colonial binary thinking and oppositional positioning. This comparative review indicates that cultural diversity can be seen as either an epistemic problem or a moral challenge. For intercultural interaction, we need to argue how prevailing concepts such as cultural diversity and cultural identity are understood in various pieces of literature and for which approach is more appropriate to intercultural interaction.

1.1 The position of culture in understandings of cultural diversity and cultural identity

Said, Bhabha, and Spivak have been known as the Holy Trinity of postcolonialism (Young cited in Moore-Gilbert, 2000). Based on discourses on difference and diversity, those three researchers have developed their theoretical foundations to contest the oppositional (or dualistic) characteristics of boundaries between oppressors and oppressed and between superior culture and inferior culture.

Said (1979) defines *Orientalism* as the West's patronising distinction between the West and the East. He argues that Orientalism has been reproduced not as a counterpart to political power, but through complicated political relationships between ex-colonies and former colonial powers. In essence, it plays a role in providing the ideological foundations for the superiority of Western values and developing the mystification of the East Asian cultures, which is called *binary oppositions of cultural representation*. In this context, Said points out the fact that Easterners tend to perceive their cultural representation based on Western perspectives rather than attempt to articulate their own authentic cultural identities. Spivak (1988) argues that such a misrepresentation does not allow Easterners to be equal agents in any cultural discourses, but instead they become (colonial) subalterns who have lost the right to speak. Then are the concepts such as ethnicity and Indigeneity made for the sake of convenience and classification? Is intercultural interaction a delusional belief? Said's answer would be *no* because he distinguishes the difference between *manifest Orientalism* and *latent Orientalism*. The latter refers to being unchanging and permanent, whereas the former refers to being gathered, collated, and amended. Said contends that Orientalism as a way of describing the Orient is bound in Eurocentrism. To articulate intercultural interaction, his dual recognition of Orientalism needs to be reviewed to confirm whether or not latent Orientalism is an alternative that breaks down the binary oppositions. The probability can be found in Bhabha's concepts of cultural hybridity and a Third Space.

Beyond cultural diversity 23

Interestingly, Bhabha (1994) criticises Said's ambivalence of Orientalism by indicating that the concept is too homogeneous, does not support cultural identity, and gives little room for resistance to colonial power. Bhabha argues, "Said's Orientalism is unified – the intentionality and unidirectionality of colonial power – also unify the subject of colonial enunciation" (p. 109). As a result, he argues that Said pays inadequate "attention to representation as a concept that articulates the historical and fantasy (as the scene of design) in the production of the 'political' effects of discourse" (p. 103). For him, Said's Orientalism neither explicitly nor consistently advocates the meanings and representations of the Third World (the Orient). Alternatively, Bhabha proposes a concept, *hybridity*, that needs to be understood as "the sign of the productivity of colonial power, its shifting forces and fixities; it is . . . the revaluation of the assumption of colonial identity through the repetition of discriminatory identity effects" (p. 159). In practice, the colonised can use hybridity to reconfigure the colonial identity in accordance with their authentic culture and language and, at the same time, they can desire to follow and stay in the colonial discourse. In this sense, hybridity is a tool for ruling as well as a means of resistance. Based on the conception of hybridity, Bhabha views,

> culture, as a colonial space of intervention and agonism, as the trace of the displacement of symbol to sign, can be transformed by the unpredictable and partial desire of hybridity. Deprived of their full presence, the knowledges of cultural authority may be articulated with forms of "native" knowledges or faced with those discriminated subjects that they must rule but can no longer represent.
>
> (p. 164)

In his later work, Bhabha (2006) defines "cultural diversity as an epistemological object" that is "adequate to the construction of systems of cultural identification" (p. 155). He argues that it causes "the common semiotic account of the disjuncture between the subject of a proposition and the subject of enunciation . . . its cultural positionality, its reference to a present time and a specific space" (p. 156). Bhabha's adoption of Lacan's dual position of the *I* in the process of communication splits the speaker (or pronominal *I*) into the signifier and the grammatical subject of the statement. The speaker will lose the *I* as a place when the other person responds to him/her (Lacan, 1964/1978). This means that the position of the *I* is not fixed in communication. In this way, Bhabha (2006) argues,

> The production of meaning requires that these two places be mobilized in the passage through a Third Space, which represents both the general conditions of language and the specific implication of the utterance in a performative and institutional strategy of which it cannot 'in itself' be conscious. What this unconscious relation introduces is an ambivalence in the act of interpretation.
>
> (p. 156)

24 *Metaphysical understanding of culture*

Bhabha's spatialisation between a speaker and an interlocutor (or the self and the other) involves visualising the unconscious and ambivalent relation that occurred in interpretations. Thus an intervention in the relation includes constructing the structure of meaning and deconstructing the cultural knowledge. This intervention "challenges our sense of the historical identity of culture" because "all cultural statements and systems" are constructed in "this ambivalent space of enunciation" (Bhabha, 2006, p. 156). This means that such ambivalent, indeterminate, and unstable movement cannot be articulated as cultural practice without an acknowledgement of the subject of enunciation in a Third Space (Bhabha, 1994, p. 55). Inversely, as a Third Space constitutes the discursive conditions of enunciation, it ensures that "the meaning and symbol of culture have no primordial unity or fixity" (Bhabha, 2006, p. 157). In this sense, revealing the identity of a Third Space is the necessary precondition for the articulation of cultural differences and cultural identity. This indicates that "hybridity is the name of the displacement of value from [cultural] symbol to sign" within cultural differences and diversity (Bhabha, 2006, p. 113). Bhabha (1994) describes the displacement of value as "the moment of panic which reveals the borderline experience" (p. 296). Consequently, Bhabha's notion of cultural hybridity supplements Said's latent Orientalism and explains the imbalanced cultural relations by regarding a Third Space as a passage where one can enter or leave and negotiate or contest. A question then arises as to how the colonised (or the colonised ethnicity) can be free from a misrepresented and fabricated Third Space or become the subject in it. According to Moore-Gilbert, Stanton, and Maley (1997), Said and Bhabha focus on the coloniser and the discourses of the dominant orders of Western society, and their criticism is focused on "the predicament and discourses of the Third World migrant to the Western metropolis", not on legitimacy and authenticity of ethnicity (p. 28). In this sense, Spivak's (1988) work, "Can the Subaltern Speak" is worth reviewing to see how postcolonialists view the position of ethnicity in a Third Space.

Spivak (1988) adopts the term *subaltern* from Antonio Gramsci (1891–1937), who was a Marxist philosopher and proposed the concept of *cultural hegemony* in order to analyse the Third World. For Spivak, the Third World refers to "subsistence farmers, unorganized peasant labour, the tribals and communities of zero workers on the street or in the countryside" (p. 84). In her later works, she extends the term to include disadvantaged constituencies within the West, including women and migrants (Moore-Gilbert, 2000). Spivak rearticulates subaltern women's histories in her works, "Can the Subaltern Speak?" (1988) and "The Rani of Sirmur" (1985). She contends that Western feminists need to consider the material histories and lives of Third World women in terms of their struggles against exploitation and oppression (Morton, 2003). By raising the question of to what extent Third World women can reveal their identity, she argues that the heterogeneity and differences cannot be homogenised with the colonised others. Like Bhabha, she criticises Said's Orientalism, which is not inclusive of subalterns and others, particularly women in the Third World. She analyses three dimensions of othering in the context of the British colonial power in India. The dimensions, which appeared in Spivak's "The Rani of Sirmur" are as follows: the first dimension is to make "the subordinate aware of who holds the power" and remind them they are the other, subordinate; the second dimension is to construct "the other as pathological and morally inferior"; and the third dimension is to realise that "knowledge and technology is the property of the powerful empirical self, not the colonial other" (pp. 64–65). This multidimensional process of othering indicates that the formation of (false) identity is inherent in the concept of othering. Spivak calls the process "epistemic violence of the discourses of the other" (1988, p. 76). The coloniser mistakenly assumes that there is a pure or essential form of the subaltern consciousness in their binary oppositions or dualism so that the truth can be retrieved, which historically constructs the subject position (Moore-Gilbert *et al.*, 1997). It is believed that the binary oppositions precipitate the epistemic fracture that causes a repetition of, as well as rupture with, colonial epistemology (Moore-Gilbert *et al.*, 1997). Then within the circle of repetition and rupture, how can the subaltern speak independently? How can they break such a vicious circle?

Spivak's answer to the questions could be either *yes* or *no*. Her answer is *yes* in that subalterns are capable of producing their own postcolonial texts, but *no* in that subalterns are not given permission to *speak* what they think is the truth. This means that subalterns can speak for themselves as long as they pay attention to the *latent*, because the *manifest* constantly suppresses subaltern voices. Spivak seems not to expand the latent in order to attack the epistemic fracture from any subaltern's perspectives because her focus is on the truth about the Third World that is always tainted with the political and economic interests of the West. Perhaps she is unaware that subaltern muteness would indicate Hindus' intrapersonal culture rather than culture written by the West. Moore-Gilbert *et al.* (1997) also support this supposition with criticism:

> If Spivak's account of subaltern muteness were true, then there would be nothing but the West (and the native elite, perhaps) to write about . . . Spivak in fact herself primarily addresses the West rather than the subaltern . . . as her privileged object of investigation.
>
> (p. 464)

As a necessary corollary, Spivak emphasises "the critic's institutional responsibility" as well as the importance of "the role of both hegemonic and oppositional intellectuals" (1988, p. 75) because "the task of recovering a (sexually) subaltern subject is lost in an institutional textuality at the archaic origin" (p. 99). She describes those intellectuals as neither "the Subject of desire and power as an irreducible methodological presupposition" nor "the subject of the oppressed" (p. 74). She also firmly refuses to accept their "role of referee, judge, and universal witness" and proposes that discursive institutions need to be considered in postcolonialism because they obliterate intellectuals' relation to the other with hegemonic vocabulary (p. 75). Instead, she argues that the produced transparency dislocates intellectuals' "interests, motives (desires) and power (of knowledge)", imputes their identity to a "dynamic economic situation" (or overdetermined

26   *Metaphysical understanding of culture*

enterprise), and unwittingly secures "a new balance of hegemonic relations" (p. 75). Consequently, her assertion indicates that (Western) intellectuals must be aware of the Western epistemological duplicity of subject position that ultimately allows subalterns to speak for themselves. If she were able to see epistemic violence not within gender-power relationships (although her criticism of the liberal feminist's narcissism articulates Western writers' discursive privilege), but in Western metaphysical conflicts with ethnicity and Indigeneity, her unintentional partial denial of *subalterns can speak for themselves* would not occur. To find out the possibility of gaining the subject position of subaltern with Spivak's epistemic violence, we need to put it in a methodological context, which is found in Hall (1989)'s *emergent ethnicity*.

1.2 Ethnicity as cultural identity: Anti-dualism

Hall (1989) argues that binary oppositions of cultural representation constantly naturalise the differences between belongingness and otherness (p. 445). He contends, "The black subject cannot be represented without reference to the dimensions of class, gender, sexuality and ethnicity" (p. 444). The black subject is constructed in historical, cultural, and political contexts, which refers to ethnicity holding *a particular culture*. An ideological contestation around multi-ethnicity or multi-culturalism builds a foundational discourse for the difference that "makes a radical and unbridgeable separation" (p. 446). At the same time, new forms of cultural practice can emerge when ethnicity can be (at least metaphysically) decoupled from the epistemic violence or the dominant discourse such as nationalism, imperialism, racism, and the state. Hall's "positive conception of the ethnicity of the margins, of the periphery" is "a recognition that we all speak from a particular place, out of a particular history, out of a particular experience, a particular culture" (p. 447). In this sense, "our *ethnic identities* are crucial to our subjective sense of who we are" (p. 447 [emphasis added]). Hall suggests a practical act:

> Fifteen years ago we didn't care, or at least I didn't care, whether there was any black in the Union Jack. Now not only do we care, we must . . . Once you abandon essential categories, there is no place to go apart from the politics of criticism and to enter the politics of criticism in black culture is to grow up, to leave the age of critical innocence.
>
> (p. 448)

The *essential categories* become clearer in his debate with Rushdie in the *Guardian* (January 1987) about *Handsworth Songs* or *The Passion of Remembrance*. His review is not about whether the films are great or not. He states, "Once you enter this particular problematic, the question of what good films are, which parts of them are good and why, is open to the politics of criticism" (p. 448). "Whether they were great or not" has no will to escape from the binary system of representation. When we are trapped in the epistemological binary

Beyond cultural diversity 27

oppositions, which is an essential category, we tend to ignore ontological and axiological questions on a matter and not to practise our meta-thinking of the epistemological assumptions.

Like Spivak, Hall (1993) attempts to reveal the essence of the binary oppositions and conceptualise an authentic ethnicity or ethnic identities. He verifies the *proneness* through analysing his encoding-decoding model of communication. His focus is on how encoding and decoding messages could lead to miscommunication. He analyses the model with three different positions that receivers will take in their decoding of meanings within cultural texts: the dominant-hegemonic position, the negotiated position, and the oppositional position:

> The dominant-hegemonic position: the viewer takes the connoted meaning . . . full and straight, and decodes the message in terms of the reference code in which it has been encoded . . . is operating inside the dominant code.
>
> (p. 209)

> The negotiated position: decoders adopt a negotiated code which acknowledges the legitimacy of the hegemonic definitions to make the grand significations (abstract), while, at a more restricted, situational (situated) level, it makes its own ground rules – it operates with exceptions to the rule. That is, the preferred reading is accepted at an abstract level, but rejected at a more personal level.
>
> (p. 210)

> The oppositional position: viewers decode the message in a globally contrary way to the hegemonic discourse, and use their own framework of interpretation.
>
> (p. 211)

These three different positions indicate that the encoding-decoding model of communication means not only that there are three different types of a receiver/viewer but also all the types could be embedded in an interpreting process between a sender and a receiver. An intellectual can also be one of the audiences who just receives a message with little misunderstanding and miscommunication, although sometimes one personally rejects it. This means that both acceptance and rejection can appear in dominant cultural and societal views. Meanwhile, one may hold an oppositional position when one is aware of a disparity between meaning structures of an encoded message and a decoded message, which causes different interest. In other words, an oppositional position contains an undertone of metaphysical conflicts or ontological tensions between a sender and a receiver. Furthermore, the ontological position of a sender/receiver becomes transcendental to the rule of dominant-hegemony for communication. In this sense, Hall's model of encoding and decoding provides the ontological foundation for intercultural interaction by presuming emergent ethnicity as the oppressed possess their own (cultural) assumptions,

28 *Metaphysical understanding of culture*

beliefs, and values, thereby holding the subject position. However, a question arises: Why does Hall not presume that the oppressor can also abandon the essential categories? If emergent ethnicity is possible, does its methodological foundation indicate that emergent identity of the oppressor is also possible in some way?

Ang (2001) argues that the frame of cultural differences (i.e., between the East and the West) should not be theorised in the age of globalisation and diaspora (i.e., a global Chineseness), but the social and intellectual space of *in-betweenness* needs to be theorised towards *togetherness-in-difference*. Ang (2001) argues for cultural identity in that age and challenges the Western (Australia) thinking that equates Chinese with Asian identity. She presumes that binary oppositions of cultural representation have been undermined by cultural globalisation and hybridisation. She states, "One of the merits of the concept of hybridisation is that it undermines the binary and static way of thinking about difference which is dominant in theories of cultural pluralism" (P. 87). Her point is that the structural ambivalence of multiculturalism discourse conceals "the binary opposition between the (white) self and the (non-white) other, but reinscribes it in a different fashion" (p. 147). As Hall (1993) articulates (black) ethnicity with his encoding and decoding model of communication, Ang has an insight into "the very condition of in-betweenness" in that hybridity "alerts us to the incommensurability of differences, their ultimately irreducible resistance to complete dissolution" (p. 17). Adopting Iris Marion Young's (1990, p. 318) concept of *being together of strangers*, she concludes, "the complicated entanglement of togetherness in difference has become a normal state of affairs" (p. 17). Her concept of togetherness-in-difference is inspired by her experiences with the transnational sense of Chinese togetherness. She also warns that the rhetoric of hybridity can be easily abused by politics and co-opted in a discourse of multiculturalism. In the context of all cultures in modernity that are "always-already hybrid" (p. 197), she positions herself as "a citizen and co-resident of this country [Australia]" and contends that the hybridity alleviates the fears of cultural loss and exclusion in a more modest and practical way (p. 158). In this sense, her notion of togetherness-in-difference refers to her translating duty "between different regimes of culture and knowledge in order to facilitate the creation of a sense of shared reality" (p. 158). She suggests,

> The concept of hybridity should be mobilized to address and analyse the fundamental uneasiness inherent in our global condition of togetherness-in-difference. This unease has been historically produced, in that we are still overwhelmingly captured by the dominant habit of thinking about ourselves and the world in terms of identity, ethnic, national and otherwise. . . In short, hybridity is not only about fusion and synthesis, but also about friction and tension, about ambivalence and incommensurability, about the contestations and interrogations that go hand in hand with the heterogeneity, diversity and multiplicity we have to deal with as we live together-in-difference.
>
> (p. 200)

Beyond cultural diversity   29

Ang's together-in-difference seems to be a synthesised concept of Said's manifest and latent Orientalism, Bhabha's cultural hybridity, Spivak's role of intellectuals and epistemic facture, and Hall's emergent ethnicity. Ang regards hybridity as a reference point of a non-dualistic approach to contemporary cultural studies (2003, p. 145). She argues that hybridity "destabilises established cultural power relations between white and black, coloniser and colonised, centre and periphery, the 'West' and the 'rest', not through a mere inversion of these hierarchical dualisms, but by throwing into question these very binaries through a process of boundary-blurring transculturation" (p. 148). In addition, her interpretation of diaspora in terms of hybridity is similar to Hall's emergent ethnicity in which "diaspora relies on the 'ethnic group' as the main constituent of the diasporic community" (p. 149). This raises the following questions: How does a process of boundary-blurring transculturation break the hierarchical dualisms? In what way can an ethnic group (or culture) (re-)gain the subject position in cultural diversity or culturally hybridised environments? And what is the process of boundary-blurring transculturation?

Both Ang and Hall use the concept of hybridity to address the limitations of binary systems and to argue for the incommensurability of differences and the irreducible resistance that upholds authentic cultural identities and ethnicities. In short, they propose the positive conception of ethnicity. Hypothetically speaking, they argue that ethnic groups can regain their subject position, distorted and interrupted by the binary systems, through non-dualistic understandings of ethnicity and cultural diversity. Metaphysically speaking, however, the relationship between the positive conception of ethnicity and ethnic groups is unstable and unsure whether the non-dualistic approach represents the ontological status of distinct ethnic identities. This unclarity is derived from a methodological issue of how two different frameworks or paradigms can co-exist without undermining each other.

1.3 A methodological approach to super-diversity

Three postcolonialists, Gilroy, Vertovec, and Amin, have elaborated on methodological understandings of cultural diversity in order to break down the hierarchical dualism to restore ethnicity and to bring it to the subject position in the context of cultural diversity.

Gilroy (1993) argues *double consciousness* for the black Atlantic as a space of transnational cultural construction and attacks contemporary forms of cultural nationalism as those diasporic people are separated by origin and at the same time, produce an explicitly transnational and intercultural perspective (or cultural hybridity). He uses the notion of the black Atlantic to "explode the dualistic structure that puts Africa, authenticity, purity, and origin in crude opposition to the Americas, hybridity, creolisation, and rootlessness" (p. 199). He describes the black Atlantic as a counterculture to European modernism engendering essentialist versions of racial identity and racial nationalism. In this way, he uses the notion to produce "an explicitly transnational and intercultural perspective" against ethnic absolutisms (p. 15). His transnational and intercultural perspective

30 *Metaphysical understanding of culture*

recognises "the value of specific and divergent local or regional developments within culture, while relating them to a metaculture" (Barson, 2010, p. 11). To go beyond the binary opposition between national and (traditional) diaspora perspectives, Gilroy (1993) places "the black Atlantic world in a webbed network [in a sense of rhizome], between the local and the global" (p. 29). His double consciousness drawn from Du Bois's intraracial differences of rural black populations indicates a split between subjectivity and race consciousness (p. 13). It is an African American's "awareness of existing simultaneously both within and outside the dominant culture" which is "one of [the] defining characteristics of black Atlantic expressive culture" (Barson, 2010, p. 10). In relation to globalised multiculturalism and its commodification of ethnicity, Gilroy adopts the metaphor of *rhizome* that represents a resilient and environmentally responsive community. He decisively emphasises authentic interaction among diasporic blacks that generates their expressive culture. He also argues that intercultural connectedness can emerge from that interaction on a rhizomatic network. Such an ontological or metaphysical understanding of intercultural interaction makes progress on the positive conception of ethnicity. In fact, the rhizomatic network not only challenges the dualistic systems and undermines cultural authority but also offers an ontic structure for ethnic authenticity, which fills the deficits of Ang's and Hall's non-dualistic understandings.

Gilroy adopts Deleuze and Guattari's (1980/1987) rhizomatic theory to justify the African diasporic cultural history that has double consciousness of a complex picture of cultural exchange and continuity. He also criticises the homogenised black Atlantic expressive culture that has been facilitated by Western essentialists or positivists. However, Matory (2012) criticises Gilroy's term "diaspora", which contains an arborescent metaphor, and argues, "the history of *a culture* involves the same unidirectional spread and temporal inequality that 'roots' suggests" (p. 106 [emphasis added]). As Matory explains, the arborescent metaphor means that there is "the unique authenticity, the unchanging nature, and the defining character of the homeland" (p. 106), which seems opposite of the rhizome metaphor. In comparison to the arborescent metaphor, he reminds us that the rhizome metaphor should refer to a unity of organism rather than of process that forms new and distinct organisms like human social groupings do. However, he does not address the fact that Deleuze and Guattari use the dualism between rhizomes and arborescences in neither an ontological nor axiological sense, but to subvert, per se (Miller, 2001). In other words, the dualism indicates that rhizomes have their own hierarchical root systems (rhizoids) to provide nutrients and water. This means that the metaphysical boundary of a culture (i.e., an independent value system) is inevitable, although it is dualistic. In this understanding, dualism can be used as a process to restore the ontological equity and axiological interaction of cultures. A critical point here is that when dualism as a process resides in rhizomatic networks, it can define cultural identity as independent and unique. While prioritising cultural exchange across territorial boundaries, Gilroy highlights uninterrupted memory of Africa. In rhizomatic networks, as he argues, a "culture does not come in temporally, geographically, or populationally bounded units", but as "our metaphors and metonyms that chop

Beyond cultural diversity 31

it up into units and map a logic of collective being and action" (p. 106). In the networks, cultures constantly and organically manifest themselves through interaction with other social units such as races, classes, genders, ethnicities, and religions. Thus Matory should have questioned how that dualistic hierarchy should be shaped for cultural diversity and how it works for interculturality. In addition, Gilroy needs to clarify the position of the memory (or ethnic or cultural uniqueness) in the networks and how its intercultural connectedness emerges in the networks. These mean that the term cultural diversity needs to be further explored in a methodological way.

Vertovec (2007) renews prior postcolonial theorists' understandings of cultural diversity in social science. Unlike other postcolonialists mentioned earlier who focus on English literary studies, Vertovec's application of the notion of *super-diversity* in social science research expands the discourse of cultural diversity to a methodological dimension. He claims that the diversity of Britain today is characterised by super-diversity that "underline[s] a level and kind of complexity surpassing anything the country has previously experienced" (p. 1024). The notion of super-diversity reflects "the proliferation and mutually conditioning effects of additional variables" including "differential immigration statutes and their concomitant entitlements and restrictions of rights, divergent labour market experiences, discrete gender and age profiles, patterns of spatial distribution, and mixed local area responses by service providers and residents" (p. 1025). The interplay of those variables indicates super-diversity. He argues that social scientists and policy makers need to take into account that the outcomes of "new conjunctions and interactions of variables" surpass the traditional ways and change the nature of various ethnic communities (p. 1025). He proposes the following nine areas that social scientific investigation of super-diversity could influence: new patterns of inequality and prejudice, new patterns of segregation, new experiences of space and contact, new forms of cosmopolitanism and creolisation, new bridgeheads of migration, secondary migration patterns, transnationalism and integration, methodological innovation, and research-policy nexus (pp. 1045–1047). He argues that such social scientific challenges, which super-diversity imposes, cannot be accepted by the conventional ethnicity studies. This is because the challenges require a methodological and theoretical change by considering "the interaction of multiple axes of differentiation" (p. 1049). He states,

> Research on super-diversity could encourage new techniques in quantitatively testing the relation between multiple variables and in qualitatively undertaking ethnographic exercises that are multisited (considering different localities and space within a given locality) and multi-group (defined in terms of the variable convergence of ethnicity, status, gender and other criteria of super-diversity) . . . the application of a revitalized situational approach . . . a set of interactions are observed and an analysis "works outward" to take account of not only the meaning of interactions to participants themselves, but also the encompassing criteria and structures impacting upon the positions, perceptions and practices of these actors.
>
> (p. 1046)

32 *Metaphysical understanding of culture*

Vertovec's methodological innovation towards super-diversity encourages social science researchers to take a look at the convergence of various social units. However, while the convergence is justified by the concept of super-diversity, it is unclear how an individual can participate in the convergence – what I call *interculturality.* Should the individual aim to undermine and ultimately abandon the traditional ways – the hierarchical dualism that perpetuates the delusion of (false) ethnicity? What methodological assumptions should researchers and educators accept to facilitate intercultural interaction inclusive of the dualism? As seen earlier, Gilroy's term "diaspora" contains both arborescent and rhizomatic metaphors, and his rhizomatic networks are inclusive of the unchanged nature of black (culture and ethnicity), although it is cognitive (memory). This means that Gilroy's theory is more methodological than that of Vertovec. Although Vertovec's super-diversity is not exclusive of the legitimacy of the variable convergence of ethnicities, his methodological innovation seems not to offer any change in methodology, but to encourage researchers to consider multiple variables and groups. Indeed, he needs to clarify his words, "the interaction of multiple axes of differentiation", in a methodological and metaphysical sense. In this context, I pay attention to Amin's concept of *convivium* as *living with difference* that offers a threshold of the methodological innovation, as the concept focuses on the interaction between people who have different cultural backgrounds.

Like other postcolonial theorists, Amin (2012) characterises today's living in the West as constitutive pluralism, hybridity, and convivial multiculture that sustains everyday conviviality in situations of intercultural co-existence. He (2013) observes minorities, migrants, and dissidents as *strangers* (or vulnerable outsiders) in European societies and questions "the conundrum of how, why and when diverse practices of intolerance, vernacular and institutional, manage to find grip in European societies that are constitutively mixed and plural" (p. 2). The concept of conviviality seems to offer a new thinking framework for cultural diversity in everyday practice. Gilroy (2004) also describes conviviality as "the processes of cohabitation and interaction that have made multiculture an ordinary feature of urban life in Britain" (p. xi). In this sense, Amin rejects prevailing sociological accounts and current policies that focus on community cohesion and mixed housing, which is based on an assumption of fixed minority ethnic identities. Alternatively, he claims that the quality of social contact and interaction needs to be built based on "identifying, for example, bridging and bonding social capital, mixed neighbourhoods and public spaces, and interaction between people from different backgrounds as the measure of good society" (2013, p. 3). He argues that the encounter between strangers has been invaded by hybridity, heterogeneity, creolisation, and multiplicity, but the current multiculturalism ignores these everyday encounters of difference. In other words, the divided plural society cannot be explained by contemporary cultural accounts that focus on customary practices of minorities. In this context, he proposes "living with difference" that is "the balance of force between the every convivial and the everyday phonotypical" by acknowledging "the value of daily encounters" that "work[s] on obdurate prejudices through civilities of engagement and collaboration" (p. 6). He argues that a new direction of policy and public services on this diverse society requires an endorsement of "every *convivium*: its tacit pluralism, its practised and deliberative nature, its daily compromises, its pragmatic negotiation of uncertainty and risk" (p. 7). Coincidentally, Vertovec (2010, p. 86) also articulates "new experience of space and contact" in social scientific investigation of super-diversity by citing Amin's (2002) words: "Habitual contact in itself is no guarantor of cultural exchange" (p. 969). Vertovec contends that Amin's hypothesis needs to be examined to identify "how people define their differences in relationship to uneven material and spatial conditions" (p. 87). At least in approaching intercultural interaction, both Amin and Vertovec agree that the interactive relationships between people who have different cultures in everyday lives and public spaces have to be investigated with a view to facilitating authentic interaction. Although both do not negate the necessity of intercultural interaction, they are unclear as to what methodological understanding is required for it. Instead, both propose new detailed categories of research objects extracted from the phenomena of super-diversity and everyday encounters of difference. While they attack dualisms, they do not address whether they need to introspect their methodology and metaphysical assumptions that may be influenced by the dualisms. This issue also appears in empirical studies that use the concept of conviviality.

For example, Wise and Velayutham (2014) investigate conviviality in everyday multiculturalism with a series of ethnographic examples under three themes: spatial ordering, connecting and bridging work, and intercultural habitus in Sydney and Singapore. Their research question is "to what extent does intercultural knowledge play a part in convivial modes of co-habitation?" (p. 410). They emphasise the importance of being aware that "there are always larger forces at work: class, structure, social fields and the distribution of forms of capital" (p. 423). They criticise a narrow view of intercultural relations (i.e., phenomenology of interpersonal contact). By adopting Amin's concept of *situated surplus*, they argue for *conviviality* that can capture something "more embodied, habitual, sensuous and affective that carries over beyond the moment" (p. 425). They do not make any specific response to *the role of intercultural knowledge*, but introduce some intercultural cases: a white employer preparing some *Halal* food for his Muslim employee, a restaurant owner in Bali who actively welcomes everyone and openly condemns fake Muslims who committed the 2002 Bali bombings, sharing suitable foods between culturally and religiously different Malay and Chinese neighbours, and a religious and/cultural debate on the fate of a dead pet mouse among Christian Chinese, Muslim Malay, and Hindu Indian children. It becomes apparent that there is no methodological innovation in the research. In fact their research is aimed at capturing various everyday activities among people who have different cultural and religious backgrounds.

1.4 Conclusion: Metaphysical tensions between cultures

Overall, postcolonialists argue that ethnicity and nationhood are constructed through binary oppositions of cultural representation, and those concepts are given specific meanings in the context of cultural diversity. They attempt to deconstruct the dualistic approach to cultures and reconstruct either independent and unique (ethnic) cultural identity or authentic intercultural interaction. In this sense, their

34 *Metaphysical understanding of culture*

arguments can be divided into three different understandings of cultural diversity. First, there are those who articulate the independence and uniqueness of individual cultures while addressing the contexts of cultural diversity. Said's *latent Orientalism* refers to an unchanging and permanent characteristic of ethnic cultures. Spivak's *othering* offers potential for the uniqueness of cultural identity that cannot be homogenised with the colonised others. Gilroy's *double consciousness of cultural exchange* also highlights the uninterrupted memory of ethnicity that determines the logic of collective being and action. Hall attempts to conceptualise authentic ethnicities and cultural identities by decoupling the concept of ethnicity from the epistemic violence produced from binary oppositions of cultural representation. Second, some other postcolonial theorists pay more attention to intercultural phenomena such as hybridity, heterogeneity, creolisation, and multiplicity, and offer transcultural concepts extracted from the ambivalence of cultural diversity. Bhabha's *Third Space* posits the ambivalent space of enunciation where the communicative and interpretive relationship between speaker and interlocutor is broken and each becomes the subject. Ang's *together-in-difference* inspired in a transnational sense indicates that the incommensurability of differences produces irreducible resistance and thus its hybridity in itself becomes a normal stage of affairs. Such transcultural concepts are used to deconstruct ideological cultural knowledge and to build new preconditions for the articulation of cultural difference. Third, there is a group that offers methodological approaches to cultural diversity. Vertovec's *super-diversity* justifies the variable convergence of ethnicities and extends the research ranges of social science to Amin's *everyday encounters of difference*. Amin argues that pluralism, hybridity, and dynamic nature of cultural diversity sustain intercultural co-existence and thus high-quality interaction is a descriptive measure of a good society. In addition, Gilroy's *diasporic cultural exchange* and *continuity* indicates that ethnic authenticity emerges when both dualism and ethnicity are viewed in rhizomatic networks, which sustain interculturality.

A pedagogical implication from those three groups of postcolonialist theories is that teachers need to restore authentic cultural identities tainted by colonial ideology and cultural hybridity and to facilitate authentic intercultural interaction by assuming the existence of distinct cultures. Their proposed non-dualistic thinking and approaches could enable teachers to open up new horizons and encourage students to hold the subject-subject relationship in intercultural interaction. However, their arguments may be metaphysically vulnerable when authentic cultural identity is justified by the ambivalence of hybridity without exploring its cultural identity. In other words, they attack the (ontological) dualism with the (epistemological) dualism, or vice versa. As Gilroy's rhizomatic networks imply, the problem of dualism is not itself, but when it is used to conceal (non-dualistic) ontology and, as a result, it ignores the possibility of axiology and has no methodological questions on intercultural interaction. In this sense, the above postcolonialists' non-dualistic approach to intercultural interaction is methodologically unstable to the extent that it is unclear whether or not authentic ethnicities or cultural identities liberated from the binary systems can be sustained in the (dualistic) education systems. Consequently, a pedagogical approach to cultural diversity requires metaphysical understanding of *other* cultures and interculturality with three dimensions:

ontology, epistemology, and axiology. This approach could address the ideological power of epistemological dualism in cultural diversity, the ontological justification for cultures that determines their uniqueness and authenticity, and the emergent properties or values from interaction between cultures. In these ways, we can disclose metaphysical conflicts and tensions between cultures that binary oppositions of cultural representation conceal. For example, liberal individualists who support binary oppositions of cultural representation may feel a fear of losing their (liberal individualism based) identity when they practise cultural values of Indigeneity – the self (precisely the egoistic cognitive horizon) merges with its environment, which causes the loss of boundaries between self and environment. On the other hand, when participating in a liberal individualist culture, Indigenous people who practise cultural identity of interrelatedness may initially aim to gain a sense of belonging in the host community and may experience extreme social loneliness because their expectation of ontic (or spiritual) mergence hardly occurs in that individualistic culture. In another context of cultural diversity, collectivistic selfishness or protectionism can be materialised and implemented to interrupt the enhancement of individuality that is perceived as a threat to the spirit of group unity and consolidation, whereas individualistic selfishness or independence espouses the logic of power (therefore, violence) against collectivistic cultures in the sense that it may threaten (individualistic) well-being and human rights. Hence the nature of metaphysical conflicts and tensions gives rise to the hermeneutic foundations for intercultural interaction. Interculturality remains latent and invisible to one's cultural horizon in a sense of institutionalised and personalised mono-cultural value systems, but becomes explicit when one is aware of situational tensions of values of both cultures. This is the reason why metaphysical approaches (i.e., ontological, epistemological, and axiological) become the necessary condition for intercultural interaction, which will be unfolded in the next chapters.

References

Amin, A. (2002). Ethnicity and the multicultural city: Living with diversity. *Environment and Planning A, 34*(6), 959–980.

Amin, A. (2012). *Land of strangers*. Cambridge: Polity Press.

Amin, A. (2013). Land of strangers. *Identities: Global Studies in Culture and Power, 20*(1), 1–8.

Ang, I. (2001). *On not speaking Chinese: Living between Asia and the West*. London: Routledge.

Ang, I. (2003). Together-in-difference: Beyond diaspora, into hybridity. *Asian Studies Review, 27*(2), 141–154.

Barson, T. (2010). Introduction: Modernism and the Black Atlantic. In T. Barson & P. Gorschlüter (Eds.), *Afro Modern: Journeys through the Black Atlantic* (pp. 8–27). Liverpool: Tate Publishing.

Bhabha, H.K. (1994). *The location of culture*. London and New York: Routledge.

Bhabha, H.K. (2006). Cultural diversity and cultural differences. In B. Ashcroft, G. Griffiths & H. Tiffin (Eds.), *The Post-Colonial Studies Reader* (2nd ed.) (pp. 155–162). New York: Routledge.

36 Metaphysical understanding of culture

Deleuze, G., & Guattari, F. (1987). *A thousand plateaus: Capitalism and schizophrenia.* (B. Massumi, Trans.). Minneapolis: University of Minnesota Press. (Original work published 1980)

Gilroy, P. (1993). *The Black Atlantic: Modernity and double consciousness.* London: Verso.

Gilroy, P. (2004). *After empire: Melancholia or convivial culture?* Oxon: Routledge.

Hall, S. (1989). New ethnicities. In K. Mercer (Ed.), *Black Film, British Cinema ICA Documents 7* (pp. 441–449). London: Institute for Contemporary Arts.

Hall, S. (1993). Encoding/decoding. In S. During (Ed.), *The Cultural Studies Reader* (pp. 90–103). London and New York: Routledge.

Lacan, J. (1978). *The four fundamental concepts of psycho-analysis.* (J.A. Miller, Trans.), New York: W.W. Norton and company Inc. (Original work published 1964)

Matory, J.L. (2012). The homeward ship: Analytic tropes as maps of and for African-diaspora cultural history. In R. Hardin & K.M. Clarke (Eds.), *Transforming Ethnographic Knowledge* (pp. 93–112). Madison: University of Wisconsin Press.

Meer, N., & Modood, T. (2012). How does interculturalism contrast with multiculturalism? *Journal of Intercultural Studies, 33*(2), 175–196.

Miller, C.L. (2001). The postidentitarian predicament in the footnotes of A Thousand Plateaus: Nomadology, anthropology, and authority. In G. Genosko (Ed.), *Deleuze and Guattari: Critical Assessments of Leading Philosophies* (Vol. III) (pp. 1113–1149). London and New York: Routledge.

Moore-Gilbert, B. (2000). Spivak and Bhabha. In H. Schwartz & R. Sangeeta (Eds.), *A Companion to Postcolonial Studies* (pp. 451–466). Oxford: Blackwell.

Moore-Gilbert, B., Stanton, G., & Maley, W. (1997). *Postcolonial criticism.* London: Routledge.

Morton, S. (2003). *Gayatri Chakravorty Spivak.* London: Routledge.

Said, E. (1979). *Orientalism.* New York: Vintage Books.

Spivak. G. C. (1985). The Rani of Sirmur: An essay in reading the archives. *History and Theory, 24*(3), 247–272.

Spivak, G.C. (1988). Can the subaltern speak. In C. Nelson & L. Grossberg (Eds.), *Marxism and the Interpretation of Culture* (pp. 271–313). Urbana: University of Illinois Press.

Vertovec, S. (2007). Super-diversity and its implications. *Ethnic and Racial Studies, 20*(6), 1024–1054.

Vertovec, S. (2010). Super-diversity and its implications. In S. Vertovec (Ed.), *Anthropology of Migration and Multiculturalism: New Directions* (pp. 65–96). London: Routledge.

Wise, A., & Velayutham, S. (2014). Conviviality in everyday multiculturalism: Some brief comparisons between Singapore and Sydney. *European Journal of Cultural Studies, 17*(4), 406–430.

Young, I.M. (1990). The ideal of community and the politics of difference. In L.J. Nicholson (Ed.), *Feminism/Postmodernism* (pp. 300–323). New York: Routledge.

2 Metaphysical aspects of culture

The previous chapter indicates that metaphysical approaches to cultural diversity can be a solution for repositioning all cultures as agents of social changes in intercultural interaction. In social science, researchers have mostly agreed with the significance of ontological and epistemological questions because ontological questions of research (e.g., what is there that can be known about it) logically lead to its epistemological questions (e.g., what is the relationship between the researcher and what can be known). On the other hand, there is some disagreement on an axiological question (e.g., whether research can be objective and value-free). For example, conventional researchers tend to hold a neutral and objective position in their research, whereas interpretivists believe that values are deeply entrenched in researchers' unconscious minds (Schuh & Barab, 2008). This contrast indicates that objectivity can be found in epistemology and also appears as knowledge that represents ontological status of concepts and objects in terms of the resistance to change. However, ontological and epistemological questions entail axiological questions that affect formulation of research questions, choice of methods, and interpretation of data (Oancea, 2016). When we focus on axiological aspects of research, a benefit is that we are able to talk to our unexamined paradigms/worldviews. Interestingly, this allows us to identify metaphysical tensions between ontological, epistemological, and axiological assumptions and facilitate in-depth methodological justification, because being aware of axiological questions merges us into the research context. In the concept of metaphysical tensions, for example, a methodology does not mean a theoretical framework or lens by which we use various methods to collect, analyse and/or interpret data, but a meta-methodology that is aimed at justifying how a chosen methodology is associated with ontology, epistemology, and axiology. In other words, a meta-methodology is an attempt to think about our ontological, epistemological, and axiological concerns in a research question. To sum up, the three dimensions of metaphysics and methodological justification can be used as the pedagogical foundations for intercultural interaction as all participants are supposed to hold the subject position.

Educational and instructional theories are constructed and linked to a particular set of philosophical assumptions (Schuh & Barab, 2008). Pedagogical strategies and methods are influenced by particular philosophical assumptions and educational theories that are implicit in instructional design (Duffy & Jonassen, 1992).

38 Metaphysical understanding of culture

In essence, a particular set of philosophical assumptions has its own ontological, epistemological, and axiological interpretations that are greatly associated with educational models and pedagogical strategies (Freimuth, 2009). Thus our reconceived understanding of such interpretations plays a crucial role in opening up new discourses of education (Freimuth, 2009). In (multicultural) education, ontology reflects cultural conventions and the resulting educational models and systems intensify those conventions (Breuker, Muntjewerff, & Bredeweg, 1999), epistemology refers to the nature of knowledge and its justification that constitute a cultural attitude towards particular knowledge and its epistemic process (Knorr-Cetina, 1999), and axiology deals with the role of values that is closely related to cultural and moral education or the metaphysical status of morality (Hinman, 2008). In sum, our views of reality (or being, existence), truth (or knowledge), and goodness (or right) determine how we perceive educational systems, pedagogical values, and instructional methods. In practice, as our metaphysical assumptions influence our examination of a specific form of knowledge (or discourse, narrative, framework), inversely, we can use them to reconceive the knowledge as a philosophical basis for further research. In this sense, a metaphysical approach to multicultural education is not performed as a predetermined set of objectives. Rather, when the three metaphysical dimensions are holistically used to build meta-questions about the essence of interculturality, we can reveal cultural horizons for intercultural interaction. In other words, our interpretations of cultural concepts, narratives, and doctrines with ontological, epistemological, and axiological dimensions can be used to reconceive a pedagogical basis for intercultural interaction. This approach is also expected to minimise teachers' unintentional intensification of a dominant culture and marginalisation of other cultures in their pedagogical practices.

2.1 Ontological justification

Ontology as a branch of philosophy within metaphysics deals with the ultimate nature of existence, being, and reality and is aimed at revealing the essence of things. In education, ontology is used to define "what are considered truths about knowledge, information and the world" (Schuh & Barab, 2008, p. 70). In English, naming something, either a physical or abstract structure (e.g., teaching and a teacher), declares its potential existence (Alexander, Chambliss, & Price, 2006). Reasoning is used to determine whether a named entity exists or not or to identify what attributes or categories that entity has (Alexander *et al.*, 2006). In a practical sense, ontology serves as "enabling knowledge sharing and reuse" (Gruber, 1995, p. 907). In knowledge sharing contexts, ontology indicates "a specification of a conceptualization" and thus becomes "a description of the concepts and relationships and can exist for an agent or a community of agents" (Gruber, 1995, p. 908). First, ontology as a conceptualisation means that the body of knowledge is represented through "an abstract or a simplified view of the world that we wish to represent for some purpose" (Gruber, 1995, p. 907). Second, ontology as a specification is used for making ontological commitments to an entity and, practically, it enables agents to share tacit knowledge as well as

Metaphysical interculturality 39

explicit one with other agents through a common ontological ground. In knowledge sharing contexts, as a consequence, ontological justification reflects educational discourses, which lays the theoretical foundations for educational models and systems that, in turn, intensify the discourses.

The notion of ontological justification shares its fundamental idea with meta-ontology that deals with ontological propositions. A meta-ontological question is not a question about the nature of the world, whether it exists or not, but a question about what to do, which is an ontological commitment about whether to adopt a given conceptual framework in question (Thomasson, 2005). Asking whether a thing exists or not itself is ambiguous because, even if there is an objectively correct answer, it will be determined by whether one accepts it or not. This position also gives a benefit to interculturality. In intercultural education, for example, a question of ontology justification for teachers is not only to be aware of their own cultural assumptions and values but also to investigate how those are structured and affect intercultural interaction, its design and implementation. In this way, ontological justification in intercultural education is a pre-requisite for teachers' ontological inquiries about the conditions of interculturality that tells them how intercultural interaction should be designed in order for all cultures to be true. In practice, it requests teachers to place all cultures in an ontologically equal position, although each has different epistemological and axiological positions in different contexts. More significantly, it encourages teachers and students to be aware of their own cultural perspectives because the ontological equality defines their positions to compensate for inequalities in epistemological and axiological positions.

Ontological justification also subverts ontological questions on education research. For example, the three layers of ontological questions on education research proposed by Alexander *et al.* (2006) can be simply subverted. The questions are (a) when researchers treat learning as an entity, does the existence of learning need to be empirically investigated; (b) to demonstrate knowledge acquisitions or achievement gains that presume the existence of learning, do researchers attempt to categorise or examine the attributes of learning; and (c) to verify the collected data, do researchers have inquiries about the correspondence between the data and the actual phenomenon in which validity is often replaced by reliability? (pp. 6–7). The subversion begins with probing into the presumptions of those questions that drive researchers to believe that knowledge acquisition is an attribute of the existence of learning. The three questions are formed to achieve research objectivity by assuming that the existence of learning needs to be empirically proved with a valid category/framework that makes a direct connection between the collected data and the phenomenon, which is formed with deductive reasoning. This means that an ontological concern of the questions is not whether learning exists or not, but how self-exclusion is implemented throughout an entire research process to achieve objectivity. This deductive reasoning has no reflection on the assumption by accepting a general belief that knowledge acquisition is an attribute of the existence of learning. Thus each question can be subverted in a reverse manner: (a) does the collected data correspond to the phenomenon as a whole or part, (b) does the chosen category/

40 Metaphysical understanding of culture

framework reflect the phenomenon, and (c) is the research question justified with the researcher's belief? These subversive questions point to self-inclusion in which the researcher is aware that the research question is based on incomplete observations and reflects a particular belief in the name of a generally accepted truth. In this sense, ontological justification is neither deductive nor inductive, but abductive in that it equates all cultures as being networked and reveals a larger space (intercultural networks) upholding all cultures. In this way, the subject-subject relationship of all participants can be sustained in intercultural interaction

When a researcher believes that he/she can be excluded from the research context, ontological reductionism operates as an ideological apparatus to conceal or ignore his/her ontological assumptions. As seen in the previous chapter, such a phenomenon is identical to the metaphysical limitations of binary oppositions of cultural representation that postcolonialists criticise. In multicultural education, it causes a common, but deadly problem that teachers unintentionally exercise othering processes in their pedagogical strategies and lesson design by excluding participants' culturally constructed selves. To avoid such ontological reductionism, consequently, ontological justification can be used as a pre-conceptual marker that leads teachers to confront the meanings of chosen or given *concepts*, to identify properties in different *contexts*, and to validate diverse perceptions and experiences related to *stakeholders*. For example, teachers can make the following inquires: (a) what are the ontological conditions that sustain the existence of a chosen concept (e.g., cultural diversity, cultural assimilation, cultural integration, cultural inclusivity) as a learning entity, (b) to what extent do teachers and students get involved in the properties of a given context (e.g., cultural differences, whiteness-dominant, non-whiteness driven, intercultural interaction), and (c) how does a stakeholder(s) (e.g., host community, immigrants, minority ethnic/religious groups, Indigenous) validate their engagement in cultural equity? These questions as ontological justification for interculturality *reveal* the conditions of the existence of interculturality in a culturally diverse environment rather than *define* the nature of being and reality predetermined by an uncritically given epistemic framework. In this sense, the ontological justification for this research focuses on the ontic structure of cultural diversity and interculturality in intercultural interaction. Furthermore, investigating ontological assumptions embedded in prevailing multicultural education models should be helpful to understand how the concept of cultural diversity is constructed within the context of a dominant culture, which will be seen in the next chapter.

2.2 Epistemological assumptions

Epistemology addresses the "origins, nature, methods, and limits of human knowledge" (Reber cited in Schuh & Barab, 2008, p. 70) and focuses on questions about knowledge justification and how to support learners in coming to know (Schuh & Barab, 2008). The three concerns of epistemology in education are *what is knowledge, how is knowledge acquired*, and *what do people know?* These concerns are related to epistemic justification, knowledge acquisition, and knowing frameworks.

2.2.1 *What is knowledge?*

Plato's theory of knowledge, known as a *justified true belief* (JTB), has prevailed for many centuries (Turri, 2012). Alexander *et al.* (2006) explain that knowledge requires both truth and falsity and this requires justification: Knowledge requires complete evidence when false propositions cannot be known. It also requires a belief in one's faith that proper justification will prove to be valid or successful. In such ways, true and belief become jointly sufficient for knowledge. If an assumption or a claim is not justified, its understanding remains a belief rather than knowledge. In educational contexts, however, epistemology builds a practical belief or a cultural attitude towards knowledge by understanding how a learner comes to know and how a knowing process can be facilitated (Knorr-Cetina, 1999). If so, how can a belief or an attitude become knowledge? In 1963, anti-JTB was demonstrated by Gettier, which most philosophers have accepted because the tripartite analysis of knowledge was shown to be incomplete. Gettier argues that one's belief is not the same as knowledge if its true proposition cannot be justified, although it may be justified and true. In other words, when a belief is both true and well supported by evidence, it becomes a JTB, but it is not sufficient to be knowledge because it can be caused by coincidence.

The responses to Gettier's challenge are varied: First, infallibilism – "justification that is incompatible with the belief's being false" (Hetherington, 2002, p. 84); second, indefeasibilism – "knowledge is genuinely undefeated justified true belief for the reasons that justify one's belief" (Turri, 2012, p. 252); and third, reliabilism – a belief is justified only through "the truth-conduciveness of a belief-forming process, method, or other epistemologically relevant factor" (Goldman, 2011, para. 1). What is meant by justification and what makes beliefs justified? It seems that additional conditions to JTB are required to count it as knowledge. Lecser (1996) argues, "One that allows the criteria for being justified to vary according to the individual's context and goals, thereby possibly making justification and knowledge more accessible than other JTB accounts" (p. 108). For example, one who has a justified belief can claim to attain knowledge when no one requires justification and, thus, one's belief is true and no additional justification is needed for one's epistemic situation (Lecser, 1996). Foley (1993) suggests that a level of justification does not refer to "a process of making up one's mind", but a "process of deep reflection" (cited in Lecser, 1996, p. 121). Turri (2012) also advocates individuals' determination of a level of justification. He argues, "A person's intellectual powers . . . are the source of epistemic justification" and "knowledge is true belief manifesting intellectual power is basically to say 'K = J > TB', where the arrow represents the relation of manifestation" (p. 258). This means, when a level of justification is made by one's true belief based on his/her intellectual powers, regardless of its methods, it becomes knowledge. As Lecser points out, eventually, one should clarify how a level of justification is aligned with one's goal that is determined by one's will.

It seems we are coming back to Gettier's anti-JTB because if a level of justification is determined by one's intellectual powers or abilities, then what is believed

42 Metaphysical understanding of culture

must be true brief until someone asks any question about its assumption. However, the similarity between Foley and Turri offers an interesting implication that it is not a matter of what knowledge is, but how justification is positioned for knowledge. While the difference between Foley and Turri appears in their recognition of the source of epistemic justification, in which Foley's is a process of deep reflection and Turri's is an intellectual ability, both reject methodologism, obsessive idealism, and scepticism towards knowledge. This means that the term justification in epistemology can be non-deontologically defined, thus a collectively perceived concept (e.g., interculturality, multiculturality, and cultural diversity) as an entity holds its own metaphysical distinction and, therefore, is culturally bound. Thus, there is no culturally free concept.

Sainsbury and Tye (2012) also argue that the role of justification ensures that a true belief is not true by accident, but justified when it instantiates its probability for action. They explain,

> In the case of probabilification, most possible worlds that are relevantly similar to the actual worlds and at which the experience is accurate are worlds at which the belief is true. So there is no difficulty in grasping how the experience can provide a reason for having the belief.
>
> (p. 162)

This means that a belief becomes an actual world when it is formed in the normal way on the basis of an experience. The premise is "there is no fundamental difference between belief content and experience content" (Sainsbury & Tye, 2012, p. 161). The content of a belief can be a set of possible worlds in which that belief is true. Consequently, a non-deontological understanding of justification allows both deontological justification and probabilification to be acceptable as methods of knowledge justification in epistemology. The difference can be explained with *externalism* and *internalism*. Internalists claim that the conditions of all knowledge production occur in the subject's psychological states because justification is a matter of duty-fulfilment (a deontological aspect) (Pappas, 2013). Duty-fulfilment is internal and its factors justify beliefs (Pappas, 2013). On the other hand, externalists present a case that "children have knowledge and thus have justified beliefs" (Steup, 2013, para. 31), but their beliefs cannot be justified in an evidentialist way – resulting from the possession of evidence (Pappas, 2013). Hence justification is external and results from reliable processes. The role of justification for externalists is "the kind of objective probability needed for knowledge and only external conditions on justification imply this probability" (Steup, 2013, para. 32). Recalling that justification has a central role in the interaction between a subject and a decision support, both externalism and internalism should be considered the sources of ontological justification rather than the validation of JTB. This means that the difference instantiates probabilification and gives rise to varied epistemological frames forming *plural worlds* or *different realities*, while epistemic justification is related to a particular cultural framework that shows which one of the worlds we belong to or how we understand the existence of the world. In intercultural interaction, then, the

Metaphysical interculturality 43

question, *what is knowledge*, is shunted to *where is knowledge that justifies our belief* that is transcendental to our habitual first-person point of view (e.g., what it is and how it works).

2.2.2 How is knowledge acquired?

Learning theories are linked to a particular set of philosophical assumptions (Duffy & Jonassen, 1992; Schuh & Barab, 2008). For example, Skinner's behaviourism is based on objectivism, rationalism, and empiricism; Ausubel's cognitivism and Piaget's cognitive constructivism are related to pragmatism, rationalism, empiricism, and idealism; Vygotsky's socio-cultural constructivism is supportive of interpretivism, relativism, empiricism, and rationalism; and Lave and Wenger's situative theory is based on ecological realism, empiricism, and rationalism (Driscoll, 2005; Schuh & Barab, 2008). An epistemological question, *how is knowledge acquired*, is directly related to assumptions and commitments of those seven philosophical perspectives of education theories with respect to worldviews.

First, objectivists and realists support an independent real, physical world, which is separate from the mind, and thus knowledge is acquired through the mind by representing and corresponding to that external reality (Schuh & Barab, 2008). Second, empiricists hold that knowledge builds from experience and thus emphasises consistency of knowledge with experience (Schuh & Barab, 2008). They reject that we enter the world with a priori ideas and concepts, and their epistemology is to formulate an argument based on evidence of experience. In variants of empiricism, positivists advocate that valid knowledge is obtained only through empirical verification, whereas realists claim that reality exists independently of observers (Ross *et al.*, 2008). Third, idealists hold the belief that a priori processes primarily acquire knowledge because all mental representations retain all knowledge and experience (Schuh & Barab, 2008). They reject the existence of the mind as an independent object because they view that reality is psychological – to be is to be perceived. Fourth, rationalists, in contrast with empiricists and idealists, equally emphasise two areas for knowledge acquisition: (a) reason as the principle source of knowledge and (b) empirical data as the privileged status of sense data. Fifth, relativism, as Schuh and Barab (2008) point out, is not a specific philosophical perspective, but a general principle that places knowledge in relationships, contexts, and individuals' meaning constructions, and there is no absolute truth to the world. Sixth, and last, pragmatists tend to share "a fallibilist anti-Cartesian approach to the norms that govern inquiry" (Hookyway, 2010, para. 1) in which they endorse "the fallibilist view that any of our beliefs and method could turn out to be flawed" (Hookyway, 2010, para. 11). They support that knowledge is a causal consequence that is derived from the interaction between humans and the world, and their focus is on "what is good for us to believe" and "what the mind could do" (Schuh & Barab, 2008, p. 72).

These seven philosophical perspectives of education theories can be re-categorised into three groups in accordance with their views on *where is knowledge* because each perspective indicates a different place of knowledge. For

44 *Metaphysical understanding of culture*

objectivists, realists, and empiricists, first, knowledge exists in reality, and they prioritise representation, correspondence, and accuracy of the mind towards reality. They tend to believe that our knowledge is a posteriori, dependent upon sense experience (Markie, 2013). For idealists and rationalists, second, knowledge exists as a form of mental status because reality is psychologically constructed. The three theses of rationalism – "the intuition/deduction thesis, the innate knowledge thesis, and the innate concept thesis" – advocate that the existence of knowledge is gained through a priori, independently of experience (Markie, 2013, para. 16). Third, relativists' and pragmatists' epistemological inquiry are not about acquiring absolute certainty, but about how to acquire "methods of inquiry that contribute to our making fallible progress" (Hookyway, 2010, para. 44). In this sense, an inquiry becomes an activity, which undermines "a sharp dichotomy between theoretical and practical judgements" (Hookyway, 2010). Consequently, this new categorisation in terms of *where is knowledge* indicates that we perceive knowledge of empirical facts about the physical world through our senses, and all forms of knowledge require some amount of reasoning such as analysis of data and making inference. Regardless of whether knowledge is constructed by human society (idealism) or through human-to-human interaction (relativism and pragmatism), a point running through these perspectives is that all knowledge would either/both come from the mind or/and pass through the mind to reality. Specifically, as seen in idealist epistemology, intuition is also believed to have access to a priori knowledge that would be constructed by human society. Furthermore, constructivists, based on relativism and pragmatism, presume that knowledge can be transmitted from an individual to another or constructed in collaboration. Hence the mind has a structure that enables us to acquire knowledge and, in this sense, the mind is metaphysically structured. This interpretation helps us ontologically justify the epistemological question *how is knowledge acquired*, in that it refers to *which mind structure do we have to acquire a particular knowledge*. This ontological justification for epistemology offers a significant pedagogical implication that knowledge exists in both ways: an objective-subjective way and an intersubjective way. Therefore, learning means what knowledge has been produced by which framework/perspective, how the mind structures work to understand that knowledge, and what knowledge we are required to have in order to create new knowledge and to change our mind structure (in Part II, I will argue how our mind is structured by adopting theories of cross-cultural psychology in line with methodological justification for interculturality).

2.2.3 *What do people know?*

The last educational question in epistemology is *what do people know*. A fundamental issue of the question is an infinite regress. Any given justification for knowledge will depend on another belief for its justification that ultimately leads to an infinite regress. In response to this regress problem, various schools of thought have arisen such as *foundationalism, coherentism, infinitism,* and *instrumentalism.*

First, foundationalists claim that when we support other beliefs based on a basic belief or a foundation, this does not need justification because the basic belief about our current mental states is infallible and indubitable (Alexander *et al.*, 2006). The basic belief is also secure because we do not have "a propositional direct apprehension of the mental states" (Pryor, 2001, p. 101). Second, coherentists hold that justification is a function that "construes coherence as a relationship between a target belief and a background system" (Lehrer, 2010, p. 171). They contend that a belief is always justified in a pattern of linear justification because it is a part of and consistent with the rest of its belief system, and thus a regression does not proceed (Audi, 2010). Third, infinitists acknowledge an infinite regress has the potential to be a valid justification because individuals have the ability to create relevant reasons when necessary (or consensus occurs) (Klein, 2010). For infinitists, all propositional knowledge is inferential. They claim,

> Some beliefs require inferential justification. No belief justifies itself. So either the justificatory path is infinite, or circular, or ends with a belief that is justified but not on the basis of another belief, or it ends with an unjustified belief.
>
> (Klein, 2010, p. 161)

Fourth, and last, instrumentalists (similar to pragmatists or Alexander *et al.*'s term *social epistemology*) hold that something is true only insofar as it works and has practical consequences. For instrumentalists, Alexander *et al.* (2006) argue,

> Truth, in essence, is what the community of practice upholds as justified . . . decisions about effective teaching practices in reading or mathematics . . . justified . . . articulated by the community of experts.
>
> (p. 9)

The focus is on *worth* that is measured by how it is effective in reality.

Those four thoughts can be divided into internal beliefs and external justification: foundationalists and coherentists hold the same view that the basis for justification is on internal beliefs, whereas infinitists and instrumentalists seek external justification for beliefs (Alexander *et al.*, 2006). This division appears in a debate between *internalists* and *externalists* that asks whether one is "justified in believing some proposition" or one's belief is "based on something that justifies it" (Pryor, 2001, p. 104). Internalists, particularly Cartesians and rationalists, are extraordinarily optimistic about the human mind, and their assumption is that introspection and reflection may be "effective agents of epistemic quality control" (Kornblith, 2010, p. 165). Although we possess the capability to be independent in our thinking or self-awareness, "the processes by which our beliefs are formed are not directly available to introspection" because the "processes are influenced by a wide range of biasing factors" (Kornblith, 2010, p. 165). Hence the internal justification for beliefs comes to the conclusion that our beliefs will be justified regardless of whether or not they are justified in a reasonable manner. On the other hand, when distinguishing between knowledge and justification, we

46 *Metaphysical understanding of culture*

notice that justification supervenes upon internal or mental facts and "if any two possible individuals are mentally alike, then they are justificationally alike" (Audi, 2010, p. 124). For externalists, internalism means, "one is justified in believing a proposition on the basis of a body of evidence only if one knows, or justifiably believes, that the evidence supports that proposition" (Audi, 2010, p. 124). For this reason, externalists reject this meta-level requirement.

The debate between internalists and externalists becomes more complicated when we ask whether there is external knowledge or internal justification. This is also endorsed by both Kornblith and Audi referenced earlier. Regardless of whether or not an infinite regress of justification is a kind of valid justification, such responses imply three perspectives of epistemology: (a) as foundationalists and coherentists claim, knowledge justification is determined or circulated in some finite number of steps by individuals based on their own relevant reasoning, experience, or beliefs; (b) an infinite regress in knowledge justification, either temporarily or permanently, will be referred to as an indwelling knowledge of individuals' either acceptance or rejection based on either pragmatic or emotional reasons; and (c) a belief does not need to be necessarily justified with its assertion of knowledge because it is impossible to permanently complete its infinite regress and thus no beliefs can be justified. Such interpretations do not mean that each response needs to be justified either for or against the regress. Rather, they imply that a belief occurs as a thinking process with a feeling or emotion attached, and justified beliefs are connected to an epistemological assumption about *how do we know what we know*. In education, an epistemological assumption is used to know what people know. In this sense, the epistemological question *what do people know* should be aimed at understanding an individual's thinking process or pattern on a matter rather than judging whether it is right or wrong. In order to reveal epistemological assumptions, then, an appropriate question would be *how do we believe what we know?* A significant point here is that this new question works in accordance with a value system as we *believe* it. When the question is applied in intercultural education, lesson design for intercultural interaction could begin with the following questions: *What makes us believe the existence of whiteness, what causes our superiority or inferiority to a particular cultural group, and what encourages us to deny the existence of interculturality?*

2.3 Axiological interaction

Ontological and epistemological assumptions in education are also highly associated with axiological and methodological assumptions (Creswell, 2003; de Gialdino, 2009). Yet at least in the education research area, axiological aspects of research are very rare. Well-known educational research methodology literature such as Creswell (2003), Johnson and Christensen (2012), Johnson and Onwuegbuzie (2004), and Maxwell (1998) do not, or only limitedly, contribute to axiological aspects of research. As seen in Alexander *et al.*'s ontological questions on educational research, this would be because the dominant trends of educational research have paid attention to understanding, interpretation, and transformation of either individual or institutional matters. In fact, the primary research focus is on the use of mixed methods to maximise objectivity of quantitative research and/or honesty of qualitative research (e.g., Creswell, 2003; Johnson & Christensen, 2012; Johnson & Onwuegbuzie, 2004; Luo, 2011; Maxwell, 1998; Savenye & Robinson, 2004). Regardless of whether intended or unintended, an epistemological process or framework entails value judgement. As seen in the previous sections, non-deontological and ontological justification, various epistemological branches, the regress problem, and an epistemic culture per se are the evidence that knowledge justification and acquisition ultimately look for meaning in the world(s) and make value judgements, which is an inescapable part of being human. Through various epistemological approaches, underlying values embedded in researchers' cultural presumptions and beliefs are mostly indirectly disclosed or entrenched in their ethics or value systems.

Each culture has a different value system, and cultural clashes of cultural diversity are seen as value conflicts (LeBaron, 2003; Turner, 2005). In fact, "the concept of value permeates our life at every step" and "we attach to them [our passions, interests, purposive action] different degrees of importance or value" (Hart, 1971, p. 29). Cultures as value systems manifest in every conflict where we make meaning and hold our values (LeBaron, 2003; Turner, 2005). More fundamentally, cultural conflicts are caused by value priorities of different cultural groups/individuals; values are often concealed and distorted in situations because people mostly unconsciously hold values as a system for non-negotiation. For example, LeBaron (2003) adopts anthropologists' cultural dimensions to explain cultural value conflicts: in collectivist settings, people prioritise "cooperation, filial piety, participation in shared progress, reputation of the group, interdependence", whereas in individualist settings, people prioritise "competition, independence, individual achievement, personal growth and fulfillment, self-reliance" (para. 42–43). The results presume that a culture manifests itself as a different value system. Turner (2005) also reports that cultural value conflicts caused by value differences appear in an institution-to-institution and a nation-to-nation context. He explains that cultural value conflicts intensify when value differences become reflected in politics. Such studies support axiological questions on cultural diversity: *What value structure does a culture have and how do different value structures cause cultural conflicts in intercultural interaction?* As Hart (1971) explicitly points out in his "Axiology – Theory of Values", "values were conceived of as independent of man", but "modern philosophy became skeptical as to the identity of the real and valuable", and because of the advancement of physical science, people have no questions about "many causal, genetic, and social determinants of values" (p. 30). Thus it can be said that the outcomes of LeBaron's and Turner's studies noted earlier indicate that a culture has its own unique value system that is deeply and invisibly embedded in the human mind, and value conflicts between different cultures inevitably appear in intercultural situations. As Hart explains, because of the rapid advance of physical science, today's scepticism towards values seems to encourage researchers to prove the affirmation

48 *Metaphysical understanding of culture*

of value or cultural differences without verifying what culture or value system drives them to conduct such studies.

Because of such scepticism towards values, axiology in education usually refers to ethics, which is often called moral education that restricts guidance and teaching of good behaviour and concerns for moral virtues such as honesty, responsibility, and respect for others. In practice, moral education decontextualises values from contexts and ideates them to reproduce and sustain a dominant culture. This ideological apparatus works unconsciously to conceal the relationship between values and (personal, cultural, historical, and social) contexts. In the learning environment, however, teachers cannot avoid considering maximisation of benefits for the greatest number of students. This is because they are required to review and design lesson components such as pedagogical strategies, learning objectives, student activities, and assessment in order to efficiently and effectively manage situational factors in the learning and teaching context or social context of education. Whether directly or indirectly, teachers experience value conflicts between designed learning objectives and curriculum requirements and have sceptical questions about concepts and meanings applied and used in their teaching. Such conflicts are differently covered by branches of ethics: normative ethics, descriptive ethics, and meta-ethics.

2.3.1 *Normative ethics*

Normative ethics (also known as prescriptive ethics) is concerned with "the best values and guiding principles of human conduct" (Fieser, 2000, p. 11). For example, "Some leading normative values are the Ten Commandments of Judaism, the Confucian principle of reciprocity that we should avoid treating others in ways we wouldn't want to be treated ourselves" (Fieser, 2000, p. 11). This description indicates utilitarianism in which it pursues the greatest happiness of the greatest number (Fieser, 2000). Normative ethics is often divided into three categories: *consequentialism, deontology*, and *virtue ethics*.

First, consequentialists argue, "the morality of an action depends on its foreseeable consequences" (John Stuart Mill cited in Richter, 2010, p. 47). They presume that a morally right action will lead to a good result. For example, utilitarianists claim that an action is right if it results in maximised pleasure and minimised pain for the greatest number of people (Sinnott-Armstrong, 2012). A difference with altruism is that the action does not lead to the sacrifice of self-interest. For hedonists, for example, pleasure is the measurement of morality in which its maximisation is the most important value that human beings should pursue (Fieser, 2000; Sinnott-Armstrong, 2012). Second, deontologists focus on an action itself, not its consequences. They argue that duties, rights, and obligations are key factors in moral judgement (Tännsjö, 2002). For example, Kantianists argue that motives, not consequences, determine the morality of one's actions because good consequences could arise by accident (Alexander & Moore, 2012). Contractarianists claim, "moral norms derive their normative force from the idea of contract or mutual agreement" (Cudd, 2013, para. 1). This is because they view a set of moral rules as a contract so that it is valid only for ones who agree to the contract and understand it. Third, *virtue ethics* focus "on traits of character rather than on criteria of right action" (Tännsjö, 2002, p. 38). A virtue is neither just a tendency nor a habit, but is "a disposition which is well entrenched in its possessor, something that, as we say 'goes all the way down' . . . is multi-track . . . concerned with many other actions . . . to be a certain sort of person with a certain complex mindset" (Hursthouse, 2013, para. 4). For example, Aristotle's *eudaemonia*, which refers to whether right actions should lead to *happiness*, can be achieved by practising virtues – the active life of the rational element – that such "disposition is to possess full or perfect virtue" (Hursthouse, 2013. Para. 9). In this sense, eudaemonia could not be subjective because it is the ultimate goal of human life.

A similarity between these three branches of normative ethics is that they prescribe morality. The fundamental question is concerned with *how should people act* and the judging standards that distinguish their characters. Prescribed morality is classified with (personal or group) benefits or intentions and makes multidimensional value judgements on a case-by-case basis. In culturally inclusive lessons, then, the three branches of normative ethics as a whole imply that, in order to maximise benefits for culturally diverse students, teachers are required to actualise opportunities for all students to learn from their diverse peers. For example, peer-to-peer interaction is not exclusive of social harmony (consequentialism), sound motivation (deontology), and rational processes (virtue ethics). Although such an inferential consequence sounds logical and reasonable, normative ethics does not give an answer to how prescribed rules or values are managed in the learning environment. This means that ethics needs to be reviewed in a methodological way and descriptive ethics offers some meaningful thoughts on this matter.

2.3.2 Descriptive ethics

Descriptive ethics uses a value-free approach to ethics. When morality refers to a code of conduct that governs a particular group of people, anthropologists observe and examine cases of actual choices in practice made by people (Gert, 2012). For example, when a human act is morally evaluated, situated ethics mainly considers the actual physical, geographical, ecological, and infrastructure state that a person is involved in and rejects particular viewpoints from a specific norm or by authority. In this sense, descriptive ethics is not a theoretical system of ethics, but a methodological approach to ethical judgement. In practice, a moral decision must be made based on critical analysis of a situation whether or not it would result in the greatest amount of happiness for a group (Fieser, 2000; Sinnott-Armstrong, 2012).

Such a utilitarian approach to ethics can be seen in *situational ethics*. Fletcher (1966/1997) observes that believers try to identify some rules based on divine commands or nature in most ethnic/religious communities. Fletcher argues that situation ethics offers a third way between legalism as absolute and antinomianism as illuminative that is *prima facie*, which "a moral agent . . . has to ask all over again in each new situation whether a particular act . . . is what love requires"

50 *Metaphysical understanding of culture*

(Fletcher, 1966/1997, p. 4). This is because moral judgement must be made by the greatest amount of love because "*Agape* [unconditional love] as absolute and all the other principles and rules are mere maxims or rules of thumb" (Fletcher, 1966/1997, p. 5). Situational ethics presumes that the end and the means simultaneously work and unconditional love should not be challenged by a society or a culture. Thus moral agents often view their internalised values that are believed to be attributes of unconditional love as more fundamental unless theories of values or of conduct are in the same line as the values.

Descriptive ethics focus on situational factors and outcomes based on the believed attributes of unconditional love for ethical judgement, whereas normative ethics focus on moral attitudes and behaviours towards prescribed rules. It seems that the latter emphasises the objectivity of ethical judgement based on subjective experiences, whereas the former emphasises the subjectivity of ethical judgement based on objective attributes. From a holistic perspective, then, such a difference deepens an axiological understanding of value engagement in a situation and ethical judgement. In other words, morality functions as an independent value system where moral agents are involved in either an objective or a subjective way, otherwise value-free or situation-free should have no value orientation. Its methodological implication is that prescribed rules or values (or the love) need to be judged and managed based on meta-ethical analyses of diverse value systems. Furthermore, its pedagogical implication is that individuals are required to participate in intercultural interaction in order to practise or realise prescribed rules or values. Yet intercultural interaction may generate conflicts with values embedded in lesson components because both value systems and the nature of curriculum operate in a normative way and are affected by situational forces. This constantly challenges both teachers and students to face scepticism about intercultural interaction.

2.3.3 Meta-ethics

Meta-ethics does not attempt to evaluate the morality of one's action, rather it investigates where moral values come from (Fieser, 2000). "One of the key issues of metaethics concerns whether moral values exist in an objective realm that is external to human society" (Fieser, 2000, p. 16). Thus meta-ethics is not independent from metaphysics, epistemology, and presuppositions of morality (Sayre-McCord, 2012). It can be further understood with its two branches: moral realism and moral anti-realism.

Moral realism holds that objective moral values are independent from subjective interpretations (Fieser, 2000). It is a cognitivist view in which "goodness is an independent of objective quality of the world" (Fieser, 2000, p. 219) and moral rights do not provide moral arguments (Tännsjö, 2002). In other words, the truth or falsity of moral statements is largely independent of subjective moral opinions, beliefs, or feelings, thus evaluated by objective features of the world. Although such a mind-independence approach is used as genuinely truth-conditional, moral realists are less interest in the facts that moral terms are bound up with various emotions and moral understanding involves moral beliefs

(Sayre-McCord, 2011). On the contrary, moral anti-realism holds the beliefs that objective moral values do not exist and moral properties are significantly mind-dependent (Joyce, 2009). This means that any moral statements do not reflect objective facts, but merely reflect sentiments, preferences, and feelings because objective moral properties do not exist. Non-cognivitists radically insist that moral statements are neither true nor false and moral knowledge cannot exist because (a) genuine morality cannot be expressed through moral statements and (b) expressions of one's own attitudes and conventions are the basis for ethical judgement (Joyce, 2009). Other branches such as moral anti-realism, extremism, and moral nihilism claim that all ethical statements must be false because there are neither objective values nor moral truths. As Joyce (2009) summarises, moral anti-realists would be seen as "moral subjectivists, or idealists, or constructivists" (para. 1). The metaphysical tensions between moral realism and moral anti-realism seem irreconcilable unless there is a third way (Finlay, 2007; Sayre-McCord, 2011).

One of the most comprehensive approaches to meta-ethics is Fieser's (2000) *meta-ethical images*, which are aimed at understanding the nature of morality. Fieser presents six meta-ethical images of morality. First is *a morally relative society* – that is, "a society that creates its own traditions and moral values" (p. 205). Second is *a higher moral reality* – that is, "a spiritual realm that houses moral truths", which is similar to Plato's unchanging spirit-like realm of the forms (p. 205). Third is *a rationally ordered universe* – that is, "everything follows a logical order and has rational purpose" because "human nature reflects the rational plan of the universe and we discover morality through human reason" (p. 206). Fourth is *divinely commanded morality*, which involves "a picture of a supremely powerful creator who authors moral standards and commands them on all people" (p. 206). Fifth is *an evolving society* that "progressively places greater emphasis on the well-being of others and less emphasis on personal interest" (p. 206). Sixth is *people expressing their feelings* that "the nature of morality, then, is largely an issue of human emotional responses, and not an issue about facts such as personal or social happiness" (p. 206). In summary, these six meta-ethical images offer us the ability to analyse metaphysics of normative and descriptive values and to understand *outward expansion* and *inward movement* of our accommodating process of values. The meta-ethical images presume that the essential meaning of ethics is transcendental to objective and subjective morality. In this sense, moral realism and moral anti-realism can merge, which allows us to pay attention to the flow of values: the former focuses on meaning of moral statements – outward expansion – whereas the latter focuses on one's attitudes and conventions – inward movement. The flow of values implies that (a) all values are ontologically equal and, therefore, all cultures are equal and (b) value conflicts and tensions in diverse cultural contexts are metaphysically understood. In practice, a serious cultural conflict could occur when one suppresses or eliminates the other one, which ignores or obstructs the flow of values by creating a value hierarchy. The oppressed may not be aware that they are oppressed or are tolerant of being oppressed at an individual level or for a short period of time. However, an outburst of their collective resistance is inevitable because the ontological equity of values has the

52 Metaphysical understanding of culture

potential to generate value conflicts in epistemological and axiological differences of values.

This review of the three branches of ethics, normative, descriptive, and meta-ethics, provides some meaningful implications for value-interaction. First, normative ethics indicates that prescribed values are sustained through the maximisation of benefits for the greatest number of people. In multicultural education, then, axiological questions would be as follows: *What are prescribed values in planned intercultural interaction* and *how are the values perceived in each culture?* Second, descriptive ethics implies that values can be studied as independent systems in social, cultural, and historical contexts. Then an axiological question would be *are all cultures compatible in understanding intercultural interaction?* Third, and last, meta-ethics allows us to deal with axiology of interculturality in terms of its epistemological and ontological aspects. An axiological question would be *to what extent are values embedded in intercultural interaction supportive of values of participating cultures?* In summary, practical applications of axiological interaction would be (a) to investigate the nature of values and (b) to understand various cultural forms of pedagogy in a comparative manner. As Nietzsche offers a generic and comparative approach to values and argues for metaphysical understandings of values (Hart, 1971), I will review Nietzsche's theory of values in Part II. For intercultural pedagogy, I will compare pedagogical theories of different cultural/religious contexts in Part III.

2.4 Conclusion: A holistic approach to multicultural education

Researchers in education have different ways to approach metaphysics. They have not only different understandings of ontology, epistemology, and axiology but also have complex arguments on each of them. For example, positivists' ontological assumption indicates that the nature of reality is fixed, stable, observable, and measurable. Their epistemological assumption presumes that knowledge can only be acquired through scientific and experimental research. On the other hand, interpretivists and critical theorists emphasise the importance of values and biases because both view the nature of reality as multiple and fluid. Both argue that knowing and reality are socially constructed by individuals and focus on understanding of the meaning of the processes/experiences. A difference between interpretivism and critical theory is that the former focuses on understanding meaning behind actions in a social context, whereas the latter examines assumptions of accepted beliefs and claims. When we apply the three dimensions of metaphysics, we can understand those three groups in a holistic way: for positivists, knowledge is objective and quantifiable, and axiology has no role of values in which they pursue value-free to be objective; by positioning the meaning-making practices of human actors (knowledge creation processes or experiences) at the centre of scientific explanation, interpretivists tend to put more weight on epistemological justification; for critical theorists, knowledge refers to ideological criticism and discussion of power relationships, and, consequently, their ontological questions play a critical role in validating the relationships. This holistic interpretation indicates that the three dimensions of educational metaphysics enable us to perceive our own perspective as an open system that is interconnected to other perspectives. Likewise, when a culture is viewed as an open system, the metaphysical interaction is necessary for our participation in intercultural interaction and interculturality. More specifically, ontological justification, epistemological assumptions, and axiological interaction help us to view a cultural framework as an open system contoured with dashed lines in the interculturally networked world. An ontological contour defines internal values (or cultural identity) and connects to external values (or other cultures and environments).

Such a metaphysical approach to multicultural education repositions minority or other cultures as equal agents of social changes in teaching and learning, which is the ontological foundation for intercultural interaction. The three dimensions of metaphysics are meaningful when they become a whole by building meta-questions about our horizons of intercultural interaction. First, ontological questions about cultural diversity include various concepts of multiculturalism (i.e., cultural diversity, cultural assimilation, cultural integration, cultural education) and social terms (i.e., host community, immigrants, minority ethnic groups, Indigenous) that need to be reviewed in terms of their ontological justification for interculturality. Second, the three concerns of epistemology in education – what is knowledge, how is knowledge acquired, and what do people know – are repositioned for intercultural commitments and changed to *where* of knowledge, *how* of mind structure, and *why* of beliefs. Third, axiological questions of interculturality based on normative, descriptive, and meta-ethics indicate that epistemological and ontological aspects of ethics have the potential for value-interaction between cultures. These meta-questions of the three dimensions of metaphysics in education are fundamentally ontological; the three dimensions open new horizons in metaphysical ways of reviewing multicultural educational models.

References

Alexander, L., & Moore, M. (2012). Deontological ethics. In E.N. Zalta (Ed.), *The Stanford Encyclopedia of Philosophy* (Winter 2012 ed.). Retrieved from http://plato.stanford.edu/archives/win2012/entries/ethics-deontological/

Alexander, P.A., Chambliss, M.J., & Price, J. (2006, April). Ontological and epistemological threads in the fabric of pedagogical research. In G. Natriello (Chair), *Promoting the Public Good through Investigations of Teaching: Challenges and Possibilities.* Symposium presented at the annual meeting of the American Educational Research Association, San Francisco. Retrieved from http://www.education.umd.edu/EDCI/hqtstudy/HQTNews.html

Audi, R. (2010). Robert Audi of Part II Twenty epistemological self-profiles. In J. Dancy, E. Sosa & M. Steup (Eds.), *A Companion to Epistemology* (2nd ed.) (pp. 108–115). Oxford: Blackwell Publishing.

Breuker, J., Muntjewerff, A., & Bredeweg, B. (1999, July). *Ontological modelling for designing educational systems.* Paper presented at Proceedings of the Workshop on Ontologies for Intelligent Educational Systems at AIE99, Le Mans, France. Retrieved from http://citeseer.ist.psu.edu/viewdoc/download;jsessionid=7326DD61AAFE ABFA52DC3A1D289C431E?doi=10.1.1.331.7057&rep=rep1&type=pdf.

54 *Metaphysical understanding of culture*

Creswell, J.W. (2003). *Research design: Qualitative, quantitative and mixed methods approaches* (2nd ed.). Thousand Oaks, CA: Sage publications.

Cudd, A. (2012). Contractarianism. In E.N. Zalta (Ed.), *The Stanford Encyclopedia of Philosophy* (Winter 2013 ed.). Retrieved from http://plato.stanford.edu/archives/win2013/entries/contractarianism/

de Gialdino, I.V. (2009). Ontological and epistemological foundations of qualitative research. *Forum Qualitative Sozialforschung / Forum: Qualitative Social Research, 10*(2), Art. 30. Retrieved from http://nbn-resolving.de/urn:nbn:de:0114-fqs0902307

Driscoll, M.P. (2005). *Psychology of learning for instruction* (3rd ed.). Boston, MA: Allyn & Bacon.

Duffy, T.M., & Jonassen, D.H. (1992). Constructivism: New implications for instructional technology. In T. Duffy & D. Jonassen (Eds.), *Constructivism and the Technology of Instruction* (pp. 1–16). Hillsdale, NJ: Lawrence Erlbaum Associates.

Fieser, J. (2000). *Moral philosophy through the ages.* California: Mayfield Publishing Company.

Finlay, S. (2007). Four faces of moral realism. *Philosophy Compass, 2*(6), 820–849.

Fletcher, J.F. (1966/1997). *Situation ethics: The new morality (Library of Theological Ethics)* (2nd ed.). Louisville, KY: Westminster John Knox Press.

Foley, R. (1993). What am I to believe? In S. Wagner & R. Warner (Eds.), *Naturalism: A Critical Appraisal* (pp. 147–163). Notre Dame: University of Notre Dame Press.

Freimuth, H. (2009). Educational research: An introduction to basic concepts and terminology. *University General Requirements Unit (UGRU) Journal, 8*, 1–9.

Gert, B. (2012). The definition of morality. In E.N. Zalta (Ed.), *The Stanford Encyclopedia of Philosophy* (Fall 2012 ed.). Retrieved from http://plato.stanford.edu/archives/fall2012/entries/morality-definition/

Goldman, A. (2011). Reliabilism. In E.N. Zalta (Ed.), *The Stanford Encyclopedia of Philosophy* (Spring 2011 ed.). Retrieved from http://plato.stanford.edu/archives/spr2011/entries/reliabilism

Gruber, T.R. (1995). Toward principles for the design of ontologies used for knowledge sharing. Presented at the Padua workshop on Formal Ontology. *International Journal of Human-Computer Studies, 43*(4–5), 907–928.

Hart, S.L. (1971). Axiology – theory of values. *Philosophy and Phenomenological Research, 32*(1), 29–41.

Hetherington, S. (2002). Fallibilism and knowing that one is not dreaming. *Canadian Journal of Philosophy, 32*(1), 83–102.

Hinman, L. (2008). *Ethics: A pluralistic approach to moral theory* (4th ed.). Belmont, CA: Wadsworth Publishing.

Hookyway, C. (2010). Pragmatism. In E.N. Zalta (Ed.), *The Stanford Encyclopedia of Philosophy* (Spring 2015 ed.). Retrieved from http://plato.stanford.edu/archives/spr2015/entries/pragmatism/

Hursthouse, R. (2013). Virtue ethics. In E.N. Zalta (Ed.), *The Stanford Encyclopedia of Philosophy* (Fall 2013 ed.). Retrieved from http://plato.stanford.edu/archives/fall2013/entries/ethics-virtue/

Johnson, R.B., & Christensen, L. (2012). *Educational research: Quantitative, qualitative, and mixed approaches.* Los Angeles, CA: SAGE publication.

Johnson, R.B., & Onwuegbuzie, A.J. (2004). Mixed methods research: A research paradigm whose time has come. *Educational Researcher, 33*(7), 14–26.

Joyce, R. (2009). Moral anti-realism. In E.N. Zalta (Ed.), *The Stanford Encyclopedia of Philosophy* (Summer 2009 ed.). Retrieved from http://plato.stanford.edu/archives/sum2009/entries/moral-anti-realism/

Klein, P. (2010). Peter Klein of Part II Twenty epistemological self-profiles. In J. Dancy, E. Sosa & M. Steup (Eds.), *A Companion to Epistemology* (2nd ed.) (pp. 156–163). Oxford: Blackwell Publishing.

Knorr-Cetina, K. (1999). *Epistemic cultures. How the sciences make knowledge*. Boston, MA: Harvard University Press.

Kornblith, H. (2010). Hilary Kornblith of Part II Twenty epistemological self-profiles. In J. Dancy, E. Sosa & M. Steup (Eds.), *A Companion to Epistemology* (2nd ed.) (pp. 163–168). Oxford: Blackwell Publishing.

LeBaron, M. (2003). Culture and conflict. In G. Burgess & H. Burgess (Eds.). *Beyond Intractability*. Boulder: Conflict Information Consortium, University of Colorado. Retrieved from http://www.beyondintractability.org/essay/culture-conflict

Lecser, J. (1996). Justified, true belief: Is it relevant to knowledge? *Auslegung, 21*(2), 107–124.

Lehrer, K.R. (2010). Keith Lehrer of Part II Twenty epistemological self-profiles. In J. Dancy, E. Sosa & M. Steup (Eds.), *A Companion to Epistemology* (2nd ed.) (pp. 168–173). Oxford: Blackwell Publishing.

Luo, H. (2011). Qualitative research on educational technology: Philosophies, methods and challenges. *International Journal of Education, 3*(2), E13.

Markie, P. (2013). Rationalism vs. Empiricism. In E.N. Zalta (Ed.), *The Stanford Encyclopedia of Philosophy* (Summer 2013 ed.). Retrieved from http://plato.stanford.edu/archives/sum2013/entries/rationalism-empiricism/

Maxwell, J.A. (1998). Designing a qualitative study. In Leonard Bickman & Debra J. Rog (Eds.), *Handbook of Applied Social Research Methods* (pp. 69–100). Thousand Oaks: Sage.

Oancea, A. (2016). The aims and claims of educational research. In M. Hand & R. Davies (Eds.), *Education, Ethics and Experience: Essays in Honour of Richard Pring* (pp. 109–120). New York: Routledge.

Pappas, G. (2013). Internalist vs. externalist conceptions of epistemic justification. In E.N. Zalta (Ed.), *The Stanford Encyclopedia of Philosophy* (Fall 2013 ed.). Retrieved from http://plato.stanford.edu/archives/fall2013/entries/justep-intext/

Pryor, J. (2001). Highlights of recent epistemology. *British Journal for the Philosophy of Science, 52*(1), 95–124.

Richter, D. (2010). *Anscombe's moral philosophy*. Maryland, UK: Lexington Books.

Ross, S.M., Morrison, G.R., Hannafin, R.D., Young, M., van den Akker, J., Kuiper, W., Richey, R.C., & Kelin, J.D. (2008). Research designs. In J.M. Spector, M.D. Merrill, J. van Merriënboer & M.P. Driscoll (Eds.), *Handbook of Research on Educational Communications and Technology* (3rd ed.) (pp. 715–757). New York: Taylor & Francis Group.

Sainsbury, R.M., & Tye, M. (2012). *Seven puzzles of thought and how to solve them: An originalist theory of concepts*. Oxford: Oxford University Press.

Savenye, W.C., & Robinson, R.S. (2004). Qualitative research issues and methods: An introduction for educational technologists. In D.H. Jonassen (Eds.), *Handbook of Research on Educational Communications and Technology* (pp. 1045–1072). Mahwah, NJ: Erlbaum.

Sayre-McCord, G. (2011). Moral realism. In E.N. Zalta (Ed.), *The Stanford Encyclopedia of Philosophy* (Summer 2011 ed.). Retrieved from http://plato.stanford.edu/archives/sum2011/entries/moral-realism/

Sayre-McCord, G. (2012). Metaethics. In E.N. Zalta (Ed.), *The Stanford Encyclopedia of Philosophy* (Spring 2012 ed.). Retrieved from http://plato.stanford.edu/archives/spr2012/entries/metaethics/

56 Metaphysical understanding of culture

Schuh, K.L., & Barab, S.A. (2008). Part 1. Foundations 7 philosophical perspectives. In J.M. Spector, M.D. Merrill, J. van Merriënboer & M.P. Driscoll (Eds.), *Handbook of Research on Educational Communications and Technology* (3rd ed.) (pp. 67–82). New York: Taylor & Francis Group.

Sinnott-Armstrong, W. (2012). Consequentialism. In E.N. Zalta (Ed.), *The Stanford Encyclopedia of Philosophy* (Winter 2012 ed.). Retrieved from http://plato.stan ford.edu/archives/win2012/entries/consequentialism/

Steup, M. (2013). Epistemology. In E.N. Zalta (Ed.), *The Stanford Encyclopedia of Philosophy* (Winter 2013 ed.). Retrieved from http://plato.stanford.edu/archives/win2013/entries/epistemology/

Tännsjö, T. (2002). *Understanding ethics: An introduction to moral theory*. Edinburgh: Edinburgh University Press.

Thomasson, A.L. (2005). The ontology of art and knowledge in aesthetics. *The Journal of Aesthetics and Art Criticism, 63*(3), 221–229.

Turner, J.H. (2005). *Sociology*. Englewood Cliffs, NJ: Prentice Hall.

Turri, J. (2012). Is knowledge justified true belief? *Synthese, 184*(3), 247–259.

3 Underlying assumptions of multicultural education

Multicultural education tends to be regarded as a naturalistic framework for understanding cultural differences and dynamics of cultural contact in a culturally diverse society and learning environment (Hidalgo, Chávez-Chávez & Ramage, 1996). Yet many researchers argue that most contemporary education systems can best be described as Eurocentric cultural and knowledge systems, and their curricula have been used to defend its ideological values and political framework (Giroux, 1988; Hidalgo *et al.*, 1996; Lander & Past, 2002; Muchenje, 2012; Stanesby & Thomas, 2012). Specifically, they argue that white privileges have been reproduced, truths have been sought by positivist approaches, and ethnic authenticity and Indigeneity have deteriorated. Basic assumptions of Eurocentric knowledge are primarily characterised by the dualisms of reason and body and subject and object (Lander & Past, 2002). Likewise, culture is also understood in opposition to nature and the nature/culture opposition facilitates an upward linear direction of scientific knowledge (Lander & Past, 2002). A process of differentiation and demarcation between *us* and *them* (or *othering*) creates cultural regulators of societal normality (Stanesby & Thomas, 2012). Such a binary cultural construction essentialises and stereotypes others as inferior in education (Lander & Past, 2002). In practice, it appears to transform other cultures and to reject them when they are perceived *relatively* unsystematic and unproductive by a dominant culture. These criticisms draw our attention to the necessity of metaphysical analyses of contemporary multiculturalism discourses and multicultural education models, in particular, why and how cultural diversity and intercultural interaction are perceived and constrained.

3.1 White privilege and multiculturalism

With Bhabha's quote, "the impossible unity of the nation as a symbolic force", Stratton and Ang (1994) argue, "national unity . . . can only be represented as such through a suppression and repression, symbolic or otherwise, of difference" (para. 1). They point out that "multiculturalism is controversial precisely because of its real and perceived (in)compatibility with national unity" (para. 1). They explain how Australia and the U.S.A. formulate multiculturalism differently: Australia conceives it as "a potential reality" that needs to be managed through "unity in diversity", whereas the U.S.A. defines it as "a utopian ideal" (i.e., the melting pot) that

58 *Metaphysical understanding of culture*

all individuals are free to create their own future (para. 77). Australian multicultur-alism, as officially expressed through the government policy, is aimed at being inclu-sive of social positions and interests of ethnic minorities within national Australian culture, whereas the U.S.A.'s multiculturalism has been politicised for an intellec-tual promotion of non-Western cultures against Eurocentric cultural hegemony, which is *Americanisation* (para. 8; para. 34). In this comparison, Stratton and Ang pay attention to how each country differently hypostatises the concept of culture and suppresses heterogeneity across cultures. They argue that such hypostatisation enhances conservative, anthropological ethno-centrism and reproduces its binary mechanism by holding the tension between the particular and the universal (para. 81). The hypostatised concept of culture refers to Hage's (1998) *whiteness* or *white supremacy* that is a "fantasy position of cultural dominance borne out of the history of colonial expansion. Not an essence that one has or does not have" (p. 20). Hage argues,

> Multiculturalism reflects the reality of Australia, the visible and public side of power remains essentially Anglo White: politicians are mainly Anglo white, customs officers, police officers and judges. At the same time, Australian mythmakers and icons, old and new are largely Anglo white, from shearers to surfers to television and radio personalities etc. This creates a lasting impres-sion that power, even if open for non-Anglos to accumulate whiteness within in, remains an Anglo looking phenomena.
>
> (pp. 190–191)

White multiculturalists perceive their nation as "structured around *a white cul-ture*" and, more critically, they view non-white Aboriginal people and migrants as "exotic objects" and "manageable objects" to be moved or removed (Hage, 1998, p. 48 [emphasis added]). Regardless of whether this occurs unconsciously or consciously, their primary justification for ruling the nation is the "credible and continuing sense of white dominance" (p. 209). White supremacy as a fan-tasy or a myth in a multicultural society indicates that its desire is not limited to *racists*. Hage pays attention to an implicit message or a promise implanted in Aus-tralian multiculturalism that white citizens do not lose anything. In this sense, he confirms that multicultural tolerance and white nationalism are two sides of the same coin because both presume that the foundation of Australia is whiteness. Differences are only acceptable within the limits of white tolerance.

Following Lacanian psychoanalysis, Hage differentiates *fantasy* as "an imag-ined 'land of the good life' pursued as a goal by the subject" and "an ideal image of the self as a 'meaningful' subject" (p. 70). In his understanding of the Lacanian concept, Hage claims that a "fantasy is propelled by a Thing, a yearned for object-cause of desire" (p. 170). What Hage stresses is that "the Thing, as far as the relationship between humans and nature is concerned, has never been domesticated nature as such" (p. 170). Even "return to nature" other than domestication is a mould based on the constant subjugation of nature (p. 170). This mechanism, Hage calls *ecological fantasy*, is a way to breed animals, which most ecologists also criticise (p. 166). It is a specific mode of being and thinking or *a white culture* that is determined by the dualism between humans and nature and it causes "the subject, as Lacan puts it, 'confuses his contemplative eye with the eye with which God is looking at him'" (p. 172). The dualism greatly benefits a functionalist consensus theory according to Stratton and Ang (1994) in which social integration is achieved through assimilation of others with dominant values. As Stratton and Ang point out, such an assimilation process fails to understand cultural diversity and to accept culturally different values. Likewise, the ecological fantasy permeates society and minority cultures and, in turn, it makes individuals tolerant of the absence of the self (or the absence of self-awareness) and the non-subject position (or unequal participation) of others in intercultural interaction. As seen in the previous chapters, the latter refers to ontological reductionism as supported by self-exclusive reflection and the former is identical to epistemic violence that is caused by binary structures of cultural representation. From a metaphysical perspective, the ecological fantasy is exclusive of metaphysical dimensions such as ontology and axiology. In the learning environment, such an anti-metaphysical approach (a) justifies multicultural education that focuses on gathering information about other cultures by concealing ontological justification towards others and (b) rationalises intercultural interaction as a simple sharing process of the gathered information by defining them as peripheral.

3.2 Contemporary multicultural education for intercultural interaction

Banks (1997) categorises multicultural education with two aspects: (a) analysing ways in which schools and educational systems as institutions sustain and perpetuate racism in society and (b) examining historical and social reasons of various forms of institutional oppression. He criticises the current mainstream-centric curriculum that (a) reinforces students' false sense of superiority (or white supremacy), (b) denies their opportunity to understand their culture from other cultural perspectives, and (c) marginalises non-mainstream students (pp. 242–243). To approach curriculum reforms in knowledge construction, Banks and McGee Banks (2010) propose the following four levels:

> Level 1: The Contributions Approach: Focuses on heroes, holidays, and discrete cultural elements, Level 2: The Additive Approach: Content, concepts, themes, and perspectives are added to the curriculum without changing its structure, Level 3: The Transformation Approach: The structure of the curriculum is changed to enable students to view concepts, issues, events, and themes from perspectives of diverse ethnic and cultural groups, Level 4: The Social Action Approach: Students make decisions on important social issues and take action to help solve them.
>
> (p. 246)

In the first and second approaches, thinking transformation is not necessary because they do not require any social action and change. On the other hand,

60 *Metaphysical understanding of culture*

the third approach is a practice of critical thinking, as diversity becomes a key strategy for non-dualistic thinking, and the fourth approach combines a transformative approach with actions for social change. Banks and McGee Banks acknowledge, "It is unrealistic to expect a teacher to move directly from a highly mainstream-centric curriculum . . . Rather, the move from the first to higher levels of multicultural content integration is likely to be gradual and cumulative" (p. 255). In this sense, they introduce various culminating activities and one of them is a tour of an ethnic community with a warning that

> a field trip to an ethnic community or neighbourhood might reinforce stereotypes and misconception if students lack the knowledge and insights needed to view *ethnic cultures* in an understanding and caring way . . . Rather the conditions under which the contact occurs and the quality of the interaction in the contact situation are the important variables.
>
> (p. 258 [emphasis added])

In this example, Banks and McGee Banks do not provide either any further examples or augments on what teachers need to do for "the quality of the interaction in the contact situation". Presumably, teachers are required to design relevant lessons, including pedagogies, learning objectives, student activities, and assessment, and facilitate authentic intercultural interaction between students. If the interaction becomes substantial, teachers can make a conscious endeavour to practise culturally inclusive teaching and learning under their professional autonomy and academic freedom, regardless of whether relevant curriculum reform is made or not. On the surface, this understanding may fit into the Level 2 Additive Approach, or it may be located somewhere between Level 2 and Level 3, the Transformation Approach, but fundamentally it doesn't correspond to any level. This is because intercultural interaction requires metaphysical instantiations of the lesson components as well as curriculum reform and institutional changes. The former can accelerate the latter by highlighting dialectical relations between self-transformation and social transformation in which habitual dualistic thinking of teachers and students reproduces binary oppositions of cultural representation, thereby enhancing the systems. This means that Banks and McGee Banks need to explain the relations between the four levels and justify how the levels are free from habitual dualistic thinking. In other words, a pedagogical issue or challenge of multicultural education is how to cultivate self-awareness and restore the subject positions of non-dominant cultures in intercultural interaction.

Like Banks and McGee Banks, Nieto (1999, 2010) also emphasises both teachers' ethnic knowledges for multicultural education and institutional reforms towards anti-racists in terms of social justice and critical approaches to learning. A different point is that Nieto, in collaboration with Bode (2008), is concerned with the interaction among stakeholders in education. Nieto and Bode argue that differences in "race, ethnicity, religion, language, economics, sexual orientation, gender and other differences" should permeate "curriculum and instructional strategies as well as interactions among teachers, students, and families and the ways schools conceptualize the nature of teaching and learning" (p. 44). To re-theorise modernist conceptions of culture, identity, and community as fixed, unchanging, and essentialist, Nieto and her colleagues insist that we need to accept those conceptions as fluid, multiple, and complex in this postmodern era and critically reflect upon curriculum, community, and diversity in an equal manner: "Whose knowledge is it, who selected it, why is it organized and taught in this way, to this particular group?" (Nieto, Bode, Kang, & Raible, 2008, p. 177). These questions indicate that Nieto potentially attempts to explore metaphysical assumptions of cultural diversity that stakeholders hold.

As argued for intercultural value-interaction in the previous chapter, education is positioned at an ontologically lower level to culture, and cultural values are always reflected in education. Banks and McGee Banks do not address the ontological position and do not situate culture in curriculum reform for anti-racism, which results in less interest in the absence of self in reflection and the restoration of the subject position of non-dominant cultures in intercultural interaction. On the other hand, Nieto *et al.* (2008) make an attempt at overcoming the limitations of dualism with metaphysical explorations – ontological and axiological questions towards each stakeholder – although she does not use the terms in her work. In short, a point of this comparison is whether we view dualism as a cultural artefact or not. Unlike Banks and McGee Banks, Nieto assigns greater independence and authority to the role of teachers by adopting Freirean perspectives that are "understood as the result of collective action undertaken by *cultures* works – students, teachers, and others in the community" (Nieto *et al.*, 2008, p. 192 [emphasis added]). She also stresses the interaction between stakeholders:

> The result of the tension between various ideologies and the conscious (and sometimes unconscious) actions undertaken by the cultural workers . . . namely, by teachers, students, and the communities of which they are a part.
> (Nieto *et al.*, 2008, p. 193)

Nieto's emphasis on the interaction between stakeholders and teachers' roles as agents of social change appears to be supportive of intercultural interaction in the learning environment. Although she does not articulate any specific mode of being and thinking as an alternative to dualism, her argument implies that creating new pedagogies for intercultural interaction should take agents (teachers and students) beyond their own cultural experiences. This can be done through the following two ways: being aware of their own mode of being and thinking and adopting other modes of being and thinking. More theoretical and practical studies on this matter are found in *global citizenship education* in the following section.

3.3 Multicultural education as a new mode of being and thinking

UNESCO (2014) defines "global citizenship education aims to empower learners to assume active roles to face and resolve global challenges and to become

62 Metaphysical understanding of culture

proactive contributors to a more peaceful, tolerant, inclusive and secure world" (p. 15). The proponents argue that today's personal identity transcends geography or political borders in the age of globalisation as seen in Amin's (2012) *convivium as living with difference*, Ang's (2001) *together-in-difference*, and Vertovec's (2007) *super-diversity*, and global citizenship or world citizenship is believed to supersede the limitations of multicultural education, which will be seen in Nussbaum's (1997; 2007; 2009) *cultivating humanity* and Rizvi's (2009; 2011) *cosmopolitan learning*.

Nussbaum (2009) argues that liberal education should aim to cultivate humanity. She argues that three abilities are required:

> First is the capacity for critical examination of oneself and one's traditions . . . further [second], an ability to see themselves . . . as human beings bound to all other human beings by ties of recognition and concern . . . the third ability . . . to think what it might be like to be in the shoes of a person different from oneself . . .
>
> (pp. 9–11)

Adopting Dewey's (1911/2009) "Democracy and Education", Nussbaum (2009) stresses the importance of the first ability, Socratic critical thinking, which is the key to a nation's transition to a democratic society that is achieved through overcoming "traditional barriers of race, class, and wealth" and educating members' "personal initiative and adaptability" (p. 56). She also stresses that the focus of criticism should be on "inadequacy of tradition for democratic life" and education must support "the struggle of reason for its legitimate supremacy" (p. 56). This is Socratic "examined life" and "unexamined life" (Nussbaum, 1997, p. 30), which is similar to Dewey's civilised mind and uncivilised mind. Due to increasingly "global interdependence" and "the impoverished norms of market exchange", the second capacity, global citizenship, which requires to us "develop an understanding of the history and character of the diverse groups", is becoming more important (Nussbaum, 2007, p. 38). She argues that today's citizens are required to learn "how to inquire in more depth into at least one unfamiliar tradition . . . focusing on an understanding of how differences of religion, race, and gender have been associated with differential life opportunities" (Nussbaum, 2009, p. 57). The first and the second abilities determine the goal of (liberal) higher education that is "a cultivation of the whole human being for the functions of citizenship and life generally" (Nussbaum, 1997, p. 9). The goal can be achieved through the third capacity, imaginative understanding, which is the ability to empathise with others and to put oneself in another's place. It seems that Nussbaum attempts to overcome the dualisms through cultivating a (new) moral virtue by highlighting more on the interconnectedness and interrelatedness between humans and nature than the separateness and independence between them. In this sense, her philosophical arguments on human relationships seem to be built based on non-dualism, not anti-dualism.

Nussbaum views those three abilities as an organic whole: critical thinking, global citizenship, and imaginative understanding. For example, studying other

Multicultural educational models   63

cultures requires a learner to develop the capacities for narrative imagination and identification, which leads one to deepen critical self-examination about one's own culture. This means that, without understanding others and oneself equally and relationally, one neither becomes a world citizen nor makes any contributions to liberal education and multicultural society. She (1997) compellingly argues, "The goal of producing world citizens is profoundly opposed to the spirit of identity politics which holds that one's primary affiliation is with one's local group, whether religious or ethnics or based on sexuality or gender" (pp. 109–110). Then how can we embed such abilities in curriculum? Nussbaum argues that Socratic criticism is a way of respecting others, which is the foundation for curriculum at least in liberal education. What she presupposes in her cultivating humanity is that humans face similar problems about morality, appetites, property, and planning their lives. This means that (emotional) identification with humanity plays an important role in her understanding of liberal education. Another assumption she presumes is that (Socratic) critical reasoning corrodes religious beliefs and promotes scepticism, which leads to the adjudication of value conflicts. In this sense, she criticises postmodern and conservative writers who undermine Socratic criticism (or the importance of reasoning). Her concept of liberal education based on cosmopolitanism certainly does not devalue local affinities, identities, or beliefs, but focuses more on an individual's primary morality, which cannot be evaded by cultural behaviours (Naseem & Hyslop-Margison, 2006). In this sense, Nussbaum argues against identity politics that undermines identification with humanity and also criticises the perceived problem of cultural relativism in which one's primary concern is one's local/ethnic group (Naseem & Hyslop-Margison, 2006).

An issue in Nussbaum's cosmopolitanism is that she does not identify characteristics and values that can be shared with various local identities (Naseem & Hyslop-Margison, 2006). In effect, she does not articulate intercultural interaction but argues that cultivating reasoning abilities is only the means. As Naseem and Hyslop-Margison (2006) point out, Nussbaum does not address the fact that many religions "reject reason and self-examination as the primary means of acquiring moral knowledge, and appeal instead to faith in metaphysical beliefs or scared text" (Naseem & Hyslop-Margison, 2006, p. 58). They also criticise that Nussbaum's cosmopolitanism creates unnecessary tensions with cultures that are unwilling to accept "its basic tenets of reason and self-examination as universal goods" (p. 58). They conclude their criticism with a suggestion that cosmopolitanism should aim to create "a global community without violating local sensibilities" (p. 59). However, it is unclear what epistemological framework and moral application should be applied in the global community and to what extent they need to be used to redeem the shortcomings. Naseem and Hyslop-Margison also need to prove that their concept of global community is culturally unbound or culturally inclusive. While I agree that critical reasoning can significantly contribute to self-examination, thereby enriching intercultural interaction, I also stress that Nussbaum's three abilities may be metaphysically and pedagogically unstable because of her expectation of critical thinking that can corrode religious beliefs. Unless she proves that her critical reasoning is value-free and intercultural

64 Metaphysical understanding of culture

interaction can be implemented without human-to-human interaction, her critical reasoning would further enhance the absence of the self in self-examination.
While I agree that the three abilities are definitely necessary for intercultural
interaction, they are insufficient, as she does not explore culturally bound individuality. In fact, she presumes that individuality should not be bound by a culture, as she believes that critical thinking is culturally unbound. This criticism
recalls Stratton and Ang's (1994) argument in which Nussbaum's cultivating
humanity is metaphysically and logically aligned with the utopian ideal of U.S.A.
multiculturalism. In essence, the three abilities appear to promote the intellectual
freedom of individuals in creating their own future, to hypostatise other cultures,
and to reproduce binary oppositions of cultural representation.

The next well-known author of cosmopolitanism is Rizvi (2009; 2011) who
argues that contemporary multicultural education should acknowledge the
intercultural and transnational nature of economic, political, and social changes
and offers related instructional methods. Rizvi (2009) presumes that the nature
of the world is "interconnected and interdependent globally" and requires
"global solutions" (p. 253). Adopting Tomlinson's (2000) complex connectivity, he (2011) argues, "In the context of growing levels of global interconnectivity and interdependence, ideological borders would also fall" (p. 225).
He (2009; 2011) argues that education should respond to contemporary conditions of globalisation and promote multiple perspectives on knowing and
interaction with others so that we may understand others and ourselves. Rizvi's cosmopolitanism recalls Gilroy's rhizomatic intercultural networks in that
both reposition minorities as equal agents for social change. Gilroy attempts
to achieve this by articulating the metaphysical structure of cultural diversity
through the rhizomatic theory, whereas Rizvi (2009) proposes an integration
of curriculum with defined pedagogical values that are "critical exploration and
imagination, an open-ended exercise in cross-cultural deliberation . . . [with]
a position that is reflexive of its epistemic assumptions" (p. 264). He develops
his concept of epistemic virtues with two instructional methods: *collaboration*
and *interrogation*. For him, collaboration needs to be "transcultural" to the
extent that it collectively develops through comparative and global processes,
and interrogation is to develop a new set of values to understand the networked
environments – mobility, exchange, and hybridisation. Rizvi (2011) synthesises
those two methods as a pedagogic approach that is aimed at encouraging people
to reveal "how the tensions between *cultures* indeed can be comprehended and
transcended", "understand others both in their terms as well as ours, as a way
of . . . how both representations are socially constituted" (p. 234 [empha-
sis added]). In this sense, his two methods are certainly more instructive than
those of Nussbaum.

Rizvi's pedagogical argument for cosmopolitan learning presumes that the aim
of education is to develop social imagination that is the key ability to understand and take action in the transformational processes. In this sense, education becomes more concerned with facilitating intercultural interaction that
transforms cultural/religious identities. He (2009) argues that transforming

Multicultural educational models 65

pedagogy is fundamentally formed by two concepts: *relationality* and *reflexivity*. Relationality refers to the ontological nature of cultural diversity that all cultures are sustained by their encounters with others and, therefore, our engagement in intercultural interaction must be reflexive. He defines reflexivity as becoming self-conscious and knowledgeable about one's own taken-for-granted assumptions. In this sense, he argues that one's transformation occurs through one's interlocking with other cultural trajectories. His two concepts are interrelated in a way that transforming pedagogy ultimately pursues both self and social transformation as an outcome of intercultural interaction. In sum, he stresses (a) the importance of self-awareness of one's own cultural assumptions, thereby understanding others; (b) the ontologically networked world; and (c) the self and social transformation as a result of intercultural interaction. His instructional methods based on epistemic virtues are aimed at encouraging students to be transcendental to their cultures and to participate in global citizenship. This means that his pedagogical discourse situates cultures in the values of global citizenship and reduced the realistic power of cultural value conflicts, which is insufficient to restore the subject position of others in intercultural interaction.

Both Nussbaum and Rizvi acknowledge the power of culture on reality and focus on the dialectic transformation of self and community. However, their transforming pedagogy presumes a culture as a subordinate concept of globalisation and justifies the transformation of self and community without cultural change. As Nussbaum promotes culturally unbound individuality based on critical reasoning as value-free, Rizvi also regards his new pedagogic work through networks as culture-free. As a result, his concept of relationality encourages stakeholders to be aware of their own cultural assumptions, whereas his concept of reflexivity encourages them to be outside of their own culture and to participate in global citizenship education, which takes cultural change out from his pedagogic work through networks. This ontological contradiction is caused by not conducting validation of proposed or embedded pedagogical values and methods from other cultural perspectives or by not disclosing the ontological justification.

3.4 Multicultural education models and their underlying values

The earlier review of the discourses of contemporary multicultural education reveals some significant issues associated with intercultural interaction, including (a) the absence of the self, (b) the non-subject position of other cultures in intercultural interaction, and (c) no considerations of culturally bound individuality and pedagogy. These outcomes further raise the need for metaphysical analysis of existing multicultural education models, in particular, why and how the epistemic dualism restricts the realisation of intercultural interaction in multicultural education and what underlying values are embedded and facilitated. In this context, I will review six multicultural educational models, including conservative multiculturalism, liberal multiculturalism, pluralist multiculturalism, left-essentialist multiculturalism, critical multiculturalism, and intercultural dialogue, which

66 *Metaphysical understanding of culture*

are identified in a taxonomic category of multicultural education proposed by Antonette (2008) and Kincheloe and Steinberg (1997), and the multiculturalism versus interculturalism of Meer and Modood (2012).

3.4.1 *Conservative multiculturalism*

Conservative multiculturalism can be described as a set of strategies and materials and it is intended to transform other cultures into a dominant culture based on race superiority and mono-culturalism (Antonette, 2008). Critics argue that the aims of conservative multiculturalism are to identify cultural differences and to teach that the differences are only appreciated and comprehended outside national boundaries (Antonette, 2008). Conservative multiculturalists consider multiculturalism as tokenistic in that such temporary phenomenon will ultimately be dissolved by the dominant culture of whiteness. Its underlying value is liberalism, which is practically aimed at broadening the diversity of individuals' lives and reducing others' perceptions that the dominant culture is white (Auster, 2004). In other words, such unquestioning superiority of the dominant culture and system institutionally determines minority groups as peripheral and marginal and ultimately merges them into the mainstream. In this sense, the function of education is to uphold and conserve whiteness (Kincheloe & Steinberg, 1997). Conservative multiculturalists advocate using moral education for a smooth transition of minority ethnic individuals to the mainstream and exploring curriculum theory and practice to cultivate individuals' tolerance for one another's contradictories (Auster, 2004). In this context, there is no room for cultural diversity.

The educational strategies of conservative multiculturalists are to keep cultural differences as relative preferences for individuals and to impede possible changes in current cultural relationships (Antonette, 2008). In this sense, "racial identification is skewed by a superficial and stereotype-ridden knowledge base" according to Antonette (2008, p. 31), which is a mono-cultural belief in the superiority of Western patriarchal culture (Kincheloe & Steinberg, 1997). Mono-culturalists also agree that "non-whites and the poor are inferior to individuals from the white middle or upper-middle class" (Kincheloe & Steinberg, 1997, p. 3), although the inferiority is rarely stated in public. It is believed that whiteness is the norm and is the invisible barometer of all other ethnicities (Kincheloe & Steinberg, 1997). Hence mono-culturalists argue that allowing ethnic minorities to practise their religious and cultural customs and values at work and school is provisional and temporary, and melting into the *Great Pot* is expected to continue (Antonette, 2008; Lander & Past, 2002). In this context, if a person belongs to a non-dominant cultural group, then one is permanently different from those who are placed within the (white) boundary (Antonette, 2008). Based on a strictly dualist approach to other cultures, conservative multiculturalists reify the distinction between white and non-white individuals by excluding non-whites in curriculum development and cultural education. In addition, they only accept skills and capabilities of non-white individuals who can bring substantive benefits to the country's economy, but in many cases, those are seen as obstacles to political and economic unification of mankind (Auster, 2004). In education,

Multicultural educational models   67

thus, minority ethnic groups are perceived as peripheral in the development of curriculum and pedagogies.

3.4.2 Liberal multiculturalism

Liberal multiculturalists use their liberalism assumption about individuals as a starting point – namely, *abstract individualism*. This liberal-democratic ideology posits as "a brute parameter of the human condition that exists and persists regardless of time or place" (Huard, 2007, p. 60). Liberal multiculturalists advocate multiculturalism on the basis of liberal values that stem from individual rights such as freedom, autonomy, and equality (Schuster, 2006). They tend to avoid both "the collectivism of radical multiculturalism and the exaggerated individualism associated with liberalism" (Schuster, 2006, para. 12). For liberal multiculturalists, cultural differences are essential for individuals and thus for individual equality (Schuster, 2006). Individuals' need for culture is a value of liberalism in which a sense of belonging and a strong cultural identity are essential for understanding and promoting individual equality (Goodin, 2006). Liberal multiculturalism is characterised by two value models: protective and self-developmental (Goodin, 2006). The protective model is "to protect *minority cultures* against assimilationists and homogenizing intrusions and the majority", whereas the self-development model is "the self-defensive liberalism of the more purely protectionist sort" (Goodin, 2006, p. 289 [emphasis added]). With the models, liberal multiculturalists emphasise "common humanity and natural equality in terms of differences in *cultures* with the eventual goal being the celebration of assumed differences and inequalities" (Sugiharto, 2013, p. 21 [emphasis added]).

According to Kincheloe and Steinberg (1997), "Such liberal ideological dynamics are grounded on an allegedly neutral and universal process of consciousness construction that is unaffected by racial, class and gender differences. These dynamics of differences are erased by the ideological appeal of consensus and similarity" (p. 11). On the surface, liberal multiculturalists promotes an inclusive strategy of teaching and learning to understand cultural differences. However, it engages in "pseudo-depoliticisation" in which cultural assimilation is unchallenged by promoting abstract individualism (Kincheloe & Steinberg, 1997, p. 13). Like conservative multiculturalists, liberal multiculturalists view whiteness as non-ethnic, but the difference is that the latter understands both whiteness and non-whiteness in terms of liberal values. For them, values such as humanity, individualism, and equality are the foundational ideas for curriculum development and multicultural education. However, they label ethnic minorities as inferior in liberal society because they perceive that minority people do not exercise the innate rights of liberal values. As a result, ethnic minorities are regarded as a resource for social events (i.e., a multicultural costume parade, face painting using international flags) and their cultural values are excluded in national identity building. In addition, cultural diversity within that liberal framework becomes compatible with moral capacities of individuals such as tolerance and autonomy. Despite their emphasis on equality, liberal multiculturalists hold the belief that social realities are fixed entities and thus they ignore collective

68   *Metaphysical understanding of culture*

differences. Like conservative multiculturalism, liberal multiculturalism, in practice, does not perceive ethnic minorities as equal participants in developing cultural curriculum and pedagogies because they are perceived as incompetent individuals.

3.4.3 Pluralist multiculturalism

"Cultural pluralism refers to a situation where different groups in society maintain their distinctive *cultures* while co-existing peacefully with the dominant group" (Anderson & Taylor, 2003, p. 245 [emphasis added]). Its fundamental assumption is egalitarianism – no culture can be superior to others (Anderson & Taylor, 2003; Muchenje, 2012; Pai & Adler, 1997). Thus such pluralists view cultural diversity as a value in itself and their emphasis is on differences rather than on an abstract universal notion of human nature and personhood. The diversity, they argue, enhances not only attitudes of tolerance, respect, and understanding towards others but also intercultural understanding for nation building (Kincheloe & Steinberg, 1997). Politically, therefore, pluralist multiculturalism is associated with attempts to protect oppressed cultures and minority ethnic groups (Muchenje, 2012).

As pluralist multiculturalism focuses on cultural differences, its priority of education is to understand cultural diversity as a value and thus to respect other cultures. In this sense, pluralists reject the liberal ideal of universal citizenship because the universality ignores particularity and difference, and they argue that an acknowledgement of cultural belonging and identity can lead to community engagement and civic participation (Grillo, 2005). For example, Young (1989) argues that "some groups will find themselves treated as second-class citizens" when citizenship rights are extended to all groups (p. 250) because "strict adherence to a principle of equal treatment tends to perpetuate oppression or disadvantage" (p. 265). In other words, as individuals are seen as citizens of the polity, he asserts that individuals should put down their particular identities and cultures and adopt the group differentiated citizenship. Young provides three specific supports for those differentiated citizens: collective empowerment through self-organisation, voicing collective approach to social policies, and voting power on related policies (p. 261). In practice, the group differentiated citizenship and the given or restored rights of minority groups would enable them to protect their cultural values and identities against homogenisation. However, critics are suspicious of the possibility that the individual citizen can enjoy rights independent of contexts such as class, race, ethnicity, religion, and gender because these specific contexts are seen as determining citizenship (Kincheloe & Steinberg, 1997). Furthermore, as Grillo (2005) points out, if we do not know how individuality is shaped in other cultures and how diverse individuality can interact with one another in a culturally diverse environment, their efforts, such as interfaith dialogue and intercultural understanding, would result in plural mono-culturalism with faith-based separatism and the absence of civic cohesion.

3.4.4 Left-essentialist multiculturalism

All forms of -*centrism*, such as Afrocentrism and Indigenous-centrism, except Eurocentrism, are the forms of left-essentialist multiculturalism that connect cultural differences and identities with a historical past of cultural authenticity (May, 1999). Left-essentialist multiculturalists address historical and current disadvantages, including racism, class oppression, sexism, and homophobia, and have the belief that gender, sexuality, race, and ethnicity hold essential, unchanging characteristics that make people who they are (Kincheloe & Steinberg, 1997). They also argue that such characteristics have been romanticised and historically modified so that social and cultural authenticity will ultimately deteriorate (Kincheloe & Steinberg, 1997).

For left-essentialist multiculturalists, multicultural education should begin with accepting the fact that cultural and historical forces shape individuals' identities and subjectivity. They uphold that ethnic knowledge needs to be studied as separate from white knowledge, and thus the aim of multicultural education is to criticise various forms of bias, stereotypes, and misinformation towards race and ethnicity (Kincheloe & Steinberg, 1997). In this way, they argue that multicultural education should promote understanding social, political, and historical problems by de-romanticising ethnic knowledge and provide students with strategies for improving social conditions. However, critics argue that left-essentialist multiculturalism "does so at the cost of overstating the importance of ethnicity and culture, and understating the fluid and dialogic nature of inter- and intra-group relations" (May, 1999, p. 21). In contemporary multicultural contexts, this criticism may be reasonable in situations in which intercultural and interreligious dialogue and cooperation are significant barometers of social cohesion. Yet such criticism should not minimise the ongoing impact of historical and collective traumas of minority ethnic groups. As Kincheloe and Steinberg (1997) point out, such moralistic reductionism tends to ignore the details of racism and other forms of oppression, and thus an integration of subjugated ethnic knowledge into the mainstream curriculum is still a legitimate action. In the context of intercultural interaction, however, this raises a question of whether such an attitude and position are part of cultural perspectives or a result of historical and collective traumas.

3.4.5 Critical multiculturalism

Critical multiculturalism challenges liberal forms of multicultural education (May & Sleeter, 2010). It integrates various critical approaches to education such as anti-racist education, critical pedagogy, and critical race theory and focuses on understanding oppression and institutionalisation of unequal power relations in education (May & Sleeter, 2010). It is often called "social reconstructionist multicultural education" that aims to transform society by achieving awareness of the social, economic, and political forces that shape society (O'Grady, 2000, p. 5). That is to say, critical multiculturalists presume that educational systems

70 *Metaphysical understanding of culture*

can provide an environment for promoting social and personal transformation. They argue that transformative education requires questioning unexamined beliefs and assumptions and thinking critically about policies and practices that cause and sustain inequality and injustice (Giroux, 1988; O'Grady, 2000). Its fundamental philosophy is to recognise humans as social beings that are shaped by socio-cultural forces and to view "social reality as mutable, dynamic, heterogeneous, discursively constructed and implicated in political and historical contexts" (Sugiharto, 2013, p. 21). In this sense, they understand a culture as "a site of conflict and struggle" and require educators to understand its relevant privilege and power relationships (Sugiharto, 2013) and to move towards the transformation of social, cultural, and institutional structures perpetuating oppression (Kincheloe & Steinberg, 1997).

Critical multiculturalism theoretically relies on Freire's critical pedagogy in which community building has to be done based on unity in diversity (Kincheloe & Steinberg, 1997). This means that critical thinking and ethical reasoning are key pedagogical strategies. Critical multicultural education examines and interrogates common humanity and natural equality constructed in a specific political and ideological context, and its aim of social transformation can be realised by the reform of cultural pathology (Sugiharto, 2013, p. 21). Specifically, students are trained to develop social perspectives by being aware of their role as historical agents; students are capable of critically examining white (male) experiences that are the invisible dominant norms measuring other cultures, and the aim of critical multicultural education is to problematise a homogeneous community grounded on consensus and its injustice and exclusionary practices (Kincheloe & Steinberg, 1997). However, if building a worldview, examining an ideology, and problematising consensus are learning processes, which are culturally bound, how can all students equally participate in the processes?

3.4.6 Intercultural dialogue

Intercultural dialogue, as a political discourse and a more practical form of cultural pluralism, offers positive qualities of cultural diversity such as encouragement of communication, recognition of dynamic identities, and promotion of unity (Meer & Modood, 2012). It pursues a group-oriented approach, focuses on cultural diversity and communities, and promotes that cultures are of value (Taylor, 1994; Parekh, 2000). It accepts pluralism by emphasising interactive diversity and cultural change (Vreede, 2009). It, as a practical and group-oriented form of multiculturalism, can be achieved by neither universalism nor relativism (Vreede, 2009). In this sense, the role of education ensures that students are able to carry out "an open and respectful exchange between individuals, groups and organisations with different cultural backgrounds or worldviews" (European Institute for Comparative Cultural Research, 2008, XIII). To achieve this, education should nurture students' "open-mindedness, a critical approach to one's own culture and a pluralist orientation to *other cultures*" (Vreede, 2009, n.p. [emphasis added]).

Unlike other multicultural models, a process of intercultural dialogue could lead to the emergence of a new culture because it regards a culture as a social construct (Vreede, 2009). An emergent culture also mounts a challenge that, according to UNESCO (2006), is "to establish and maintain the balance between conformity with its general guiding principles and the requirements of specific cultural context" (p. 10). This presumes that the conflicts and tensions between universalism and cultural pluralism and between difference and diversity are inevitable (UNESCO, 2006). Thus intercultural dialogic education emphasises the universality of human rights and supports cultural differences at the same time. In practice, participants need to have not only (a) a deep understanding of their own culture but also (b) the ability to explain their own culture from other cultural perspectives. However, not all cultures prompt such capabilities. Another concern is that intercultural dialogic education does not embrace religious characteristics that greatly influence a person's belief, attitude, perception, and behaviour towards other religions and cultures.

3.5 Conclusion: Metaphysical issues and challenges of multicultural education models

As discussed in the previous chapter, ontology, epistemology, and axiology are deeply associated with educational models and pedagogical strategies. To conclude this chapter, I will reconstitute the landscape of the six multicultural education models with the three dimensions of metaphysics in order to open up new discourses of multicultural education.

3.4.1 Ontological justification for cultural diversity

As argued, the ontological concerns are the absence of the self and the non-subject position of other cultures in intercultural interaction.

For those who support conservative multiculturalism and liberal multiculturalism education, self-awareness becomes externally driven and is not accompanied by self-reflection because white knowledge (or Angle-Saxon Protestant/Western European Christians knowledge) is the only source of knowledge, and ethnic knowledge as subjugated knowledge is less important or supplementary to sustaining whiteness. Thus they view cultural diversity as a temporary phenomenon, and intercultural interaction means teaching others in a way that is sensitive to individuals' rights. This means that the universal values of human rights based on individual freedom and individual liberty can only be applicable to those who learn and practice abstract individualism (Huard, 2007; Schuster, 2006). As a result, intercultural interaction does not come into existence through holding the subject position of other cultures, but the forced assimilation of others.

For supporters of pluralist multiculturalism and intercultural dialogue, on the other hand, the ontological concerns appear significant because learning about other cultures and one's own culture are equally important. They define the nature of knowledge within the context of cultural diversity and emphasise the

72 *Metaphysical understanding of culture*

values of cultural diversity towards building an inclusive society. In particular, intercultural dialogic education is more group-oriented than the other education models because it stresses interaction and communication skills among different cultural communities. Hence they acknowledge that the subject position of other cultures is critical to intercultural interaction. However, both self-reflection and self-awareness could remain externally driven because individuals' capabilities of interaction and communication with different cultures are the source of knowledge, and ethnic knowledge is only valid when it facilitates such capabilities.

In left-essentialist multicultural education and critical multicultural education, the self-reflection and the subject position become more important. Knowledge is understood as a constitutive component of social reality and a form of identity within specific social contexts and power relations. In particular, critical multiculturalists, based on critical pedagogy and transformative education, emphasises critical examinations of cultural assumptions sustaining and reproducing inequality and injustice. However, self-awareness becomes vague and indistinct because self-transformation is only valid when it leads to social change.

Consequently, those six multicultural educational models tend to either ignore or conceal their ontological assumptions of cultural diversity or confine their metaphysical assumptions to personal capabilities and/or social ones. Their ontological discourses are confined to the binary oppositions between nature and culture, between cultures, and/or between society and self rather than articulate the relationships. In essence, cultural diversity cannot be fully investigated by a positivist sense of scientific approaches because other cultures have no Western sense of individuality and socialisation (i.e., holistic and monistic cultures). In this sense, the intercultural dialogic model would be more practical than the other models. However it needs to be more explicit in understanding the relationships between cultures and culturally bound individuality. Otherwise, its pluralistic approach will rely too much on individuals' communicative ability that is believed to be culturally unbound and thus, other cultures are not given an opportunity to express their subject position in intercultural interaction. Norms, processes, and methods used in an intercultural dialogic process should not be regarded as culture-free.

3.4.2 Epistemological assumptions and processes

An epistemological assumption found in conservative multiculturalism and liberal multiculturalism is dualistic reductionism of cultural identity in which whiteness, as an invisible barometer of normality, determines curricular content and pedagogical strategies, thereby shaping instructional methods and human relations. In this sense, education is used to identify and remove or minimise non-white characteristics against white ones.

On the other hand, left-essentialist multiculturalism and critical multiculturalism focus on historical and current social disadvantages to include both white and non-white people in ethnic knowledge. Both are aware of social, economic, and political forces that shape individuals and society and pursue social transformation to remove racial and ethnic inequality. In doing so, left-essentialists attempt to invert traditional stereotypes and truth claims, whereas critical theorists strive to cultivate critical thinking and ethical reasoning in individuals. Their epistemological process is to strengthen cultural authenticity of minority groups in order to realise their equal power in a society by reversing the binary opposition rather than de/reconstructing it. In practice, their epistemological process aims to minimise whiteness by enhancing non-whiteness because it is believed that equal participation between white and non-white people is impossible unless social transformation occurs. Ironically and in a metaphysical sense, this may be achieved through a dualistic epistemic process in which what non-white people have done against white people is to what white people have done against non-white people. As a result, self-reflection of non-whiteness is omitted or less emphasised, which is unsupportive of realising the ontological position for intercultural interaction that white and non-white need to be equal agents.

Unlike the previous four multicultural education models, both pluralist multiculturalism and intercultural dialogue models focus on interaction and communication between white and non-white individuals for a cohesive community or nation. In these models, a primary educational concern is on nurturing the capacity of individuals to act independently and to make their own decisions about intercultural understanding and respect. In this sense, the role of education is to promote egalitarianism and individualism, which are believed to enable individuals to understand cultural diversity as social assets and mutually deepen intercultural dialogue. Its epistemological process towards cultural diversity is used to encourage both white and non-white participants to contemplate society as a living community and the common problems both face. The process is arranged based on optimistic faith in the power of individualism that can neutralise cultural and religious differences in intercultural interaction. As a result, intercultural dialogic educators tend neither to problematise whiteness nor to examine intercultural interaction as culture bound. In practice, there would be no question about its communicative process per se. This means that the process can lead to alienate other cultures from the mainstream because some cultures (e.g., Islam and Confucianism) do not distinguish between individual identity and cultural/religious identity and have no a Western sense of individualism. As a result, the process can be perceived as pluralistic mono-culturalism, and a Western sense of individualism is often considered ruthlessly selfishness or an anti-social attitude.

3.4.3 Axiological interaction of cultures

The underlying values of conservative multiculturalism and liberal multiculturalism are enlightenment and individualism, which are ideologically used to advocate whiteness. In a context of multicultural education, the values are restricted to reinforce strongly (ethnic) independent and reasonable individuals who are capable of contributing to economic and public life. Hence the role of education is to nurture students to become such individuals. This is also found in the other multicultural models, but their approaches to such individuality are more critical and responsible: Proponents of critical and left-essentialist multiculturalism emphasise the critical and reasonable abilities of individuals, whereas those

74 *Metaphysical understanding of culture*

of intercultural dialogue require individuals to be more responsible, reflective, and skilful in intercultural/interfaith communication. Unlike all of these models, only pluralist multiculturalism shows flexibility by welcoming additional values for *differentiated citizens* (i.e., collaboration or collaborative individuals) other than individualism. However, the additional values are only accepted and valid if those are proved to be effective to cultivate such citizenship.

Overall, each education model has a different image of individuality in terms of roles, functions, and responsibilities in society. Their underlying values of individuality also determine their ontological positions in understanding cultural diversity and justify appropriate epistemological processes for intercultural interaction. There are three different understandings of individuality in those six models. As seen earlier, the core value of conservative and liberal multiculturalism is *abstract individualism*. While promoting individuals' equity and freedom, they are likely to acknowledge influences of social, political, and economic conditions on individuals. On the other hand, critical and left-essentialist multiculturalism put more weight on social conditions that are believed to cause oppression and discrimination. In this context, *morally responsible individuals* are understood as the foundations for reforming and changing social systems in a more equal and inclusive way and thus social justice is achieved. Lastly, pluralists and intercultural dialogic multiculturalism expect individuals to be *rational, reflective, and moral* towards mutual interaction between individuals. In this sense, social transformation is relatively less emphasised in education.

In the learning environment, each model appears to promote different values of individuality, but the common metaphysical reference points are ontological dualisms between white and non-white cultures, between individual transformation and social transformation, and between reflective and non-reflective individuals who make dual commitments in intercultural interaction. For example, reflective individuals are the subjects of education and the meaning of learning, whereas non-reflective individuals are the objects of education and the aims of teaching. Such approaches are hardly seen in most non-Western cultures/religions, which will be addressed in Part III.

References

Amin, A. (2012). *Land of strangers*. Cambridge: Polity Press.

Anderson, M.L., & Taylor, H.L. (2003). *Sociology: The essentials*. London: Thomas Wadsworth.

Ang, I. (2001). *On not speaking Chinese: Living between Asia and the West*. London: Routledge.

Antonette, L. (2008). Liberal and conservative multiculturalism after September 11. *Multicultural Review, 12*(2), 29–35.

Auster, L. (2004). How the multicultural ideology captured America. *The Social Contract, 14*(3), 197–208.

Banks, J.A. (1997). *Educating citizens in a multicultural society*. New York: Teachers College Press.

Multicultural educational models 75

Banks, J.A., & McGee Banks, C.A. (2010). *Multicultural education: Issues and perspectives* (7th ed.). Hoboken, NJ: John Wiley & Sons, Inc.

Dewey, J. (2009). *Democracy and education: An Introduction to the philosophy of education*. New York: Macmillan. (Original work published 1911)

European Institute for Comparative Cultural Research. (2008). *Sharing diversity: National approaches to intercultural dialogue in Europe* (Report). Retrieved from: http://www.interculturaldialogue.eu/web/files/14/en/Sharing_Diversity_Final_Report.pdf

Giroux, H.A. (1988). *Teachers as intellectuals: Toward a critical pedagogy of learning*. Granby, MA: Bergin and Garvey. Retrieved from http://teacherrenewal.wiki.westga.edu/file/view/Rethinking+the+Language+of+Schooling.html

Goodin, R.E. (2006). Liberal multiculturalism: Protective and polyglot. *Political Theory, 34*(3), 289–303.

Grillo, R. (2005). *Backlash against diversity? Identity and cultural politics in European cities*. Centre on migration, policy and society [working paper no. 14]. University of Oxford. Retrieved from http://www.compas.ox.ac.uk/fileadmin/files/Publications/working_papers/WP_2005/Ralph%20Grillo%20WP0514.pdf

Hage, G. (1998). *White nation: Fantasies of White supremacy in a multicultural society*. Annadale, NSW: Pluto.

Hidalgo, R., Chávez-Chávez, R., & Ramage, J.C. (1996). Multicultural education: Landscape for reform in the 21st century. In J. Sikula, T.J. Buttery, & E. Guyton (Eds.), *Handbook of Research on Teacher Education* (pp. 761–778). New York: Macmillan.

Huard, R.L. (2007). *Plato's political philosophy: The cave*. New York: Algora Publishing.

Kincheloe, J.L., & Steinberg, S.R. (1997). *Changing multiculturalism: New times, new curriculum*. London: Open University Press.

Lander, E., & Past, M. (2002). Eurocentrism, modern knowledges, and the 'Natural' order of global capital. *Nepantla: Views from South, 2*(2), 245–268.

May, S. (1999). Critical multiculturalism and cultural difference: Avoiding essentialism. In S. May (Ed.), *Critical Multiculturalism: Rethinking Multicultural and Antiracist Education* (pp. 11–41). London: Falmer Press.

May, S., & Sleeter, C.E. (Eds.) (2010). *Critical multiculturalism: Theory and praxis*. New York: Routledge.

Meer, N., & Modood, T. (2012). How does interculturalism contrast with multiculturalism? *Journal of Intercultural Studies, 33*(2), 175–196.

Muchenje, F. (2012). Cultural pluralism and the quest for nation building in Africa: The rationale for multicultural education. *Journal of Sustainable Development in Africa, 14*(4), 70–81.

Naseem, M.A., & Hyslop-Margison, E.J. (2006). Nussbaum's concept of cosmopolitanism: Practical possibility or academic delusion? *Paideusis, 15*(2), 51–60.

Nieto, S. (1999). *The light in their eyes: Creating multicultural learning communities*. New York: Teachers College Press.

Nieto, S. (2010). *The light in their eyes: Creating multicultural learning communities* (2nd ed.). New York: Teachers College Press.

Nieto, S., & Bode, P. (2008). *Affirming diversity: The sociopolitical context of multicultural education* (5th ed.). Boston: Allyn & Bacon.

Nieto, S., Bode, P., Kang, E., & Raible, J. (2008). Identity, community and diversity Retheorizing multicultural curriculum for the postmodern era. In F.M. Connelly, M.F. He & J. Phillion (Eds.), *The SAGE Handbook of Curriculum and Instruction* (pp. 176–197). Thousand Oaks, CA: Sage.

76 Metaphysical understanding of culture

Nussbaum, M.C. (1997). *Cultivating humanity: A classical defense of reform in liberal education*. Cambridge, MA: Harvard University Press.

Nussbaum, M.C. (2007). Cultivating humanity and world citizenship. In Forum for the Future of Higher Education (Ed.), *Forum Futures 2007: Exploring the Future of Higher Education* (pp. 37–40). Cambridge, MA: Forum for the Future of Higher Education. Retrieved from https://net.educause.edu/ir/library/pdf/ff0709s.pdf

Nussbaum, M.C. (2009). Tagore, Dewey, and the imminent demise of liberal education. In H. Siegel (Ed.), *The Oxford Handbook of Philosophy of Education* (pp. 52–64). New York: Oxford University Press.

O'Grady, C. (Ed.). (2000). *Integrating service learning and multicultural education in colleges and universities*. Mahwah, NJ: Lawrence Erlbaum Associates.

Pai, Y., & Adler, S.A. (1997). *Cultural foundations of education*. Upper Saddle River, NJ: Prentice Hall.

Parekh, B. (2000). *Rethinking multiculturalism: Cultural diversity and political theory*. Houndmills/London: Macmillan Press.

Rizvi, F. (2009). Towards cosmopolitan learning. *Discourse: Studies in the Cultural Politics of Education, 30*(3), 253–268.

Rizvi, F. (2011). Beyond the social imaginary of 'clash of civilizations'? *Educational philosophy and theory, 43*(3), 225–235.

Schuster, A. (2006). Does liberalism need multiculturalism? A critique of liberal multiculturalism. *Essays in Philosophy, 7*(1), Article 15. Retrieved from http://commons.pacificu.edu/cgi/viewcontent.cgi?article=1231&context=eip

Stanesby, C., & Thomas, E. (2012). Seeing the invisible, and confronting culture: From pre-service teacher to graduate. In J. Phillips & J. Lampert (Eds.), *Introductory Indigenous Studies in Education: Reflection and the Importance of Knowing* (pp. 56–77). Sydney, Australia: Pearson.

Stratton, J., & Ang, I. (1994). Multicultural imagined communities: Cultural difference and national identity in Australia and the USA. *Continuum: The Australian Journal of Media & Culture, 8*(2). Retrieved from http://wwwmcc.murdoch.edu.au/readingroom/8.2/Stratton.html

Sugiharto, S. (2013). Critical multiculturalism and the politics of identity in academic writing. *K@ta, 15*(1), 19–24.

Taylor, C. (1994). The politics of recognition. In A. Gutmann (Ed.), *Multiculturalism. Examining the Politics of Recognition* (pp. 36–46). Princeton: Princeton University Press.

UNESCO. (2006). *UNESCO Guidelines on intercultural education*. Retrieved from http://unesdoc.unesco.org/images/0014/001478/147878e.pdf

UNESCO. (2014). *Global citizenship education: Preparing learners for the challenges of the twenty-first century*. Retrieved from http://unesdoc.unesco.org/images/0022/002277/227729E.pdf

Vertovec, S. (2007). Super-diversity and its implications. *Ethnic and Racial Studies, 20*(6), 1024–1054.

Vreede, E. (2009). *Education for an intercultural dialogue*. World Public Forum Dialogue of Civilizations. Retrieved from http://wpfdc.org/161-education-for-an-intercultural-dialogue

Young, I.M. (1989). Polity and group difference: A critique of the ideal of universal citizenship. *Ethics, 99*(2), 250–274.

Part I Conclusion: Multicultural education towards intercultural interaction

Postcolonial theorists indicate that cultural diversity and ethnic cultures should not be understood with binary oppositions of cultural representation. They argue that contemporary intercultural (often transcultural) phenomena are characterised by hybridity, heterogeneity, creolisation, and multiplicity, and these concepts contain both commensurability and incommensurability between cultures. They pay attention to the latter, which engenders irreducible resistance to the coloniser, which is ontological. Postcolonial theorists strive to restore ethnic/cultural authenticity and its unchanging nature by arguing for non-dualistic approaches and articulating the subject position of other ethnic groups. In sum, Said's latent Orientalism and Bhabha's Third Space offer an ontological foundation to support authentic (cultural) identity of subalterns or ethnic groups; Spivak's epistemic violence of othering processes, Hall's encoding and decoding communication model, and Ang's together-in-difference clarify how we are trapped in the binary systems and justify why we need to pay attention to other metaphysical aspects; Gilroy's double consciousness on the rhizomatic network, Vertovec's super-diversity and methodological innovation, and Amin's every conviviality and cultural exchange build a methodological basis for value-interaction of cultures. In particular, Gilroy's rhizomatic network lays the metaphysical foundations for both the culturally diverse world and cultural authenticity. Overall, metaphysical approaches to cultural diversity and intercultural interaction that those theorists hold can be characterised with a non-dualistic or holistic approach. However, it is unstable to use in the learning environment because there is a lack of evidence linking the proposed approaches to ethnic authenticity. In other words, as the attention is on understanding cultural hybridity as an intercultural phenomenon with postcolonial insights, strictly speaking, as a transcultural phenomenon, it is unclear whether their approach is still valid in a reverse way, which is to understand cultural diversity from (ethnic) cultures. Furthermore, its methodological approach is vague on whether cultures can interact with each other without undermining each other's cultural values, although the literal meaning of cultural hybridity is less concerned with intercultural interaction itself. Alternatively, I have argued for the three dimensions of metaphysics as a non-dualistic, holistic approach to cultural diversity and interculturality: ontological justification, epistemological assumptions and processes, and axiological interaction.

78 *Metaphysical understanding of culture*

First, ontological justification is a meta-ontological approach that minimises the impact of ontological reductionism by focusing on ontic structures of each culture, cultural diversity, and intercultural interaction. Second, epistemological assumptions and processes focus on epistemic frameworks that justify where knowledge is and how it is acquired. In other words, while epistemic justifications help us find true knowledge, its framework per se implies that we belong to one of the cultural worlds. A question, *where is knowledge that justifies our belief,* requires ontological justification for that epistemology that refers to *a particular (cultural) mind structure,* which is more than cognitive abilities, *that allows us to acquire that knowledge.* This understanding leads us to think of *how people believe what they know.* Third, axiological interaction is based on an acknowledgement of value conflicts. Normative ethics indicates that values need to be managed and multi-dimensionally judged in the learning environment, but descriptive ethics raises the issue that value judgement varies from situation to situation. For both, morality functions as an independent value system, and interaction between diverse value systems always occur in intercultural situations. Intercultural interaction causes value conflicts, which should not be ignored in culturally inclusive education. In this sense, as *meta-ethical images* imply, value conflicts need be understood epistemologically and ontologically, as well as semantically in a comparison of different value systems.

Consequently, the three dimensions of metaphysics are required to incorporate in interculturality and cultural diversity. This non-dualistic, holistic approach allows us to understand each culture as an open system that makes intercultural interaction possible and to detect emergent values from intercultural interaction that can be irreducible to each culture. For example, the ontological structure of a culture can be described as an open system contoured with dashed lines in the interculturally networked world. An ontological contour indicates the connections between the values of a culture and the values of other cultures, and the connected relationships are the epistemological foundations for intercultural interaction in the networked world. Also, the three dimensions of metaphysics are effective in revealing the metaphysical nature of the networked world when we ask meta-questions about our cultural horizons, thereby participating in the horizons of other cultures. In this way, the metaphysical approach to cultural diversity is to minimise our (unintentional) epistemic violence caused by binary oppositions of cultural representation and ontological reductionism supporting self-exclusive self-reflection. Based on this metaphysically holistic approach to interculturality, Chapter 3 has provided a critical review of contemporary multicultural education discourses and models.

Bhabha and Stratton and Ang criticise white privilege that is reproduced through binary oppositions of cultural representation. Hage defines its reproduction mechanism as ecological fantasy, a dualistic mode of being and thinking, which restricts individuals to self-exclusive self-reflection and unequal participation in intercultural interaction. In contemporary multicultural discourses, I have reviewed the two streams *dimensions of multicultural education* with Banks and McGee Banks' sequential levels of approaches and Nieto's critical perspectives in socio-cultural understanding and *cosmopolitanism* with Nussbaum's cultivating humanity and Rizvi's cosmopolitan learning. Banks and McGee Banks formulate the four levels of approaches to multicultural education: content integration, knowledge construction process, prejudice reduction, equity pedagogy, and empowering school culture and social structure, and they argue that these levels ultimately lead students to be agents of social changes. Nieto defines multicultural education as a process that refers to an ongoing, organic development of individuals in a social-political context through critical pedagogies. Her critical pedagogy draws upon experiences of students involving relationships among people and takes them beyond their own experiences and develops critical thinking about diversity. Like Nieto, Nussbaum highlights the non-dualistic nature between humans and nature and provides philosophical foundations for (universal) humanity education through the enhancement of critical reasoning and self-examination. Similarly, Rizvi defines a set of epistemic virtues in the context of global interconnectivity that can be cultivated through collaboration and interrogation. Both Nussbaum and Rizvi agree that the virtues are expected to result in individuals' transcultural experience and self-reflectivity.

It has appeared that all of the theorists agree that dualism or our habitual dualistic thinking is the key barrier to multicultural education because it results in ontological reductionism that removes the interfaces of multiple perspectives and causes the absence of metaphysics in education. In practice, it operates as an ideological apparatus that interrupts the functions of ontological justification for epistemology and axiology in education by privatising and romanticising individuality and mythicising the relationships between self-transformation and social transformation. Metaphysically, then, a new mode of being and thinking needs to be considered as an alternative to dualism and its potential has been seen in Hage's ecological fantasy, Stratton and Ang's criticism on multiculturalism, and Nieto's critical pedagogy. These theorists emphasise the significance of awareness of our own mode of being and thinking and acceptance of other modes of being and thinking. This insight is enhanced in global citizenship education in theoretical and practical ways. For example, Nussbaum's cultivating humanity focuses on the importance of critical reasoning that initiates self-examination and even corrodes religious beliefs, whereas Rizvi's transforming pedagogy for cosmopolitan learning is driven by two instructional values: relationality and reflectivity. Both presume that critical reasoning and instructional methods are value-free, which causes an ontological contradiction. In other words, they place individuality and pedagogical values outside cultural networks by being unaware of the fact that emergent values arising from intercultural interaction can lead to changes in both concepts and values. Such a metaphysical issue becomes concretised in contemporary multicultural education models.

The review of the six multicultural education models has also shown the absence of metaphysics in education that is facilitated by dualism as a dominant worldview: *conservative dualism* of conservative and liberal multicultural education, *moderate dualism* of critical and left-essentialist multicultural education, and *liberal dualism* of pluralists and intercultural dialogic education. First, conservative dualism differentiates qualities of cultures in a hierarchical relation with a denial of ontological and axiological values of others in reality by predefining what true

80 *Metaphysical understanding of culture*

reality is – whiteness. For them, cultural diversity refers to an ideological means that can hide white superiority and non-white exclusiveness. Second, moderate dualism becomes less exclusive by recognising and encompassing others in their epistemological process towards morally responsible participation in individual (not *the self*) and social transformation. Such values are predefined by reflecting cultural diversity in terms of liberal egalitarianism and communitarianism. Third, liberal dualism is no longer critical to cultural diversity and acknowledges it as a social and economic asset. Equal participation is promoted for a culturally inclusive and socially cohesive society, and the competence of individuals becomes a mediator between idealistic society and cultural diversity.

In the learning environment, consequently, these dualisms justify competency assessment regardless of individuals' cultural backgrounds and swinging between two party systems. For example, in Australia, the Howard Government (Liberal) endorses the principles of civic duty, cultural respect, social equity, and productive diversity, whereas the Hawke Government (Labor) supports cultural identity, social justice, and economic efficiency (Koleth, 2010, see the reference list in the introduction in this volume). The dualisms facilitate enhanced epistemological instrumentalism that promotes the capabilities of individuals without developing the inherent rights of human beings such as community ownership of human rights. In the learning environment, such dualism-based multicultural education is aimed at sustaining the way that society is organised by placing cultural diversity in a political domain and/or personal sector and by systematically (often aggressively) assimilating non-white individuals into the white curriculum. Such outcome-driven deductive approaches do not modify and manipulate the curriculum to allow non-white or all individuals to participate in learning. There seem to be no substantial efforts to understand metaphysical tensions and conflicts between cultures, to identify ontological structures of cultural diversity and each culture, and to initiate a pedagogical discourse on intercultural interaction. While the dualisms of cultural representation seem to have evolved, the criticism and pedagogical discussion are at a standstill. While criticising the limitations and dangers of dualisms, we have overlooked the fact that minds, values, and methods are also culturally bound. The three dimensions of educational metaphysics as a meta-methodological form certainly alert us to the negligence, but seem insufficient unless we consider developing a new mode of being and thinking for authentic intercultural interaction and test it in the learning environment.

Part II
Interculturality and its methodology

Part II Introduction:
Intercultural interaction

Culture is often understood in two different ways: "Culture as the folk-spirit having a unique identity, and culture as cultivation of inwardness of free individuality", have prevailed in Western context until recently (Velkley, 2002, p. 13). The former meaning has been used as an extension of colonial power. Its ideological reproduction has been made through binary oppositions of cultural representation. It is a thematically fixing approach to a (non-white) culture as an epistemological object that determines "a true or proper or scientific sense of culture" (Nowotny, 2006, para. 4). As argued in the previous part of this study, such an approach has a critical metaphysical problem – that is, to conceal or ignore the ontological equality of cultures and the axiological interaction between cultures – and as a result, authentic intercultural interaction does not occur in the learning environment. In this sense, the concept of culture needs to be open to metaphysical discussions by posing a question: *How does a culture form a particular individuality?* This metaphysical question not only tackles binary oppositions of cultural representation by assuming the ontological equality of all cultures but also opens up possibilities for teachers to design intercultural interaction. As argued in the introduction chapter, *culture*, as a mode of being, enables human beings to hold a particular cultural framework to understand the world, and *a culture*, as a particular metaphysical framework, enables human beings to hold a unique collective worldview and value system. Thus intercultural interaction in the learning environment refers to *the mutual interaction of different worldviews* that is inevitably metaphysical. A culturally bound value system or framework would be a worldview that determines individuals' cultural identity in social contexts, and its power, deeply embedded in one's unconscious mind, is persistent.

In his philosophical study of culture, Kagan (1996/2009) views culture as the form of human existence and argues its social and historical mechanism, which implicitly distinguishes between culture and a culture as I have argued. According to him, products from human activities are objectified as external materials (or substances) and thus are transferred to the next generation, and human beings become social agents by learning values embedded into the products and are capable of producing new products. He describes such a cultural mechanism as a container of *social genes* and explains why human beings become agents of social creation/production in history. Such an interpretation of culture can obtain an

84 *Interculturality and its methodology*

epistemic position in metaphysics. In the field of critical theories, Tubbs (2005) argues that every culture has its own specific educational meaning, which can be seen through speculative philosophy, because a culture refers to "the way in which an idea or an experience, in being known, re-forms itself in this being known" (p. 219). Based on Adorno's critique of the *culture industry*, he also warns that without a notion of culture (as both culture and cultures), ideas are anchored in dogma because we tend to only use culture as *an ideology of ideology*. He argues first that the "politicisation of the dialectic between image and reality" dissolves our recognition of illusion through duplicated products and their images; second, representation liquidates the opposition between image and reality, and "this liquidation both creates and feeds its own needs" through consumption of every product that is "always already a representation of the needs of empirical reality"; and third, the liquidation of conflicts results in individuals' conformity to this entire mechanism that replaces our consciousness and thinking (pp. 219–224). This process explains why we perceive culture as a representation of reality because all forms of our thinking are confined to that mechanism that its representation resides in. Tubbs defines this process as *the absence of relation* because the mechanism has become a substitute for relation. This directly supports the two points that I have argued in the previous part: the absence of self-consciousness in self-reflection and the non-subject position of other cultures in intercultural interaction. Inversely, when we realise that our reflection needs to reflect the relationships with ourselves and all participants are equal agents of intercultural interaction, we can be aware that the mechanism generates binary oppositions of cultural representation. Furthermore, the mechanism explains why we are compelled to perceive pedagogical values and instructional methods as culturally unbound, which was my third point. This means that interaction between pedagogical values and cultural frameworks needs to be part of intercultural interaction in the learning environment. Those three points can be further discussed in accordance with the three dimensions of educational metaphysics.

First, cultural identity as a metaphysical recognition of our thought reformation in and for itself requires ontological justification for our engagement in our own culture and other cultures. As a culture appears as a perception or representation of reality, we need to investigate three things: the essential form of culture that preserves relation, the mind structure that causes our thoughts or worldviews, and the reality or the world structure that actuates social genes. Second, intercultural interaction requires restoring the ontologically equal position of *other cultures* to ensure their equal and full participation. This is associated with methodological concerns in which the correlation and relationship between cultural realities and our minds need to be verified in interactional interaction. To articulate a methodological approach to intercultural interaction, prevailing methodologies such as methodological individualism, holism, and relationism need to be critically reviewed. Third, metaphysical understanding of culture embeds the concepts of social change agents and creativity in history. To realise authentic intercultural interaction, then, our participation needs a holistic approach to interculturality. The approach is a form of philosophical hermeneutics in which transcultural experiences will occur in intercultural interaction and that experiences will have

Interculturality 85

an immense influence on our pedagogical changes and topological changes in the culturally networked world. Those three arguments will be unfolded in the next three chapters.

References

Kagan, M.S. (2009). *Philosophy of culture*. (Korean version) (H.S. Lee, Trans.). Saint Petersburg: Petropolis LLP TK. (Original work published 1996)

Nowotny, S. (2006). *"Culture" and the analysis of power*. (A. Derieg, Trans.). Retrieved from http://translate.eipcp.net/strands/01/nowotny-strands01en

Tubbs, N. (2005). The culture of philosophical experience. *Journal of Philosophy of Education, 39*(2), 217–233.

Velkley, R. (2002). *Being after Rousseau: Philosophy and culture in question*. Chicago: University of Chicago Press.

4 Interculturality
Values, minds, and realities

This chapter aims to argue why a culture represents a value system and how values are structured in our minds, relations, and society. First, the fundamental metaphysical form of culture is a set of values for the ontological equality of all cultures in intercultural interaction, which will be argued through reviewing Nietzsche's (1872/1968) argument of the Dionysian and Apollonian worlds and his concept of *a table of values*. It is known that Nietzsche offers a philosophical foundation for deconstructing our metaphysical myths and ideological aspects of cultural frameworks. As Gemes (2001) explains, Nietzsche has been cited as a model of deconstruction, and his genealogical endeavours have been used as a paradigm of disclosing the origin in both sympathisers and critics of postmodernism (e.g., Habermas, Barthes, Lyotard, Foucault, & Derrida). In brief, Nietzsche argues that our perceptions are a table of values that is created through our Apollonian world, which obstructs the Dionysian demands, the flow of energy. This metaphysical interpretation indicates that a culture is composed of a set of values or a value system. For him, values are interconnected and form multiple cultural realities, yet the Apollonian separates us from our dynamic and creative engagement in value-interaction. In this sense, Nietzsche's concept of a table of values can be extended to intercultural value networks by connecting the ontological complexity with multiple realities. Our ontological complexity is known as *self-construal* in cross-cultural psychology and *intersubjectivity* in philosophy. The concept of self-construal has been clinically tested through priming frameworks (e.g., independent self vs. interdependent self), whereas intersubjectivity has been argued for multiple realities (e.g., Popper's three worlds of knowledge and Habermas's theory of communicative action on the Lifeworld). Both will be also reviewed in this chapter.

4.1 Values: Primordial unity

Nietzsche's (1872/1968) dialectic relationship between the Dionysian and the Apollonian not only attacks dualism that ignores ontological relations but also justifies how existentiality is determined by relations. To reach the true nature of the world, he stresses the revival of the Dionysian world. He argues that a fusion of the Dionysian and the Apollonian worlds forms dramatic arts or tragedies in which the Greeks never considered the two worlds (gods) to be opposites or

88 *Interculturality and its methodology*

rivals. He contends that an infusion of reason into ethics (or Socratic rationalism) undermines the foundational structure of tragedy and conceals the fact that both the worlds are interacting with each other. He presumes that the interaction is the root of power. Nietzsche (1872/1968) says,

> This is my Dionysian world of the eternally self-creative, the eternally self-destructive, this mystery world of the twofold delight, this my "beyond good and evil", without aim, unless the joy of the circle is itself an aim, without will, unless a ring feeling goodwill towards itself . . . This world is the will to power.
>
> (p. 550)

Nietzsche interprets the Dionysian world as "a monster of energy" and names it "the will to power". He attempts to define its ontic properties with a contradictorily affirmative episteme, which needs to be understood as a dialectically dualistic, non-linear monist approach. The means that the energy is perceived as the relationship of both worlds in reality. This appears in his description of the characteristics of the world:

> This world: a monster of energy, without beginning, without end; an immovable, brazen enormity of energy, which does not grow bigger or smaller, which does not expend itself but only transforms itself . . . as energy throughout, as a play of energies and waves of energy at the same time one and many, increasing here and at the same time decreasing there; a sea of energies flowing and rushing together, eternally moving, eternally flooding back, with tremendous years of recurrence, with an ebb and flow of its forms.
>
> (Nietzsche, 1872/1968, p. 550)

The focus is not on whether or not the energy itself is a noumenal substance, but on its ontological foundation with a continual and spontaneous flow of energy. The two worlds are not transcendental to each other, but co-exist. In other words, energy is power, beyond the concepts of being powerful and powerless, that sustains forms of existence. In practice, the revival of the Dionysian world means that we become aware of the relational nature of human beings. Structurally, our awareness of the Dionysian nature (Nietzsche calls this *primordial unity*) integrates the Dionysian and the Apollonian because the Apollonian nature, as the universe exists in order and harmony, is also emphasised in the Dionysian world. This integration discloses an epistemic restriction. With the Apollonian world only, for example, we tend to believe that only things that we understand exist and, as a result, other metaphysical concerns, in particular, ontological ones, are subjugated to the needs of (ideological) reasoning. Then how should we deal with the Apollonian nature while being aware of the Dionysian nature?

Nietzsche (1882/2001) reminds us that we deconstruct and (re)construct values through *naming*. Nietzsche develops his doctrine of the will to power based

Values, minds, and realities 89

on the notion of naming because realists also create the (Apollonian) world by naming. He argues:

> You call yourselves realists and hint that the world really is the way it appears to you.
>
> Only as creators! . . . How foolish it would be to suppose that one only needs to point out this origin and this misty shroud of delusion in order to destroy the world that counts for real, so-called "reality". We can destroy only as creators. – But let us not forget this either: it is enough to create new names and estimations and probabilities in order to create in the long run new "things".
>
> (p. 69)

For Nietzsche, naming can be used to deconstruct the delusional duality between the self and the world, go beyond the linguistically objectified world, and pay attention to our mysterious emotional experiences. Metaphysically, thus, the relation between our existence and the world (not between ourselves and the world) is disclosed through naming new things. He also stresses that the will to power highlights the subject in a hierarchical relation with others, which refers to a value system. In this sense, naming characterises a regression of the Dionysian world to the Apollonian world. Nietzsche (1882/2001) describes the doctrine of the will to power as follows:

> Benefiting and hurting others are ways of exercising one's power over others; that is all one desires in such cases. One hurts those whom one wants to feel one's power, for pain is a much more efficient means to that end than plea-sure; pain always raises the question about its origin while pleasure is inclined to stop with itself without looking back.
>
> (p. 38)

The will to power manifests itself when one exercises one's power over others to either enhance or diminish one's life or affirm or deny one's fate. In this manifesta-tion, the root of human beings is disclosed. That is, the will to power becomes the basic nature of all living things and the fundamental life-drive of humans because a set of values (or a cultural framework) determines existence. In this way, we perceive the world as a specific value system. Nietzsche's insight enlightens us to realise the fact that values are always temporal and interactive from the Dionysian perspective (not as the opposite to Apollonian, but as the ontological foundation, the flow of energy). If we are unaware of this nature, we consciously and uncon-sciously reproduce and enhance our Apollonian disposition infused by dualistic socio-cultural practices or a particular cultural framework that encourages us not to have an interest in the primordial unity. Nietzsche (1882/2001) argues,

> Whatever has value in the present world has it not in itself, according to its nature – nature is always value-less – but has rather been given, granted

90 *Interculturality and its methodology*

value, and we were the givers and granters! Only we have created the world that concerns human beings!

(p. 171)

Valueless of nature indicates that we can redefine the world predefined by values through creating new names. More precisely, redefinition can be done through revealing new values that our will to power has concealed. This appears in his description of *a table of values*. He argues that a table of values hangs over all enlightened people and they know how it works:

> Power is the standard of all value. In establishing what he [Nietzsche] refers to as a table of values, it is who is valued, then what actions are valued, and then what things are valued. And recall, values are created by individuals.
>
> (Peery, 2008, p. 27)

Everyone has a different value table, but the common ground between people is the act of esteeming and/or creating values that shape and transform reality. Nietzsche affirms that what makes people great is the act of valuism, not their beliefs. Inversely, an Apollonian approach to culture(s) blinds people to their value tables and, as a result, cultural diversity and interculturality are perceived as political mirages. Thus redemption can be achieved through our will to transform values (or rename or reveal them). Nietzsche (1891/2010) describes redemption as follows:

> You want reward for virtue, and heaven for earth, and eternity for your today? And now you upbraid me for teaching that there is no reward-giver, nor paymaster? And truly, I do not even teach that virtue is its own reward. (p. 76) . . . To redeem what is past, and to transform every "It was" into "Thus would I have it!" – that only do I call redemption! (p. 113) . . . The past of man to redeem, and every "It was" to transform, until the Will says: "But so did I will it! So shall I will it-" – This did I call redemption; this alone taught I them to call redemption – Now do I await my redemption – that I may go to them for the last time.
>
> (p. 157)

For him, the will is more fundamental and essential than goals and objectives. Thus the feeling of power is not an individual's independent choice or free will, but reversely, is determined by the collective will through a shared value system. Individuals perceive and experience values, beliefs, and the basis of principles and practices via mutual agreement and its historical prevalence in community. This basis of a common sense of purpose becomes explicit in moral systems. Yet the Apollonian world gives an illusion that each of us has an independent value system, which supports ideological cultural realism and hides the power of taken-for-granted values. This is criticised by Nietzsche's prophet, *Zarathustra*: "A thousand goals have there been thus far, for a thousand peoples have there been. Only the fetter for the thousand necks is still lacking; there is lacking the one goal. As yet humanity has not a goal" (1891/2010, p. 52). This implies that values, regardless of individual or collective will, have no goal and no reward. Nevertheless, we or realists still "want to be paid besides", "reward for virtue", and pursue religious rewards – "eternity for your today" (p. 52). Even through nature has no value on its own, we bestow values on ourselves and develop them as a belief system due to our habitual use of dualism. Nietzsche (1872/1968) criticises,

> What determines rank, sets off rank, is only quanta of power, and nothing else . . . Order of rank as order of power, war and danger the presupposition for a rank to retain the condition of its existence . . . What determines your rank is the quantum of power you are: the rest is cowardice.
>
> (p. 457)

We create values by naming and continue to create a rank order, which does not exist in the actual world, but the rank manifests itself in ordinary consciousness and everyday behaviour. Only vulnerable individuals do not recognise the concealed structure of values, but fetishise the values. Peery (2008) succinctly interpreted Nietzsche's question of rank:

> Only we have created the values goodness, beauty, and truth. We have called things "good", "beautiful", or "true". And we have created, and continue to create or re-create, an order of rank among things; rank is never "in the world", so to speak. Philosophers and theologians, according to him, along with the militarists, have been the primary creators of orders of rank.
>
> (p. 27)

Adopting Heidegger's interpretation of Nietzsche's revolutionary thinking, Peery (2008) reminds us, "Values are constantly in flux, never stable, constantly changing – never absolute, objective, permanent, eternal, or certain. Values, and primarily moral values, form the foundation, the basic structure of any human culture, the driving force of history" (p. 27). In other words, the dialectic relation between the Dionysian and the Apollonian allows us to become agents of change by revealing how values are structured and interact with other values. Nietzsche seems not to highlight the fact that naming is a social process predetermined by a collectively shared value system as the Apollonian legitimises and sustains the world. Yet his insight on the dialectic relation between the Dionysian and the Apollonian worlds justifies how individuals engage in valuism for their existential hermeneutics. To revive the primordial unity for our ontological position as agents of the energy flow, we need to be aware of how our minds are structured to interact with a set of values.

4.2 The multilayered self

Our culturally predefined thinking frameworks are constantly enhanced by our engagement in various social, economic, and political institutions and systems.

92 Interculturality and its methodology

It would be difficult for us to participate in intercultural interaction unless we examine how we engage in our own value system. Otherwise, as we are obsessed with the Apollonian world, we perceive our given cultural values as universal ones and reproduce them through our habitual thinking and behaviour. As seen earlier in Nietzsche's argument, values incarnated as a cultural framework form our minds and work to sustain cultural formation and cultural identity. This is pedagogically significant, as intercultural interaction essentially draws on transformational learning. When intercultural interaction occurs, we see new values that reveal larger parts of the world that, in turn, reshapes our minds. This educative process should be a philosophical goal of intercultural interaction. In this context, I will review cross-cultural psychology, which helps us see what mind structures we have and how they work in cross-cultural contexts.

The study of self-construal has been conducted in the field of cross-cultural psychology, which seeks psychological human universals across cultures based on a premise that *the self* as a socio-cultural process exemplifies psychological and social phenomena (Gardner, Gabriel, & Lee, 1999; Harb & Smith, 2008). "As such, self-construal refers to the way these knowledge structures are constructed within a fluid, flexible, and dynamic matrix" (Harb & Smith, 2008, p. 178). Its fundamental assumption is that the self is construed within a cultural matrix. Cross-cultural psychologists describe the distinction of self-construal between Eastern and Western cultures in terms of how the self is defined in relation to others: autonomous entity versus socially embedded (Gardner *et al.*, 1999), independence versus interdependence (Harb & Smith, 2008), idiocentric versus allocentric (Suh, Diener & Updegraff, 2008), and independent self-view versus interdependent self-view (Kühnen, 2009). These studies demonstrate empirical evidence of accessibility of self-construal and shifts of self-construal in judgement and thinking when priming techniques are applied. They argue that manipulation of self-construal is possible when cross-cultural research and social cognition research meet (Kühne, 2009). Social cognition research indicates that "chronic and temporary sources of construct accessibility are functionally equivalent", whereas cross-cultural research indicates that "the self is one of the critical mediators for *cultures'* influence on thinking and judgment" (Kühne, 2009, p. 304 [emphasis added]). In this context, it is presumed that subjective cognitive constructs can mediate between cultural contexts and individuals' behaviour (Gardner *et al.*, 1999). This dialectic relation can be understood as "cultural beliefs shape self-construals", and, in turn, "self-construals may shape the behaviour of the individuals within *a culture*" (Gardner *et al.*, 1999, p. 321 [emphasis added]). Empirical evidence can be seen in Schwartz's (1992) value inventory research between individualists' values and collectivists' ones. He demonstrates that interdependence-primed individualist participants endorse collectivists' values at a much higher rate than those of collectivist participants and a reversed outcome also appears in independence-primed collectivist participants. He claims that value endorsement is mediated by self-construal and a shift of self-construal occurs when a different value system is applied. However, as Gardner *et al.* (1999) point out, only chronic activation of a priming framework can result in a permanent shift of self-construal. This is also consistent with a priming study of independent self and relational self conducted by Suh, Diener, and Updegraff (2008). These researchers claim, "The priming effects are transient and momentary, whereas the cultural influences are enduring" (p. 12). This implies that self-construal has its own structure and perpetuity to sustain its uniqueness and independence, and intercultural interaction leads to a shift of self-construal either temporarily or permanently.

Harb and Smith (2008) divide the self into four levels based on prior studies such as Brewer and Gardner's (1996) three sources of self-representations, including individual, interpersonal, and group, and Turner, Hogg, Oakes, Reicher, and Wetherell's (1987) hierarchical classification. The four levels are focal-personal, relational, collective, and humanity, and each corresponds to individual, group, and species hierarchy. They describe the following: first, a personal self holds personal, unique, and independent identity by differentiating one from others; second, a relational self identifies an interpersonal self that is construed by binary relations in family or a small group; third, a collective self is an interchangeable exemplar of larger in-groups that incorporates the norms and roles of a group; and fourth, humanity or a humane self is the supra structure in which the self is defined by its properties of humankind – that is, distinguishable from other living things.

In this multi-levelled self-construal, I pay attention to relationships between the levels that could legitimise the power of culture on the self. There are two relationships that directly relate to personal and group identity or cultural identity as a whole. First, a relational self and a collective self affect the formation of a personal self by which either independence or interdependence is more practised depending on cultural forces over either individual or group. Second, binary relations between either independence or interdependence and a collective self highlight either the recognition of an individual in one's individual relationships or as a representative of one's group. This distinction results in either horizontal- or vertical-oriented collective selves. Such an analysis indicates that a culture (or a cultural framework) plays a significant role in the formation of the self, which does determine our perception of humankind (hence a humane self). Such cross-cultural psychologists' research outcomes offer some instructional implications. For example, a student activity can be designed to provide a cultural shift experience. Such priming techniques for the mutual interaction between different value systems or cultures could increase awareness of others' expectations. However, the techniques may further stereotype ethnic groups because of the following two metaphysical reasons.

First, cross-cultural psychologists tend to view a personal self and a humane self as unique, fixed, and unchangeable entities. Also, they view the independence and interdependence frame as a universal one without being aware that it predetermines one's ontological foundation. As we have seen, Nietzsche criticises our obsession with the Apollonian world or ontological dualism. The independence-interdependence frame is not free of that criticism, as it rejects the necessity of ontology by simplifying complexity and diversity of ontological structures. As agreed by many researchers, priming techniques presume that participating individuals are "members of Eastern and Western *cultures* [who] are capable of displaying both kinds of self-construals, as might be expected given

94 *Interculturality and its methodology*

the universality of both the goals of autonomy and belongingness" (Gardner *et al.*, 1999, p. 321 [emphasis added]). In priming techniques, in this sense, intercultural interaction relies too much on the intellectual capacity of individuals. As a result, both a relational self and a collective self are confined to predetermined cultural frames (i.e., Said's criticism of Western Orientalism: the West's view of Asia), and the existence of the world can only be defined and described by mentalities of independence-self individuals. This is identical to the epistemological restrictions of the Apollonian world towards the Dionysian world and Tubbs's criticism of the absence of relation. Such limitations are derived from removing the ontological structure from self-construal and, thus, presuming that a personal self and a humane self are value-free. Second, the independence-interdependence frame could undermine the power of culture, which happens in favourite individualistic and collectivistic cultures. For example, individuals who hold an interdependent self could experience difficulty articulating their values without being given any contextual or situational references because of their contextual, relational, and collectivistic cultural characteristics. Also individuals who hold an independent self would believe that they would be less affected by socio-cultural contexts because they are more familiar with egocentric and individualistic values.

Consequently, cross-cultural psychology certainly benefits intercultural interaction by providing empirical evidence that a shift of self-construal is possible by applying a different value structure, and different levels of self-construal hold cultural values as a multilayer self-organising system. In this sense, the self needs to be understood as *the multilayered self* in the intercultural context. In the learning environment, teachers can incorporate the multilayered self in each stage of intercultural interaction by encouraging students to think of their self – namely personal, relational, collective, and humane – in diverse cultural contexts. This activity should presume that multiple cultures equally co-exist with different ontic structures and that diverse selves in the self are interacting with each other. In practice, teachers should ensure that students are aware that they might feel various emotions such as superiority or inferiority to other cultures because their own cultural resistance unconsciously occurs. Teachers also need to remind students of the aim of intercultural interaction that is to bring their unconsciously embedded value systems into their cognitive processes, although this takes a long period of time and requires much effort. Theoretically and pedagogically, on the other hand, teachers need to provide evidence that cultures are ontologically equal. While the multi-levelled self-construal indicates that an individual has a different mind structure that is constructed by a culture, it does not explicitly justify how multiple cultures co-exist and form multiple realities.

4.3 Multiple realities

The concept of multiple worlds/realities can be found in a critical rationalist, Popper's (1972) three worlds of knowledge, and a critical theorist, Habermas's (1981/1984) theory of communicative action on the Lifeworld. Interestingly, both theories are related to epistemological and ontological shifting processes

Values, minds, and realities 95

that correspond to the multi-levelled self-construal. I will review these theories to articulate the concept of culturally mediated multiple realities and how we understand the world as cultural realties or multiple worlds.

Popper's three worlds are the physical, mental, and objective worlds of scientific knowledge. He describes them as follows:

> World 1 is the physical universe. It consists of the actual truth and reality that we try to represent, such as energy, physics, and chemistry. While we exist in this world, we do not always perceive it and then represent it correctly.
>
> World 2 is the world of our subjective personal perceptions, experiences, and cognition. It is what we think about the world as we try to map, represent, and anticipate or hypothesis in order to maintain our existence in an every changing place. Personal knowledge and memory form this world, which are based on self-regulation, cognition, consciousness, dispositions, and processes.
>
> World 3 is the sum total of the objective abstract products of the human mind. It consists of such artifacts as books, tools, theories, models, libraries, computers, and networks.
>
> (Popper, 1972, pp. 73–74)

Popper argues that World 3 exists even when World 1 is destroyed and World 2 is forgotten. World 3 is similar to Plato's world of *Ideas*, although Popper asserts that Plato's world is divine, unchanging and his World 3 is man-made and changing (Johansson, 2005). This is ontological pluralism. In this sense, Faure and Venter (1993) reinterpret World 1 as "an expression of his metaphysical realism", which is "an independent observable world", and argue that World 2 and 3 interaction does not render the world, but "genuine conjectures about reality" (p. 44). This means that truth or falsity can be determined in World 3 only, which rejects both positivism and metaphysical idealism (Faure & Venter, 1993). In essence, Popper (1972) argues that World 1 and 2 interaction is an alternative to Cartesian dualism in which the physical states and the mental states interact with each other, and World 2 and 3 interaction occurs through our engagement in World 3 objects and events, which also leads to a change of World 2. When a World 3 object or event is instantiated in the mind, which means it becomes a World 2 object or event, the intercommunication between minds and/or mind modification occurs through either direct communication or intermediate World 1 objects, and then a modified mind becomes a new World 3 object (Johansson, 2005). For Popper, this process is the growth of our knowledge in a way that some World 3 ideas permeate other minds and generate derivatives. This evolutionary perspective justifies how World 3 objects emanating from our minds become *social* via World 2 (Johansson, 2005).

Popper's description of World 3 encompasses the possibility that intersubjectivity can be materially extended to objectivity. In his three worlds, intercultural interaction occurs as an intersubjective event of World 3, and we participate in World 2 and 3 interaction. World 3 initially determines the interaction, and then its outcomes change World 2 and 3. This is how new knowledges are constructed, and we participate in a change of the world. This process implies that

96 *Interculturality and its methodology*

the aim of intercultural education is to disclose the relations between World 2 and World 3 or intersubjectivity. If we focus on each world (or output of each world) rather than the relations (new), knowledge construction would not occur and, as a result, education becomes mere skill acquisition. This indicates that intersubjectivity needs to be understood with our multilayered self for individuals' transformative engagement: A relational self and a collective self are associated with World 2, and a collective self and a humane self are related to World 3. As a collective self connects our multilayered self as a whole to both World 2 and 3, its nature turns out intersubjective. Yet this intersubjectivity is different from what Popper defines. For him, World 3 is a set of intersubjective meanings and its objects are intersubjectively testable. He defends this by stating, "Now I hold that scientific theories are never fully justifiable or verifiable, but that they are nevertheless testable. I shall therefore say that the objectivity of scientific statements lies in the fact that they can be inter-subjectively tested" (2002, p. 22). He takes World 3 objectivity as a product of intersubjectivity and stresses its testability. In other words, he introduces intersubjectivity to morality in order to emphasise scientific examination of consequences of moral judgement.

His intersubjectivity causes a metaphysical problem in understanding cultural identity and cultural formation in which he cannot claim that we have different cultural identities and cultural formations. This is because his intersubjectivity presumes that we are experiencing the same reality, thereby ignoring that (a) the multilayered self constitutes experiences and (b) (culturally) different self-construal causes different experiences. In short, his intersubjectivity cannot justify how different cultural realities co-exist. Popper's critical rationalism holds the belief that social science should not be rooted in metaphysics and is best conceived as a set of empirical questions through scientific investigation (logical positivism) (Holub, 1991). For him, in this sense, culture or religion may only be meaningful in ethics because it cannot be fully explained within the sum of our empirical knowledges, probably through scientific investigation. Interestingly, critical theorists have also attempted to formulate intersubjectivity and argue that there is more to intersubjectivity than determining realities, as it is grounded in a set of objective conditions (Burbules & Rupert, 1999). This is why Habermas's theory of communicative action is significant, as it explains how our rationality is logically structured.

In his *communicative actions*, Habermas (1981/1984) distinguishes social actions, strategic actions, and communicative actions (pp. 85–101). First, social actions refer to actions by people in society in relation to other people; strategic actions occur where objectives are fulfilled. Second, strategic actions are further divided into concealed strategic actions and open strategic actions. The former involves deception and perlocutionary aims at either unconscious or conscious levels, whereas the latter involves an action through illocutionary aims. Third, communicative actions reach a shared understanding about either facts or norms or feelings and have three (or four) validity claims: (a) objective validity (the facts), (b) subjective validity (beliefs and thoughts), and (c) intersubjective validity (being dependent on a circumstance). In addition, (d) fourth validity claim, which is not a validity, but a similar one, is comprehensibility, which is implicit in any desire for one's communicative action to be taken seriously. In his understanding, these claims are independent of any ideology or any situatedness and offer different perspectives on the attempt to reach shared understandings. Habermas's belief is that we have the ability to decide the rules of language, which means we arrange a limited number of words in an unlimited number of ways in order to figure out the world that a statement is indicating, which is called *communicative competence*. In this sense, rationality via language is achieved through communicative competence that thus refers to the right kind of discourse for a situation.

However, people can conceal their actual goal in communication, which is not communicative, but strategic, to achieve predetermined results rather than shared understandings. Hence shared understandings through communicative actions are inclusive of subjective, objective, and intersubjective domains. This presumes that rationality has a universal structure that is culturally unrestricted in terms of those four validity claims of communicative actions. This implies that every culture can be understood with its subjective, objective, and intersubjective claims to truths (fundamentally values). Then we should ask, why are all people not capable of undertaking such communicative actions in terms of building a shared understanding? Is this because people do not take their communication action seriously as Habermas's fourth validity implies? Furthermore, how is it possible that rationality is culturally unbound, while our engagement in either or both strategic or/and communicative actions is culturally bound? Habermas responds to these questions with his concept of Lifeworld. He argues that the world where communicative actions occur is the Lifeworld. He defines it as a large collection of unstated assumptions, beliefs, and values in a same Lifeworld. He also stresses that the Lifeworld is not a composition of subjective, objective, and intersubjective worlds, but a shared understanding in a situated context. Cultural, social, and personal levels of the Lifeworld hold its rationalisation through transformation processes from traditions, moral and legal principles, and experience to abstract concepts and cognitive structure. At a structural level, the rationalisation occurs in institutional systems (initially connected with cultural worldviews and increasingly disconnected), interpersonal relations (prominent in the relation between personality and society), and individual activities (the renewal of tradition in the relationship between culture and personality). At a functional level, the rationalisation occurs through specific institutions and discourses (i.e., political institutions and education). The rationalisation is the result of the conversion of its implicit worldviews into explicit terms.

In summary, the Lifeworld is a place where we have shared understandings and taken-for-granted assumptions, where we develop our narrative identity, and where we construct our lives and make the lives of our communities meaningful. Habermas claims that the Lifeworld has gradually been subjected to communicative rational consensus rather than just accepted on a traditional basis since the Renaissance. However, as he stresses, capitalists systems (i.e., economic and political-bureaucratic systems, systems of money and power, the marketplace) have progressively taken over the control of communicative rational consensus and have colonised the Lifeworld. In this sense, discourse ethics or critical hermeneutics is significant in that we can re-establish its integrity from its being subordinated to money and power systems. Unlike Popper's hermeneutics of the three

98   *Interculturality and its methodology*

worlds, Habermas's Lifeworld legitimises the co-existence of multiple cultures and justifies the validity of intersubjectivity for interaction between the worlds. However, his Lifeworld does not answer two questions: Why don't all people have the same capability of undertaking communication actions and in which way is rationality that supports culturally bound strategic and communicative actions not culturally bound? Instead, it seems that he absolutises rationalisation and even deifies it as he argues that communicative rational consensus can take over the interaction between intersubjectively formed and perceived cultures or *inter-intersubjectivity.*

For Habermas, shared systems through rationalisation can stabilise patterns of our action and mind structures acquired in various institutional entities (e.g., family, church, neighbourhood, and school) (Bohman & Rehg, 2011). For Popper, meanwhile, World 3 as "the sum total of the objective abstract products of the human mind" is "to account for the objectivity of scientific criticism, creativity and the relationship between the mind and the body" (Percival, 1996, p. 5). In other words, Habermas systematises communicative competence for individuals' participation in publicly shared understanding, while Popper articulates socially shared meaning in connection with prior knowledges. Both are driven by the problem of self-grounding that the objective world, as the repository of objective meanings, concepts, and knowledge, provides the basis for realism. As a result, Popper claims that the structure of our engagement in the multiple worlds is universal and value-free, whereas Habermas views that rationality is not culturally bound and culture can be understood with a composite of its subjective, objective, and intersubjective claims to truths. This is not because of their theoretical limitations, but their total indifference to how people in different cultures perceive and interact with the world. In an intercultural sense, their indifference is a result of ontological dualism that promotes the superiority of the mind to the world, knowing to being known, and individuality to relation, although they do not radically separate them from each other.

4.4 Conclusion: A methodological value

Adopting Nietzsche's concept of a table of values, it can be argued that values are our ontological foundations whereby our will to power and primordial unity are exercised. The Dionysian nature indicates that power is not an individual's independent choice or free will, but the flow of energy that connects values to each other. This indicates that intercultural interaction is fundamentally and structurally value-interaction. However, our engagement in values is complicated because value networks are composed of multiple (cultural) realities or worlds that result in the multi-levelled self-construal and, in turn, the self-construal sustains and develops the multiple realities. In the review of cross-cultural psychology, we have seen that the self is construed like a matrix under a particular culture (system) and, conversely, self-construal is an interpretive framework for understanding a culture. As I have argued, self-construal theory does not facilitate intercultural interaction because it rejects the diversity of ontological structures

Values, minds, and realities   99

and accepts the independence-interdependence frame as universal and value-free. Cross-cultural psychologists presume that the mind structure is the world and, as a result, the deprivation of axiology is attached to the self, which compels minority or other cultures to accept so-called universal values. Although their priming techniques offer some instructional benefits, they eventually mythicise the intellectual capacity of individuals by not paying attention to the relationships of the multilayered self.

I have argued for multiple (cultural) realities of the world or multiple worlds by reviewing Popper's three worlds of knowledge and Habermas's theory of communicative action on the Lifeworld. Popper's World 3, the sum total of the objective abstract products of the human mind, indicates that the world is independent of individuals and exercises its own power over our minds. Intersubjectivity, as objects of World 3, allows us to observe our engagement in culture (values) and understand new meanings in intercultural interaction. Yet his intersubjectivity does not justify the fact that we have different cultural identities and cultural formations because it presumes that we are experiencing the same world. On the other hand, Habermas emphasises the intersubjective world by focusing on its emergent feature, which is the Lifeworld as a large collection of unstated assumptions, beliefs, and values. In the Lifeworld, culture plays a pivotal role in allowing people to share a same Lifeworld in which it works for people to be subjected to communicative rational consensus. Surely, Habermas's theory justifies how multiple cultural identities and cultural formations co-exist. Such multiple realities imply that our approach to the world is subject to our understanding of the relations between cultures/worlds. However, neither theory is explicit about intercultural interaction due to their ontological dualism that prioritises the individual's epistemic knowledge over ontological relations and axiological interaction. Ontological dualism dismisses the necessity of metaphysical understandings of the worlds because it does not see mutually feedback and feedforward relations between our multilayered minds and cultural realities. As a result, we fail to recognise inter-intersubjectivity of different cultures.

Consequently, we have seen that the three domains (cross-cultural psychologists' self-construal, Popper's three worlds, and Habermas's Lifeworld) indicate that cultural frameworks, the multilayered self, and multiple cultural realities are interconnected and interrelated, although they have certain metaphysical limits to intercultural interaction in which they attempt to revert back to the prominence of the Apollonian world by neutralising their methodological values.

References

Bohman, J., & Rehg, W. (2011). Jürgen Habermas. In E.N. Zalta (Ed.), *The Stanford Encyclopedia of Philosophy* (Winter 2011 ed.). Retrieved from http://plato.stanford.edu/archives/win2011/entries/habermas/

Brewer, M.B., & Gardner, W. (1996). Who is this "We"? Levels of collective identity and self-representations. *Journal of Personality and Social Psychology, 71*(1), 83–93.

Burbules, N.C., & Rupert, B. (1999). Critical thinking and critical pedagogy – Relations, differences and limits. In T.S. Popkewitz & L. Fendler (Eds.), *Critical Theories in Education* (pp. 45–66). New York: Routledge.

100 Interculturality and its methodology

Faure, M., & Venter, A. (1993). Karl Popper's critical rationalism. In J. Snyman (Ed.), *Conceptions of Social Inquiry* (pp. 37–67). Pretoria, South Africa: HSRC Press.

Gardner, W.L., Gabriel, S., & Lee, A.L. (1999). "I" value freedom, but "we" value relationships: Self-construal priming mirrors cultural differences in judgment. *Psychological Science, 10*(4), 321–326.

Gemes, K. (2001). Postmodernism's use and abuse of Nietzsche. *Philosophy and Phenomenological Research, 62*(2), 327–360.

Habermas, J. (1984). *Theory of communicative action. Volume One: Reason and the rationalization of society.* (T. McCarthy, Trans.). London: Heinemann. (Original work published 1981)

Harb, C., & Smith, P.B. (2008). Self-construals across cultures beyond independence-interdependence. *Journal of Cross-Cultural Psychology, 39*(2), 178–197.

Holub, R.C. (1991). *Jürgen Habermas: Critic in the public sphere.* New York: Routledge.

Johansson, S. (2005). *Origins of language: Constraints on hypotheses.* Amsterdam: John Benjamins Publishing.

Kühnen, U. (2009). Culture, self-construal and social cognition: Evidence from cross-cultural and priming studies. In A. Gari, K. Mylonas & A. Gari (Eds.), *Q.E.D. From Herodotus: Ethnographic Journeys to Cross-Cultural Research* (pp. 303–310). Athens, Greece: Athens: Atrapos Editions.

Nietzsche. F. (1968). *The birth of tragedy.* (W. Kaufmann. Ed. & Trans.). New York: Vintage Books. (Original work published 1872)

Nietzsche. F. (2001). *The gay science.* (W. Kaufmann. Ed. & Trans.). New York: Vintage books. (Original work published 1882)

Nietzsche. F. (2010). *Thus spake Zarathustra.* (W. Kaufmann. Ed. & Trans.). New York: Penguin Books. (Original work published 1891)

Peery. R.S. (2008). *Nietzsche, Philosopher of the perilous perhaps.* New York: Algora Publishing.

Percival, S.R. (1996). The Metaphysics of scarcity: Popper's world 3 and the theory of finite resources. *The Critical Rationalist, 1*(2), 1–28. Retrieved from http://www.tkpw.net/tcr/volume-01/number-02/v01n02.pdf

Popper, K.R. (1972). *Objective knowledge: An evolutionary approach.* Cambridge: Oxford University Press.

Popper, K.R. (2002). *The logic of scientific discovery.* London and New York: Routledge.

Schwartz, S.H. (1992). Universals in the content and structure of values: Theoretical advances and empirical tests in 20 countries. In M. Zanna (Ed.), *Advances in Experimental Social Psychology* (pp. 1–65). Orlando, FL: Academic Press.

Suh, E.M., Diener, E., & Updegraff, J.A. (2008). From culture to priming conditions: Self-construal influences on life satisfaction judgements. *Journal of Cross-Cultural Psychology, 39*(1), 3–15.

Turner, J.C., Hogg, M.A., Oakes, P.J., Reicher, S.D., & Wetherell, M.S. (1987). *Rediscovering the social group: A self-categorisation theory.* Oxford, UK: Blackwell.

5 Interactive methodology for intercultural interaction

In the previous chapter, methodology appeared as an important issue in which the theory of self-construal, the three worlds of knowledge construction, and the communicative action in the Lifeworld tend to neutralise values embedded in their methodological approaches. Such a tendency can restrict intercultural interaction to an epistemic frame, which ignores the fact that methodology is also culturally bound. For example, if teachers believe pedagogy as value-free and culture unbound, they unconsciously promote predefined values, as they are not free from professional responsibilities. Pedagogy is practised in line with values and norms, while instruction is concerned with knowledge and skills (Biesta & Miedema, 2002). Thus, without exploring underlying assumptions and values of pedagogy they have chosen or practised, teachers cannot achieve pedagogical innovation (I will argue this in Part III). Likewise, methodological appropriateness of intercultural interaction is needed, which will be done through a critical review of existing methodological approaches in education in this chapter.

In general, methodological approaches to social science offer a deeper insight into metaphysical issues of cultural realism. For example,

> Whilst empiricists pursue "the Enlightenment urge to categorise and count" in the service of prediction and control, the interpretive tradition's desire to recover the authentic experience which "harks back to the romantic movement" and its rejection of routinisation and instrumental rationality.
>
> (Murdock, 1997, p. 178)

This empirical and interpretive methodological debate is based on their "reactions to High Modernity" (Murdock, 1997, p. 178). Similarly, methodologies used in cultural studies and education research, have different ontological and epistemological assumptions for social and cultural life, which helps us understand metaphysical aspects of culturally diverse realities. The most predominant methodologies in social science are known as methodological individualism, methodological holism, and methodological relationism. In this comparison, I will focus on appropriateness of each methodology for interculturality in value networks. I will also adopt the concept of nodes from *the theory of distributed knowledge* into this comparison because it is a pedagogical theory for the networked world.

102 *Interculturality and its methodology*

5.1 Metaphysical assumptions of methodological individualism, holism, and relationism

The three methodologies can be summarised as methodological individualism assumes *self-in-social-vacuum*, methodological holism supports *society-independent-of-self*, and methodological relationism upholds *self-in-social-relations*. Methodological individualism assumes that individuals are agents of history and social changes, whereas methodological holism presumes that "the causes of social processes must be sought outside individuals" (Di Iorio, 2013, p. 2). The distinction is determined by whether or not a social system exists independently of individuals. On the other hand, methodological relationism overarches theoretical perspectives of methodological individualism and holism and clarifies a meta-theoretical base in social psychology (Ritzer & Gindoff, 1992). It also defines social behaviour as the outcome of individuals' involvement in structural social relations (Tsekeris, 2010).

First, methodological individualism adopts that "synthetic expressions . . . [are] a collection of individuals, beliefs, attitudes, actions of individuals, unintended effects deriving from their actions, and systemic", and posits that these collective entities only exist as observable objects with empirical data (Di Iorio, 2013, p. 2). For the proponents of methodological individualism, a whole is a pseudo-systemic or a reality that individuals experience. Hence they tend to reject the substantiality of culture determining individuals' identity and thoughts. Although they do not reject ontology, they endorse it only based on nominalism and reject realism (Di Iorio, 2013). For them, objects are manifestations of their existence, and their properties are merely words for communication (Di Iorio, 2013). Hence the ontological position of methodological individualism is that only individuals are real in the social world, and the epistemological position subscribes to the notion that "what we know about social phenomena stems from our knowledge about individuals, their actions, and their interaction" (Ritzer, 2001, pp. 143–144). In this sense, methodological individualism is found in conservative multiculturalism and liberal multiculturalism education models, as the proponents regard cultural diversity as a provisional or temporary phenomenon and adopt dualistic reductionism in which education is used to remove or minimise ethnicity and Indigeneity.

Second, methodological holism denotes "the totality of all the properties or aspects of a thing", and its aim is to explain all relationships (Di Iorio, 2013, p. 86). Relations are believed to form a cultural reality as an emergently structured whole (Di Iorio, 2013). Hence to understand a whole, we must approach a whole, not its parts. In other words, a focus should be on how a whole determines the nature of parts and how parts are interrelated and interdependent (Ritzer, 2001). In this sense, social-cultural phenomena are understood only in terms of "social wholes" (Ritzer, 2001, p. 114). A whole can be intuitively recognised based on the strong belief that intellectually and intuitively capable individuals can visualise its essence (Di Iorio, 2013). Methodological holism can be found in left-essentialist multiculturalism and critical multiculturalism education models, as both models presume that cultural realities and identities are socially

Interactive methodology 103

constructed and they prioritise social transformation as a whole over individual transformation. Yet the proponents do not fully discard methodological individualism (or positivists' approach) in which they argue that cultural processes are reducible to actions of individuals (see Chapter 3).

Third, methodological relationism presumes that individuals, groups, or society are defined by their socio-cultural relationships. Ontological relationism is based on the premise that "what is real is the relationships among individuals, groups, and society" (Ritzer, 2001, p. 144). The proponents of epistemological relationism argue that knowledges and concepts of the socio-cultural world must be formulated in terms of relationships between individuals, groups, and society (Ritzer, 2001, p. 144). Relationism is often likened to a networked system in which things are what they are depending on their location and movement in a network, and thus there is neither a fixed nor constant position (Fuchs, 2001). Unlike methodological holism, methodological relationism equally emphasises both self-reflexivity and socio-cultural formation (Tsekeris, 2010). Self-reflexivity can be described as a self-self (or intrapersonal) relationship that is a precondition for participating in dialogic interaction with changing socio-cultural environments. On the other hand, socio-cultural formation focuses on theoretical modelling and empirical analysis of a network. Yet this dualistic approach may cause an issue in which interaction between self-reflexivity and socio-cultural formation is presumed value-free. Pluralist multiculturalism and intercultural dialogic education models may also be seen as partially involved with methodological relationism. Yet the primary concern of the models is on intercommunication between white and non-white individuals towards a cohesive community or nation, not in the networked world of interculturality. Thus they tend to restrict intercultural interaction to participating individuals' epistemic processes separating individuality from interculturality and return to methodological individualism to promote individual egalitarianism and abstract communitarianism.

In sum, methodological individualism corresponds to synthetic expressions of subject-object relations and focuses on interaction between individuals and their activities, which enhances abstractions for their actions; methodological holism presupposes that individuals are required to accommodate themselves to a social whole that regulates or influences their behaviour and minds; methodological relationism assumes that relations between individuals, groups, and society are the only true entity of all phenomena. In intercultural interaction, methodological individualism is not or is less concerned with relationships in a sense of the ontologically networked world; methodological holism does not address the relational structure of a whole that determines individuals' thinking and behaviour; methodological relationism does not presume that a whole-part relationship is culturally bound. These differences are caused by different images of agents that each methodology pursues. Methodological individualism defines an individual as an independent being, methodological holism as an interdependent being, and methodological relationism as a morally subjugated being to a network. In the perspective of the three dimensions of educational metaphysics, inversely, all these images are needed for intercultural interaction: the individual needs to be an independent being as to decision making, an interdependent being to be

104 *Interculturality and its methodology*

aware of the ontologically networked world, and a morally responsible being to interact and collaborate with others and for the world.

Such a synthetic understanding of individuality undermines the subject-object order and encourages participants to focus on "ontological complicity – or mutual possession" (Bourdieu & Wacquant as cited in Tsekeris, 2010, p. 140). Yet it is still methodologically insufficient to apply in intercultural pedagogy in that (a) participants' cultural perceptions of the networked world can determine their ontological positions in intercultural interaction, (b) new values emerging from intercultural interaction can redefine interaction processes and methods, and, therefore, (c) knowledge construction and values embedded in teaching and learning activities have to be examined based on the nature of the networked world. These concerns are partially addressed by connectivists' *theory of distributed knowledge*.

5.2 Nodes of connectiviism

The theory of distributed knowledge proposed by Downes (2005) and supported by Siemens (2008) is that "the learning of knowledge – is distributive, that is, not located in any given place", but "consists of the network of connections formed from experience and interaction with a knowing community" (Downes, 2005, para. 3). Distributed knowledge on digital networks is embedded in multimedia such as audio, video, text, animation, and images, which generates new knowledge domains including interaction, interface, functionality, accessibility, and user experience. In this context, Siemens (2008) argues that both knowledge and learning "rest in diversity of opinions" and defines this distribution with a new term, *connectivism*. Downes (2005) also argues that learning refers to meaningful activities that are embedded in networks and this embedment occurs through interaction, sharing, collaboration, production, and communication, which means learning is no longer regarded as a separate activity. In this sense, distributed knowledge is in constant change, and, as a result, validity and accuracy of knowledge are also not fixed as it appears through learners' discovery of a new network (Kop & Hill, 2008).

This discovery activity refers to *connectivism* that is theoretically associated with methodological individualism in terms of objectivism and pragmatism and methodological holism in terms of interpretivism (Kop & Hill, 2008). In connectivism, knowledge exists outside the mind (objectivism) and each learner constructs his or her own mental model through negotiation and interpretation (pragmatism and interpretivism). Pedagogically, thus connectivism shares its principles with constructivism in which learning on networks requires individual learners to build their own cognitive frameworks through socio-cultural interaction (Kerr, 2007). In this sense, connectivism fits at an instructional level (Verhagen, 2006). As an instructional theory, the theory of distributed knowledge provides new learning considerations for networked learning environments. As connectivism adapts to a changing technological landscape, it presumes that learning occurs when learners participate in nodes on networks (Verhagen, 2006). Thus, as Siemens (2008) argues, "the capacity to know is more critical than what is actually known . . . [and] the ability to see connections between fields, ideas, and concepts is a core skill" (para. 24). In practice, learners connect to nodes or a set of networks to find information or participate in a networked community to share or create information. This connectivity may lead them to modify their prior experience and beliefs and to reconnect to another set of networks to share it with others and/or seek further information. In the networks of distributed knowledge, consequently, such a knowledge connection becomes the nature of learning.

This review of the distributed knowledge theory indicates that connectivism does not address how learning is constrained by nodes, as they presume that learners will choose a node at their own will. This causes a problem in claiming it as either an instructional theory or a learning theory. Indeed, the networked learning environment has a great impact on learning and teaching, but without clarifying how interaction between nodes and learners' dispositions generates knowledge construction, connectivism becomes a concept indicating connectivity in that environment. Kerr's (2007) theoretical criticism also indicates that connectivism needs to provide either a mental model for learners or a conceptual framework for instructors because it does not articulate how interaction between learners and nodes is predefined by the nature of networks. As Kop and Hill (2008) explicitly point out, connectivism certainly provides some principles of *how to design* curriculum in a digitally networked environment, but it is insufficient to answer *how to teach*. In his practical criticism on connectivism, Verhagen (2006) also points out that learners will miss critical learning opportunities from peer learners and instructors because connectivism moves learners away from peers and instructors to nodes in the networks. This means that connectivism is unconcerned with "how connections to networks may be interpreted in relation to physical maturation or the changes that occur over time via a person's exposure to, and interaction, with the social world" (Kop & Hill, 2008, p. 3).

In essence, by placing learners outside the networks of distributed knowledge, connectivism promotes some particular kinds of individuality that individuals are supposed to be independent from networks to be able to freely access any nodes and to be intellectuals to identify nodes and connect themselves to them based on their own self-interest. However, an individual's engagement in nodes cannot be done without acknowledging three facts: nodes form a set of networks, the networks as a whole sustain the relations of nodes, and our minds are changed as per a change of the relations of nodes as our minds are structured by the networks. This means that we are always in the networks, as if we are in a ship that is permanently sailing in an ocean, as there is no land. Consequently, we can confirm that connectivism needs to pay attention to such interconnectedness and interdependence between nodes (values), minds, and the nature of networks.

5.3 Conclusion: Interactive methodology

Dewey's (1922/1983) *habits of mind*, Bourdieu and Wacquant's (1992) *social field*, and Bruner's (1999) *situated view of mind* can be hybridised into the concept of nodes. Dewey (1922/1983) argues, "Our individual habits are links in forming the endless chain of humanity" (p. 19). Bourdieu and Wacquant (1992) define a

106 *Interculturality and its methodology*

social field as "a network, or a configuration, of objective relations between positions" (p. 97), and Bruner (1999) argues that community creates meanings that are embedded in the human mind, and its culture provides frames to understand and communicate with the world. These concepts are complementary to each other and point at interconnectedness and interrelatedness between our minds and the worlds. As a result, they allow us to see how our cultural values are connected and to have the ability to think about ourselves and interact with people from other cultures. Likewise, the relationships between our minds and nodes or simply *value-interaction* affect our social-cultural formations and relations, which results in a topological change of networks as well as our minds. In effect, the networked world intrinsically animates value-interaction between individuals/ cultures via self-reflexivity and sustains cultural realities via sets of value networks that we are metaphysically participating in. Furthermore, value-interaction emits a new set of values that produces a new ecology of the mind as it changes value networks. In this understanding, every culture has its own interculturality, and our engagement in value networks means that we are interacting with others and ourselves, which is metaphysical. A problem will occur when we are obsessed with a delusional idea that we are ontologically independent of value networks. In an epistemological sense, the independence is only needed for perceiving interculturality because its actuation is a form of already interpreted networks. In this way, we can return to value networks, otherwise a change in value networks remains an impossible dream and cultural historicity is demolished.

Such a holistic understanding of the networked world enriches connectivism. Although it is not explicit, it can be said that connectivism's epistemology is consistent with constructivism in which individuals' construction of mental learning models occurs by engaging in nodes (Kop & Hill, 2008). In essence, both connectivism and constructivism presume that individuals stay outside of value networks. Connectivism emphasises one's willingness to participate in nodes, whereas constructivism limitedly reflects the nature of value networks in mental models of learners (e.g., Piaget's assimilation and accommodation processes and Vygotsky's zone of proximal development presume that learning is mediated by multiple realities via the human mind. See Chapter 9 for further details). Like methodological individualism, however, this epistemological connectivism does not discover relationships between learners and networks because it is presumed that learning quality in the networked world is directly determined by individual learners' abilities. This is the reason why connectivism needs methodological holism in which learners' willingness to make a connection with nodes is determined by a set of value networks where their cultural framework is formed, which is supposed to be ontological connectivism. In this way, learning refers to an extension of value networks (a cultural framework) through (a) learners' awareness of how their thinking is affected by nodes where they participate and (b) learners' rearrangement of relations of nodes that they are supported to reach their full potential. The nature of such an extension is methodologically holistic, as leaners identify their ontic position through values embedded in nodes and change relations of nodes by discovering new values, which should be called axiological connectivism. Such a metaphysical integration of (enriched) connectivism justifies the co-existence of methodological individualism, holism, and relationism in the networked world and explains an ecological change of value networks through learners' connection, disconnection, and reconnection of nodes or a set of networks.

Such an integration offers a new metaphysical position for each methodology in the networked world: methodological holism justifies the ontological foundations for the world that is interconnected and interrelated – *ontological justification*. Methodological individualism defines a relationship and develops an epistemic process between independent learners and networks – *epistemological assumptions and processes*, and methodological relationism facilitates value-interaction of interculturality – *axiological interaction*. Such a conceptual integration through defining positions of each methodology in the networked world for interculturality indicates that the three methodologies are metaphysically interactive, which can be named as *interactive methodology* (IM). IM in intercultural interaction makes the three methodologies interactive by exerting vigilance over three -isms: cultural intellectualism, cultural voluntarism, and cultural emotionalism.

First, IM rejects reductionist interpretations of methodological individualism. Reductionists believe that phenomena that occurred in value networks are completely reducible to individuals, and, as a result, individuals can discover properties of value networks through intellectual practice (or *cultural intellectualism*). Instead, IM accepts both personal and social epistemology in which what we know about cultural phenomena is derived from our knowledge about our mind structures, actions, and interactions with others. Personal epistemology identifies and evaluates how one's beliefs interact with values embedded in nodes, whereas social epistemology construes knowledge as a collaborative achievement through interaction between epistemic agents who exercise causal influence on their beliefs. Second, IM shares ontological holism with methodological holism in which value networks cannot be understood by values per se, but need to be approached as a whole because values are interconnected and interrelated. Yet IM criticises ontologically dualistic approaches to methodological holism that indicate actions of individuals determine cultural interaction and not vice versa, and, as a result, the individual's will is the ultimate principle of value networks (or *cultural voluntarism*). Third, IM supports ontological relationism in which relationships are truly real. It also upholds epistemological relationism in which our knowledge of the world is formulated and this is determined depending on which part of the networked world we stand on. However, IM criticises methodological relationism's ignorance of causal interaction between minds and values and its unawareness that emergent values can change relationships. In practice, it rejects the fact that emotions are prioritised to hide their personal gain, and emotional exhibition is patternised to only conserve current relationships (or *cultural emotionalism*)

Such an interactive integration of the three methodologies with the three dimensions of metaphysics (a) lays the ontological foundations for interaction between cultures as sets of value networks, (b) exercises a non-dualistic approach to self-transformation and social transformation, and (c) facilitates learners' participation in ecological (inter)cultural formation. This means that our being is

108 *Interculturality and its methodology*

fundamentally metaphysical and our engagement in intercultural interaction is methodologically hermeneutic. Realistically, if we have superiority over others, this means that we are obsessed with a particular epistemology that legitimises cultural hegemony and prevents us from being aware that we are all parts of the networked world.

References

Biesta, G.J.J., & Miedema, S. (2002). Instruction or pedagogy? The need for a transformative conception of education. *Teaching and Teacher Education, 18*(2), 173–181.

Bourdieu, P., & Wacquant, L. (1992). *An invitation to reflexive sociology.* Chicago: The University of Chicago Press.

Bruner, J. (1999). Culture, mind and education. In. B. Moon & P. Murphy (Eds.), *Curriculum in Context* (pp. 148–179). London: Paul Chapman Publishing and The Open University.

Dewey, J. (1983). *Human nature and conduct. In The middle works of John Dewey.* Carbondale: Southern Illinois University Press. (Original work published 1922)

Di Iorio, F. (2013). Nominalism and systemism: On the non-reductionist nature of methodological individualism. CHOPE Working paper No. 2013-07. http://dx.doi.org/10.2139/ssrn.2289318

Downes, S. (2005, December 22). An introduction to connective knowledge. Stephen's Web. Retrieved from http://www.downes.ca/cgi-bin/page.cgi?post=33034

Fuchs, S. (2001). *Against essentialism: A theory of culture and society.* Cambridge, MA: Harvard University Press.

Kerr, B. (2007). *A challenge to Connectivism.* Transcript of Keynote Speech, Online Connectivism Conference. University of Manitoba. Retrieved from http://ltc.umanitoba.ca/wiki/index.php?title=Kerr_Presentation

Kop, R., & Hill, A. (2008). Connectivism learning theory of the future or vestige of the past? *The International Review of Research in Open and Distance Learning, 9*(3). Retrieved from http://www.irrodl.org/index.php/irrodl/article/view/523/1103

Murdock, G. (1997). Thin descriptions: Questions of method in cultural analysis. In J. McGuigan (Ed.), *Cultural Methodologies* (pp. 178–192). London: Sage.

Ritzer, G. (2001). *Explorations in social theory: From metatheorizing to rationalization.* London: SAGE Publications.

Ritzer, G., & Gindoff, P. (1992). Methodological relationism: Lessons for and from social psychology. *Social Psychology Quarterly, 55*(2), 128–140.

Siemens, G. (2008). *Learning and knowing in networks: Changing roles for educators and designers.* Paper 105: University of Georgia IT Forum. Retrieved from http://it.coe.uga.edu/itforum/Paper105/Siemens.pdf

Tsekeris, C. (2010). Relationalism sociology: Theoretical and methodological elaborations. *Facta Universitatis Series: Philosophy, Sociology, Psychology and History, 9*(1), 139–148.

Verhagen, P. (2006). *Connectivism: A new learning theory? Surf e-learning themasite* Retrieved from http://elearning.surf.nl/e-learning/english/3793

6 Philosophical hermeneutics for intercultural interaction

The previous two chapters can be summarised as verifying interculturality as a reality with the three dimensions of metaphysics in order for us to be aware of our own cultural boundaries and to mutually interact with other cultures in value networks. Particular metaphysical frameworks are predominant across multicultural education models and reproduced through socio-cultural activities, institutions, and historical engagements. For intercultural interaction, a challenge is not only to criticise frameworks that we hold but also to investigate interculturality embedded in our cultural frameworks. Otherwise, we cannot prevent ourselves from viewing cultural diversity and intercultural experiences as merely contingent by-products that are only constructed by individual actions. In this sense, our interpretation (or hermeneutics) of interculturality should be pre-critically metaphysical with the aim of disclosing ideological aspects of cultural frameworks and articulating intercultural interaction through refining the three dimensions of metaphysics. In doing so, a methodological approach to intercultural education is to find out how values interact with the mind (ontological justification), how intercultural interaction is structured in value networks (epistemological assumptions and processes), and how emergent values of intercultural interaction affect a topological change of networks (axiological interaction).

Modern hermeneutic theories (i.e., Heidegger's being-in-the-world, Gadamer's fusions of horizons and effective-historical consciousness, Kuhn's paradigm shift, and Deleuze and Guattari's rhizomatic theory) focus on our engagement in situations and our interaction with others and develop systematised understandings and dialogues. In particular, hermeneutic theories quoted in education are used to articulate educational changes and to justify the necessity of transforming educational systems. Classic hermeneutics refers to the study of the interpretation of texts by assuming that texts have definite meaning (Sammel, 2003). It is found in the areas of literature, religion, law, and so on. On the other hand, contemporary hermeneutics refers to the study of the theory and practice of interpretation, particularly in religious studies and social philosophy (Cohen, Manion, & Morrison, 2005), and hermeneutic phenomenology assumes "the lived experiences (phenomenological) are already meaningfully (hermeneutically) experienced" (Sammel, 2003, p. 160). Indeed, human life per se is neither the subject as an a priori nor a completely independent subject, but a hermeneutic process within dynamic and diverse relationships and associations with others and environments.

110   *Interculturality and its methodology*

In our daily lives, we find ourselves in "meaningful places" rather than mere "abstract space", and our involvement is "part of our being-in-the-world that roots in a conception of the world as an ethos" (Drenthen, 2011, p. 124). In other words, hermeneutics as an interpretative process of our meaningful lives underlines all human activities in that "human beings exist inasmuch as they draw the meaning of their lives from the objects and experiences that they encounter" (Hainic, 2012, p. 230). Methodologically, hermeneutics is also known as a qualitative research method and it is a study of interpreting collected data (Cohen *et al.*, 2005), whereas philosophically (or phenomenologically), it is a theory to understand the goal or meaning of human life and a matter of universal significance (Gadamer, 1960/2004).

"Gadamer's hermeneutic phenomenology makes the ontological assumption that meaning is constructed intersubjectively within a historical horizon, reality therefore, does not exist independently, but rather is a process of how these parties negotiate meaning" (Sammel, 2003, p. 161). In brief, it aims to deconstruct stultified thinking and to provoke new horizons. Gadamer's metaphor of a fusion of horizons refers to limitations of recognising and experiencing truths and also implies possibilities of epistemic extensions. This is clearer in a comparison with Nietzsche that appears in Mootz (2006): "Nietzsche is wary of the stultifying effects of horizontal relationships within a cultural horizon, whereas Gadamer invites the educative effects of vertical relationships between past horizons and the present" (p. 100). Nietzsche employs rhetoric to search for appropriate means of persuasion, while Gadamer draws on rhetoric to approach people with open horizons to mutual understanding. Gadamer contributes to postmodern destruction of metaphysics grounded in "the hermeneutical situation of limited horizons reaching understanding in a moment of fusion" (Mootz, 2006, p. 101). Nietzsche's critical philosophy presumes that (cultural) reality is hermeneutically structured and Gadamer's philosophical hermeneutics acknowledges that "[cultural] tradition is a linguistically structured and contested medium through which understanding takes place" (Mootz, 2006, p. 105). As we always engage in cultural horizons, philosophical hermeneutics can be used to encourage us to face our own "prejudiced fore-structure of understanding as a participant within a cultural perspective" (Mootz, 2006, p. 100), where intercultural interaction can be initiated and formulated.

In this chapter, by focusing on the concept of intersubjectivity in Gadamer's fusion of horizons, Kuhn's paradigm shifts, and Deleuze and Guattari's rhizomatic theory, I will argue that an occurrence of interculturality as emergent is inherent in intercultural interaction because no one has ever escaped from socio-cultural construction of realities or value networks. In the process, I will argue that a constructed (cultural) reality becomes a form of *interobjectivity* (or inter-intersubjectivity) of interculturality because of the metaphysical interaction of different cultures that exerts power over our multilayered self and perceived multiple realities. My conclusion will be that our involvement in (or doing to) intersubjectivity and (doing with) engagement in interobjectivity, which is *hermeneutic duo circles*, facilitates our hermeneutic participation in intercultural interaction in value networks, and we perceive emergent values that push our linguistic boundaries of value networks. I believe that such a methodological concept will demonstrate that intercultural value networks are decentralised, rhizomatic, and built upon new ways of thinking about and transforming society. Ultimately, this chapter will be dedicated to providing a methodological approach to intercultural interaction. My methodological approach to intercultural value networks will unfold through five themes – namely values, intersubjectivity, interobjectivity, emergent values, and axiological mapping.

6.1 Values: Fore-structure of understanding

The foundation of Gadamer's philosophical hermeneutics inherits from Heidegger's *being-in-the-world*. Heidegger uses the concept of *Dasein* to refer to the experience of being (*Sein*) and the existential form of human beings (Heidegger, 1953/2010). Dasein must confront mortality (being-toward-death) and ultimate aloneness (Heidegger, 1953/2010). Thus this hermeneutics of Dasein means that the existence of human beings can be disclosed not by our transcendental subjective consciousness but by our being-in-the-world. In his hermeneutic phenomenology, Heidegger understands consciousness within "historicity" and "temporality", unlike Husserl who defines it as "transcendental subjectivity" (Palmer, 1968, p. 125). When removing the individual subject (you or whomever) from consideration, Husserl argues that isolating oneness from the live experience stream is transcendental subjectivity, whereas Heidegger argues for human being-in-the-world that cannot transcend over one's own historicity and temporality (Palmer, 1968). Gadamer and Heidegger argue that Dasein is always *a being engaged in the world*. The *always* here should refer to *ontologically*, not epistemologically or axiologically, in a sense that the fundamental mode of being cannot be subjective or objective, but a revelation by projection into and engagement with the epistemic, aesthetic, and moral worlds, which opposes the Cartesian abstract agent and, as a result, challenges our existence. This makes sense of their claim that hermeneutic phenomenology is not an understanding technique of text, but the revelation of human and world existence. As "I" am always a being engaged in the world, Dasein exists, Dasein and existence are one, and the world and Dasein are one. This means that Dasein and existence are structurally inseparable. The world here refers to neither the natural environment nor an objective reality against subjective consciousness, but a thing beyond subjective and objective frames. The world becomes a mesh of life where meanings are understood and generated. In this sense, the world itself refers to the ontological structure of existence, "which concerns ways of being, are differentiated by virtue of their apophantical and hermeneutical referents" (Mills, 1997, p. 42), where every process of understanding occurs against our culturally and historically embedded pre-understandings. Gadamer (1960/2004) explains how our prejudices as pre-understandings hold historicity as follows:

> In fact history does not belong to us, but we belong to it. Long before we understand ourselves through the process of self-examination, we understand ourselves in a self-evident way in the family, society and state in which

112 *Interculturality and its methodology*

we live . . . The self-awareness of the individual is only a flickering in the closed circuits of historical life. That is why the prejudices of the individual, far more than his judgements, constitute the historical reality of his being.

(p. 245)

An individual's prejudices do not mean that he or she has bias or *doxa* when understanding things and judging his or her own values, but refer to the expressions of his or her own existence. Thus, "Existential understanding . . . is an understanding of the ontological structures of existence, that is, what it is to be Dasein, and existential understanding is a person's self-understanding, that is, an understanding of her/his own way to be or what s/he is" (Mills, 1997, p. 43). This indicates that prejudices, as pre-understandings, are necessary conditions for interpretive understandings of a participatory historical event. In this point, both Heidegger (1953/2010) and Gadamer (1960/2004) criticise the Cartesian subject-object dualism which means that a human being as a subject understands the (external) world mediated through an object and condemns that the inseparable relation is broken by myths of subjectivism and methodologism. For Heidegger and Gadamer, understanding is not an active cognitive process of a conscious being that grasps and manipulates things as objects, but it is understanding the world that is constituted by our hermeneutic responses and experiences. In this sense, the concept of being-in-the-world rejects subjectivism and methodologism and understands human beings in terms of their temporality, historicity, process, and relationship (Palmer, 1968).

Gadamer expands such an interpretation into the fore-structure of understanding for mutual understanding, which is the *hermeneutic circle*. A fore-structure pre-exists based on a meaningfully associated structure found in the world that is our own (cultural) value systems beyond the Cartesian subject-object dualism. Like Heidegger, Gadamer's fore-structure of understanding does not refer to a cognitive by-product or attribute, but refers to a preliminary structure that allows us to interpret and understand the world. That structure is an understandable and revisable presupposition that holds the coherence of existence and can be a metaphysical framework where values are embedded in our social practices – that is, in a culture. In intercultural interaction, then, we can presume that interculturality denotes a new cultural and living experience that occurs in association with a fore-structure of our cultural understanding. This means that fore-structures of understanding our own culture and other cultures are predetermined by values embedded in the fore-structures. This interpretation is consistent with a metaphor of the Iceberg model of culture (i.e., Hall, 1981; Schein, 1985; Selfridge & Sokolik, 1975). A set of values is a form of deep culture so that values are mostly invisible to those who have a different culture (a value system) unless intercultural value-interaction occurs. As seen in Chapter 4, this is also supported by Nietzsche's concept, *a table of values*, in which we manipulate values through *naming* and our self-awareness of the Dionysian energy, the flow of values, requires us to identify how values are interacting with one another. In other words, our being-in-the-world is revealed through practising deconstruction and reconstruction of values in intercultural interaction through naming. In interculturality, both Gadamer's fore-structure of understanding and the Iceberg model share the same assumption that values flow and values as a whole refers to the networked world. Consequently, one interprets the world based on one's fore-structure, and the fore-structure is a representation of one's culture as a particular set of value networks. Hence intercultural interaction begins with self-awareness about understanding one's own fore-structure through values forming one's own culture in comparison with fore-structures of other cultures and the nature of the networked world. This approach refers to an intrapersonal experience. Then we need to investigate further about how intercultural interaction occurs as interpersonal and collective experiences in the networked world.

6.2 Intersubjectivity: A fusion of horizons and paradigm shifts

An individual sees neither beyond his or her perception nor a thing from multiple perspectives. This can be seen with a person who has an attachment to a region, race, culture, or social class (Rees, 2003). On the contrary, those who are aware of their own confinement to things are able to extend their horizons by participating in a hermeneutic conversation regarding an event. In this way, a fusion of horizons rejects objectivism and absolute knowledge, and horizons are transformed according to Ricoeur (1973/1981). Ricoeur argues,

> This [fusion of horizons] is a dialectical concept which results from the rejection of two alternatives: objectivism, whereby the objectification of the other is premised on the forgetting of oneself; and absolute knowledge, according to which universal history can be articulated within a single horizon. We exist neither in closed horizons, nor within a horizon that is unique. No horizon is closed, since it is possible to place oneself in another point of view and another culture . . . But no horizon is unique, since the tension between the other and oneself is unsurpassable.
>
> (p. 75)

This argument implies that Ricoeur rejects Husserl's self-foundational philosophy and Cartesian definition of the self on immediate and transparent consciousness and views that the self is only understood within-the-world. His point is that one cannot exist in a closed horizon, but is always situated in a context and constantly interacting with the world. Likewise, it is impossible to remove oneself from one's own culture – values, beliefs, assumptions, and ways of thinking. If one believes that one has no horizon, one may be confined to things surrounding oneself and be obsessed with them or unable to see relative, related values of others. A critical point here is that expanding or transforming our horizons is the way that we interact with the world. In Gadamer's (1960/2004) words, this refers to the *multiplicity of horizons* that includes "narrowness of horizon, or the possible expansion of horizon, of the opening of new horizons" (p. 302), and hence "we move and moves with us" (p. 304). Although it seems that Gadamer does not

114   *Interculturality and its methodology*

explicitly address its precondition, an expansion or transformation of horizons is based on the premise that we involve intersubjective experiences that are forms of collective consciousness. This means that a fore-structure of understanding has a shared structure of existence in a particular situation. Otherwise, a fusion of horizons could not be an interpersonal experience. Contrarily, as seen in Habermas's Lifeworld and Popper's World 3 in Chapter 4, concepts appearing in our minds are either identical to the world or at least representations of the world. Thus if we believe that we directly contact the world without any mediation of collective consciousness, a fusion of horizons remains an intrapersonal experience. As Ricoeur (1973/1981) argued, "Pretension of the subject to know itself by immediate intuition, it must be said that we understand ourselves only by the long detour of the signs of humanity deposited in cultural works" (p. 87). Consequently, a hermeneutic approach to intercultural interaction is an understanding of the self being involved in intersubjective objects in a cultural context. In this sense, we can reject both an egocentric universe and true self as a permanent and autonomous entity and regard our collective mind as a culturally organic system (or the world-centric self) – that is, *always* interacting with the unity of all selves where intersubjectivity occurs. Then we can see that our horizons are always anchored in hermeneutic situations.

As a fusion of horizons occurs by an in-depth understanding of others' viewpoints, intercultural hermeneutics always challenges our cultural frameworks. This means that a fusion of horizons causes not only a shift from one way of thinking to another but also supervenes an expansion of one's cultural framework that brings humanity into contact with interculturality. Yet Gadamer's fusion of horizons does not explicitly address such a phenomenon that intersubjectivity can be reshaped as a result of intercultural interaction. Presumably, this is because his primary focus is on ontological relationships between individual agents and the world via horizons, and this leads to ignoring the possibility that a fusion of horizon has the potential to reveal a new whole world or a new cultural horizon that can reshape collective consciousness. Fortunately, this collective interaction is quite explicit in Kuhn's notion of paradigm shift. Kuhn (1996) defines *a paradigm shift* as "a transition between incommensurables, the transition between competing paradigms cannot be made a step at a time, forced by logic and neutral experience" (p. 150). A paradigm shift occurs when

> all crises begin with the blurring of a paradigm and the consequent loosening of the rules for normal research. . . . Or finally, the case that will most concern us here, a crisis may end with the emergence of a new candidate for paradigm and with the ensuing battle over its acceptance.
>
> (Kuhn, 1996, p. 84)

The concept of paradigm shifts refers to epistemological relativism in which we cannot compare which paradigm is better because "each paradigm will be shown to satisfy more or less the criteria that it dictates for itself and to fall short of a few of those dictated by its opponent" (Kuhn, 1996, p. 109). Kuhn also argues for a new paradigm in a sense of epistemological relativism:

> These fundamental inventions of a new paradigm have been either very young or very new to the field whose paradigm they change . . . the puzzles that constitute normal science exist only because no paradigm that provides a basis for scientific research ever completely resolves all its problems.
>
> (p. 89)

This means that a paradigm would be incommensurable with a different paradigm because there is no common measure for assessing different theories, and the reason in the choice of a paradigm is subjective. Other scholars also understand paradigms in line with such epistemological relativism. For example, Horner and Westacott (2000) define a paradigm as "a theoretical framework, a set of assumptions, an orientation toward specific problem solving practices, and a rule for how these problems should be approached and proposed solutions appraised" (p. 113). Liu and Matthews (2005) also argue that a paradigm is not the same as the total sum of concrete truth, but is "a general orientation for human reflection", which is a general hypothesis (p. 390). Such understandings indicate that paradigm shifts are conditioned by three facts that (a) all paradigms are ontologically networked, (b) this networked world allows an epistemological shift between a new paradigm and an old paradigm, and (c) we participate in paradigm shifts by revealing pre-understandings of our own cultural framework, which is a set of value networks. For example, if we understand all (prominent and potential) paradigms as a whole, we can be aware of our collective pre-understanding, which is an indicator that our cultural framework is connected to the networked world. As we choose a paradigm, or we are attracted by a paradigm, there should be a higher framework that works as the foundation for our choice, or is chosen regardless of whether our choice is correct or not. In other words, the higher framework refers to our cultural framework that is always there to project itself onto us, and we perceive it as our perceived world – an image of the whole world – that makes us think and behave within a particular framework. In intercultural interaction, this ontological connection indicates that all cultures are fundamentally connected by the world, and we participate in the world with our collective pre-understanding determined by our cultural framework.

Such a metaphysical understanding of the world discovers that the interculturally networked world is composed of an ontological world (value networks), an epistemological world (paradigm shifts), and an axiological world (cultural frameworks). Thus our collective pre-understanding is always connected with other collective consciousnesses. We can only experience this connection when we engage in intercultural interaction by disclosing our multilayered self's engagement in a situation, which means we are required to introspect and disclose our own value table in intercultural interaction. In this sense, a paradigm shift refers to a change in collective thinking and collaborative practice, whereas a fusion of horizons refers to a change in individual thinking and practice. In the

116 *Interculturality and its methodology*

interculturally networked world, a fusion of horizons implies that there is inter-subjectivity between different individuals within a shared framework or a culture, whereas paradigm shifts require *inter-intersubjectivity* between different cultures (I prefer to name it *interobjectivity*, and its further justification is presented in the following section). This distinction helps us understand the ontological foundations for paradigm shifts and fusions of horizons in that both are positioned in the networked world. If we assume that both concepts cannot co-exist in the same world, we have to isolate agents in one collective consciousness and regard intercultural interaction as a merely intrapersonal experience. In a hermeneutic process, then, we can compare values embedded in cultures (a sense of inter-subjectivity) in terms of how each culture is opposite to or harmonised with other cultures in a particular situation (a sense of inter-intersubjectivity). This means that we should understand the concept of intersubjectivity as a kind of perspective-taking of others or putting oneself in the place of another rather than achieving understanding (Duranti, 2010, pp. 14–15). Furthermore, intersubjectivity as the primary source of multiple-reality is the basic quality of co-existence with others, which allows us to be aware of the presence of others and other cultures in particular forms. Now we can expect that our perspective-taking initiates intercultural interaction, yet we do not know how interculturality emerges from our perspective-taking. This is because the concept of intersubjectivity only indicates the fact that values are already interconnected and form multiple realities, but does not explain why we tend to get trapped in mono-cultural thinking or restrictively practise perspective-taking. The concept of interobjectivity helps us find the next clue.

6.3 Interobjectivity: Effective-historical consciousness and plurality of audience

Human life is bound to historical movement. As we continuously test prejudices in our understanding, horizons of the present are also continuously in a process of being formed. In Gadamer's (1960/2004) sense, all horizons arise from what is historically pre-given. Inversely, when a new horizon is arising, its historically effective consciousness is also working. A new horizon requires us to unfold its effective-historical consciousness, as our consciousness is embedded in a particular historical and cultural context. Gadamer's concept of *effective-historical consciousness* is "not a particular attitude or frame of mind", but "the consciousness that we belong to when we are engaged in the event of understanding – an event that grounds our world of perceived causes and effects, and ourselves as historical subjects" (Mitscherling, 2009, para. 16). Historicism is rejected in effective-historical consciousness when historians disregard their own historicity and attach to particular values. Gadamer (1960/2004) argues, "historical objectivism conceals the fact that historical consciousness is itself situated in the web of historical effects" and "they [historical objectivists] let the 'facts' speak and hence simulate an objectivity that in reality depends on the legitimacy of the questions asked" (p. 300). When we appreciate and understand something like a piece of artwork, a religious scripture, a literature, or a cultural event, a horizon built

Intercultural hermeneutics 117

by a particular historical consciousness will be open, regardless of whether we are aware of it or not. This means that the historicity of a work and our historical consciousness become structurally intermingled with each other during our understanding. This understanding can be regarded as a fusion of two different historical horizons – a past historical horizon and a present historical horizon. This is the reason why understanding is not the meaning that we objectively extract from text, but we interpret meaning in text based on our preconceptions, which is our historically built consciousness.

As we cannot be transcendental over our historical consciousness, "our own past and that other past toward which our historical consciousness is directed help to shape this moving horizon out of which human life always lives and which determines it as heritage and tradition" (Gadamer, 1960/2004, p. 303). This does not mean that a horizon can be acquired by transposing our consciousness into a historical situation. Rather, we need to be aware of our own horizon that allows us to transpose ourselves into a situation. Transposing ourselves means that we are able to get out of ourselves by being aware of otherness and put ourselves in a position of other. This approach is ontological because the transposing realises the existence of others and discloses relationships between horizons. It requires us to make a special effort to acquire a historical horizon that allows us to face our own particularity and that of the other and see how it (transposing ourselves) "involves rising to a higher universality" (Gadamer, 1960/2004, p. 304). In this sense, individuality cannot be ontologically independent from otherness, but an individual's historical consciousness is effective based on interaction with others. This is the point where the mind-body dualism and abstract individualism are deconstructed. Furthermore, such an understanding process, where historical consciousness of text and a comprehender's historical consciousness are interacting, can only be said to be objective. Significantly, both consciousnesses are not adversarial in nature, but "together constitute the one great horizon that moves from within and that, beyond the frontiers of the present, embraces the historical depths of our self-consciousness" (Gadamer, 1960/2004, p. 303). This relationship between both consciousnesses also becomes a self-organising entity because "historical consciousness is aware of its own otherness and hence foregrounds the horizon of the past from its own" (Gadamer, 1960/2004, p. 305). This implies that the (ontological) hermeneutic approach projecting a historical horizon is different from a horizon of the present in which the former is only "one phase in the process of understanding", cannot be "solidified into the self-alienation of a past consciousness", and "overtaken by our own present horizon of understanding" (Gadamer, 1960/2004, pp. 305–306). This process of understanding enlivens and animates a past consciousness through mergence of a horizon of the present. Moreover, a historical horizon is projected and at the same time superseded by a mergence of horizons. In this way, such a mergence becomes historically effected consciousness. Gadamer's effective-historical consciousness, as a result of a fusion of (historical) horizons, connotes its collective understanding or intersubjectivity by a group of people and/or individuals.

However, there is still a danger of reductionism in which intersubjectivity returns to individuals' consciousnesses unless it is placed in an intercultural process

118 *Interculturality and its methodology*

for *inter-intersubjectivity*. This is because Gadamer regards the unity of historical horizons as the output of intersubjectivity within an individual person's collective consciousness, not in a manifestation of relational unconsciousness. The latter is the fundamental structuring property of intersubjective interaction in individuals of a group (or a culture). Intersubjective experiences create meanings, not based on an individual's independent reasoning but on inter-intersubjectivity that refers to an ongoing social/cultural construction of reality. In inter-intersubjectivity, *we* participate in group-to-group and culture-to-culture, although *I* am not personally interested in that. In other words, intersubjectivity (intercultural interaction) of cultures produces inter-intersubjectivity (interculturality), and, conversely, the latter constantly confines our historical consciousnesses to the former. In this sense, inter-intersubjectivity interobjectively works. As Sammut, Daanen, and Sartawi (2010) argue, "human relations are not essentially characterized by intersubjective relations but rely on the non[un]-conscious engagement in practices that occur within a social field that is phenomenally objective for subjects" (p. 451). Inversely, intersubjective relations can hide the fact that the existence of interobjectivity and its power shape our thinking, and we tend to think about what we are given rather than think of what (relation) causes such thinking. This explains why left-essentialist multiculturalism and critical multiculturalism is metaphysically vulnerable to ethno-centrism or plural mono-culturism, as I have argued in Chapter 3.

The concept of interobjectivity fastens the intercultural nature of culture (or the flow of values) in such a way that this meta-collaboratively constructed reality can hold the highest level of self-construal, humanity or a humane self, in culturally diverse contexts and also can determine the relational characteristics of the multilayered self. As Moghaddam (2003) argues, "The concept of interobjectivity leads to a focus on collaboratively constructed objectifications of the world to different degrees shared within and between *cultures*, out of which arises intersubjectivity" (pp. 221–222 [emphasis added]). It would be an extended version of Gadamer's historical consciousness that focuses on its collectiveness and the diversity of intersubjectivity in the networked world. Yet as Moghaddam (2003) argues, we have to be aware that intersubjectivity tends to reflect reductionistic, individualistic biases that do not address power inequalities. Moghaddam explains, "Groups have unequal levels of influence on shaping interobjectivity, with majority groups enjoying greatest influence" (p. 221). In a methodological sense, in multiple cultural realities, intersubjectivity is exclusive of the feedforward and feedback relation between intersubjectivities, whereas interobjectivity can evolve into intercultural identity. In essence, intersubjectivity does not disclose differently shaped worlds between cultures or multiple cultural realties and does not respond to cultural inequalities in intercultural interaction. Consequently, applying intersubjectivity only in intercultural interaction, we cannot see how cultural diversity and interculturality are perceived and understood by other cultural frameworks.

Without interobjectivity, like most multicultural educational models, intercultural education becomes focused on either an individual capability or settles on the line of demarcation between culture and life. Without interobjectivity,

Intercultural hermeneutics 119

furthermore, the context of intercultural interaction representing how different cultures are interconnected with each other will be neglected. This relational characteristic of interobjectivity is explicit in Gracia's *plurality of audience*. Investigating relationships between audience and a text, Gracia (1996) classifies the plurality of audience in two ways: "distributively, as a plurality composed of single persons who become or may become acquainted with a text in their individual privacy; or collectively as a group which understands a text" (p. 148). This classification has an ontological implication of a collective understanding of a text in that "a plurality of individual persons can come together as a whole and act collectively as audience" (Gracia, 1996, p. 148). When individuals are connected with a collective understanding of a text via their relationships with others, this plurality of audience indicates that a group understanding of a text and a personal understanding of a text are epistemologically connected, which is intersubjectivity. This connection itself is evidence that that group understanding is ontologically relational to other groups. This ontological relation manifests as being intercultural and extrapersonal, which is interobjectivity. Interobjectivity is transcendental to a personal understanding, but not transcultural, in which case it is meta-cultural to interculturality. Such dual structures of hermeneutics explain why incompatible values (or yet-to-be-connected assumptions) between cultures/groups (or Gadamer's otherness or postcolonialists' incommensurability of differences) widen the ontological distance between cultures.

Consequently, effective-historical consciousness should be viewed not only as a result of a fusion of horizons at an individual level but also as a result of inherent intercultural interaction between cultural groups at a collective unconscious level. In this way, intersubjectivity and interobjectivity are inherent in interculturality, and we are able to grasp two types of values as one embedded in our cultural horizon and the other arising from intercultural interaction. In turn, the emergent values as a new whole determine our intersubjective understanding of the networked world.

6.4 Emergent values: Linguisticality and universality

The concept of interobjectivity is directly associated with emergent properties of intercultural interaction in which it expresses the universal linguisticality of humanity's hermeneutic relation to the (networked) world. For Heidegger and Gadamer, linguisticality as a mediator of the past and the present enables us to face up to temporal and spatial limitations, while different historical horizons enable us to merge horizons and to be dialogic. Like Nietzsche's Apollonian world, Heidegger (1962/2009) argues that language modifies our perceptual processes through phenomena of names, and as the house of being, language constructs our unique understanding of being and allows us to have the capacity for ontological inquiry. Heidegger (1962/2009) states,

> Genuinely and initially, it is the essence of language to first elevate beings into the open as beings. Where there is no language – as with stones, plants, and animals – there is also no openness of beings and thus also no openness

120 *Interculturality and its methodology*

of non-beings, un-beings, or emptiness. By first naming objects, language brings beings to word and to appearance.

(p. 145)

In effect, language is ontological as well as an invented tool or a sign system, as a means of communication. In hermeneutics, "Language . . . no longer an objective body of words which one manipulates as objects . . . not to be seen as expression of some inner reality" (Palmer, 1968, p. 139). An ontological aspect of language discloses not the speaker, but *the being* of the world that is neither a subjective nor an objective phenomenon – as disclosure of what is real for men (Palmer, 1968). According to Gadamer (1960/2004), word (*onoma*) refers to a proper name in Greek or Nietzsche's *naming* and a name holds *the being* of a person who calls or responds. As the ontological bearer and the house of being, language discloses what human beings are supposed to be in a situation. It is the world by which we are defined with language, and our statements are to reveal being, not (egocentric) ourselves, which is identical to Heidegger's linguisticality. Palmer (1968) explains,

Heidegger's turn toward the increasing emphasis on the linguisticality of man's way of being, and his assertion that being leads man and calls him, so that ultimately it is not man but being that shows itself, are of course incalculable significance for theory of understanding.

(p. 155)

Understanding one's way of being-in-the-world is to place language in living contexts, which articulates one's existential understanding. This approach undermines temporal reasoning and conceptual manipulations of objects in the world as peripheral and ignores the fact that language discloses *a world* that is not the same as the environmental scientific world or universe (Gadamer, 1960/2004). In understanding ontological hermeneutics, the world and language are transpersonal matters rather than restricted to the subject-object dualism, and language is closer to objective in the sense that the world is "the shared understanding between persons . . . what makes it possible is language" (Palmer, 1968, p. 206). In this sense, Gadamer's linguisticality shares its underlying concept with Nietzsche's table of values. For interculturality, then, linguisticality is the house of intersubjectivity and interobjectivity in that *I* and *you* engage in intersubjective processes through understanding meaning, and *we* participate in the revelation of interobjectivity through understanding relationships. This means that the linguisticality of named values enables us to develop participatory and collaborative actions in intercultural interaction and empowers us to articulate our interobjective experiences, which is the universality of hermeneutics as a process in Gadamer's term and the flow of values in Nietzsche's term.

Human beings exist in language that is a medium where people and the world meet and "manifest their original belonging together", and this speculative process points to "a universal ontological structure" (Gadamer, 1960/2004,

Intercultural hermeneutics 121

pp. 469–470). Indeed, hermeneutics is very speculative that our reflective interpretations involve movement, suspension, and openness in which it broadens our horizons within what is understood through language. In this sense, Gadamer (1960/2004) asserts that hermeneutics is a universal way of being that constitutes ontological relations associated with an ontological commitment – an interpretation. The universality of hermeneutics is based on the premise that speculative awareness, as a universal characteristic of being, enables being (Dasein) itself to obtain openness and move beyond the confines of the subject-object dualism. Speculative awareness is dialectical, which points to the ontological structure of an experience in which "historical consciousness knows about the otherness of the other, about the past in its otherness, just as the understanding of the Thou knows that the Thou as a person" (Gadamer, 1960/2004, p. 354). This speculative movement of hermeneutics has a universal ontological language in which a historical consciousness involves the mediation between the past and the present and therein language plays a role as its universal medium. A universal ontological language indicates that our conceptual frameworks are centred on our fundamental categorisation and relationisation of things. In this way, an interpretation reveals a universal ontological structure, which allows hermeneutics to become a universal aspect of philosophy (Gadamer, 1960/2004, pp. 470–471). The universality of hermeneutics also indicates that all human beings are ascriptive to a speculative mode of language so that mutual understandings between different cultural behaviours, meanings, and historical experiences are possible.

Speculative hermeneutics is "the coming into language of meaning" (Gadamer, 1960/2004, p. 476) and aims to reveal the fact that what is between people is the world (or a relational approach). In other words, being-in-the-world and language are connected within a speculative mode. Adopting Palmer's (1968, p. 156) words, language is "a realm of interaction" where "the community of understanding" is constructed. The community of understanding, which is an emergent thing from a hermeneutic experience of being-in-the-world, operates as interobjective and, at the same time, as intersubjective returns to individual horizons. In this recursive, a realm of interaction where hermeneutic experiences occur reveals collective and relational understandings of interculturality, which maintains the inseparable relationship between being and language and sustains ontological connectedness and epistemological/axiological interaction on being-with-others. In this sense, speculative hermeneutics rejects an individualistic/atomistic approach that objectifies and alienates others within the subjective-objective dualism.

An hermeneutic experience of the world as "already resident in language[,] transcends all relativities and relationships in which beings might show themselves" (Palmer, 1968, p. 206). The linguistic transcendence here indicates the power of language as a realm of interaction that sustains our own linguistic world and interpersonal realities. Palmer (1968) argues,

> The power of language to disclose transcends even time and place, and an ancient text from a people long extinct can render [the] present with the

122 *Interculturality and its methodology*

most amazing exactness[,] the interpersonal linguistic world that existed among those people. Thus our own language worlds have a certain universality in this power to understand other traditions and places.

(pp. 206–207)

Indeed, Gadamerians strive to prove that their hermeneutics is ontological, not methodological, which facilitates fusions of horizons by revealing ontic structures of agents. As Gadamer (1960/2004, p. 304) emphasises, agents are required to cultivate openness to be dialogic beings by being aware of linguisticality and universality. This is because "to restrict hermeneutics to the domain of the human sciences [for methodology] is to distort its universal nature" and "the truth it seeks can never be fully captured by language", but through an open-ended dialogic process (Hoffmann, 2003, pp. 98–99). However, as our understanding is initiated and possibly determined by our own cultural framework, a delusion will appear that our own culture is superior to others or vice versa. Such an unconscious response must be ensured from the outset of interaction by our speculation on the emergence of interobjective interculturality. This implies that Gadamerians are unaware of how the tradition of ontological discourse ideologically reinforces a dominant culture and excludes other cultures by their negligence on emergent values arising from intercultural interaction. This calls for both considerations of epistemological and axiological aspects of interculturality in which the co-existence of others should be accepted and acknowledged within a shared intercultural ontic structure – that is, a new set of value networks. Otherwise, a fusion of horizons remains a person's subjective experience, which interculturality degenerates into an unforeseen contingency and event from cultural activities of individuals only. In this sense, an epistemological process of interculturality should serve to reveal and sustain ontic structures for dialogic beings while it seeks emergent values; an axiological process of interculturality reassures intercultural interaction that constantly updates relationships between cultures and brings emergent values into individuals' horizons. Otherwise, intercultural interaction will be trapped in language for a dominant culture and the universality of intercultural hermeneutics does not occur. In this sense, intercultural hermeneutics explores our engagement in intersubjectivity and interobjectivity. Such hermeneutic duo circles are ultimately aimed at grasping an emergent whole, a new interculturality, in the interculturally networked world, which is irreducible to each culture that reconceives each culture, each participant, and interculturality. This is distinguishable from Gadamerians' (philosophical) hermeneutics, which clarifies the rules governing interpretations by exploring the structure of individuals' (universal) consciousness or intersubjectivity.

6.5 Axiological mapping: Rhizome and situatedness

Heidegger's ontological view of knowing is based on criticism of Cartesian epistemology, the identity of knower-known: the subject is given to the knower as the only certain thing and the object as known is an experience of the subject.

In the knower-known dualism, "knowing" is understood as "the primary way of interacting with things" (Çüçen, 1998, para. 8). In a hermeneutic circle, on the contrary, knowing is an ontological realisation of one's own being in and towards the world, and this results in "the primordial knowledge of things present-at-hand which is ready-to-hand" (Çüçen, 1998, para. 10). As Heidegger (1953/2010) views "knowing" as an ontological basis, a "phenomenon of knowing the world" should not be understood as external, but as "a relation between subject and object which contains about as much truth" (p. 60). However, such an ontological approach does not facilitate our perception of an emergent whole because the ontological foundation of knowing has the following two intentions. First, its aim is to reject the Cartesian view of phenomenon of knowing the world, which indicates that one is aware of the ontic structure of oneself towards the world. However, one may be trapped back in subjectivism unless one is aware that the ontic structure is associated with both intersubjectivity and interobjectivity where one's multilayered self engages in multiple realities. Furthermore, if one is unaware that value networks are changing, subjectivism also appears. Second, Gadamerians reject objectivism and methodologism in order to emphasise the unlimited continuity of hermeneutic circles and the cultivation of dialogic beings. This rejection can lead to rejection of interobjectivity in which it is believed that we have direct contact with relational multiple realities and the whole world has no impact on that contact. Because of those intentional constraints, an emergent whole (interculturality) is not seen as a new reality, but a synthetic expression referring to a collection of individual parts. As a result, agents cannot be agents of history. Hence emancipation only occurs within an individual's capacity for exerting willpower over *knowing* rather than in an ongoing hermeneutic process through exploring collective and relational mechanisms of intercultural interaction. Our everyday understanding of the world is essentially value-laden, which constantly affects our thinking and behaviour by enhancing or manipulating our multilayered self. In this sense, intercultural knowledge refers to a transformation of our multilayered self. In other words, it is to understand our diversity of self-construal, such as independent, collective-interdependent and relational, by engaging in emergent values and to cultivate/transform our mind structure. Here we are confronted with a difficult challenge: On what grounds do values appear and interact with each other and how can axiological interaction be articulated in value networks?

Rhizomes are used to represent culture (more precisely values) as a map, not a tracing – arborescent culture – or to create a more dynamic mapping of the relationship between centres and margins to illustrate a whole. For example, Deleuze and Guattari (1980/1987) describe Western and Eastern culture as follows: "The West: agriculture based on a chosen lineage containing a large number of variable individuals. The East: horticulture based on a small number of individuals derived from a wide range of 'clones'" (p. 18). The focus is a rhizome of intertextual connectivity where values reside and, in this sense, a rhizome becomes a new ontological model (Chisholm, 2007): "A rhizome is not a metaphor but a virtual ecology of mind, a real becoming-rhizome of philosophy" (Chisholm, 2007, para. 11). Deleuze and Guattari (1980/1987) use a term "rhizomatic"

124 *Interculturality and its methodology*

to oppose an arborescent conception of knowledge and define a rhizome as "ceaselessly established connections between semiotic chains, organizations of power, and circumstances relative to the arts, sciences, and social struggles" (p. 7) . . . "has no beginning or end; it is always in the middle, between things, interbeing, intermezzo" (p. 25). The notion of arborescence represents dualistic categorisation and hierarchical and linear connections, whereas the notion of rhizome represents the co-existence of history and culture as a map. Deleuze and Guattari (1980/1987) outline the concept of rhizome with six principles, including *connection* (all points are immediately connectable), *heterogeneity* (rhizomes mingle signs and bodies), *multiplicity* (the rhizome is flat or immanent), *asignifying rupture* (the line of flight is a primary component, which enables heterogeneity-preserving emergence or "consistency"); *cartography* (maps of emergence are necessary to follow a rhizome); and *decalcomania* (the rhizome is not a model like the tree, but an "immanent process") (pp. 7–14). In particular, the fifth and sixth principles elucidate "a rhizome is not amenable to any structural or generative model" (p. 12). Deleuze and Guattari define those two principles as follows:

> The cultural book is necessarily a tracing: already a tracing of itself, a tracing of the previous book by the same author, a tracing of other books however different they may be, an endless tracing of established concepts and words, a tracing of the world present, past, and future.
>
> (p. 26)

It seems that Deleuze and Guattari insufficiently address the emergent attributes of rhizomes because of their pluralistic and deconstructive approach to knowledge production. Yet their statements, "the rhizome resists territorialisation" and "a rhizome may be broken, shattered at a given spot, but it will start up again on one of its old lines, or on new line" (p. 9), imply that emergent attributes always happen on rhizomatic networks. As a rhizome moves and flows by redirecting around barriers and its broken sections continue to grow, *it always renews the entire network*. In other words, emerging nodes (a set of values) offers the possibility to make a connection between the multilayered self and multiple realities in which intercultural interaction should result in an expansion of value networks as our minds are attached to a set of values in the networks. However, if the rhizomatic theory indicates that knowledge no longer moves upon a diffused axis, but is subject to dispersion, then how can we trace the movement of that distribution? As argued with the theory of *distributed knowledge* in Chapter 5, could it be that the only thing we can do is to find nodes (or a community) based on our interests?

In value-interaction in the networked world, we perceive multiple realities depending on our existential situation. Even though we tend to believe the world as a single unit, this belief itself indicates that we are just a part of the world as it has already been networked. In this networked world, values per se are pre-historical and post/trans-historical because we tend to hold values as eternal ones at present and ignore that values flow. In our cognition, then, value-interaction sprouts only when we confront different values. This is an ontological awareness of the fuzziness of situatedness, and its endless task of interpretation is given to human beings according to Gadamer (1960/2004). This means that such ontological hermeneutic situatedness requires us to be aware of the fact that we are always projected onto its ongoing process that determines interculturality. Structurally, interculturality as a yet-to-be-revealed or part of an already interpreted world is ill structured, and ill-structured and well-structured situations are interacting with each other on the duo circles of intercultural hermeneutics – an emergent whole (interobjectivity) and an already interpreted world (intersubjectivity). In this sense, the circles are symbolic-situated systems that reveal that our cognition is constantly affected and challenged by an infinite loop between ill-structured and well-structured situations. To identify a particular set of values or a pattern in symbolic-situated systems that appear arbitrary and complicated, values need to be understood through a situated structure. In other words, a symbolic system as a defined situation (interculturality as an already interpreted world) is used for our cognitive interaction with a situated-system, which provides essential properties of an emergent symbol system (interculturality as an emergent whole). In this way, value-interactions as symbolic-situated systems presume that we are always within a (networked) situation (via values) and agents of axiological mapping, which is an expansion and transformation of a set of value works and reveals larger parts of the networked world.

6.6 Conclusion: Value networks

In this chapter, I have critically argued how intercultural interaction is conceptually and theoretically supported in philosophical or ontological hermeneutics. With the five dimensions: values, intersubjectivity, interobjectivity, emergent values, and axiological mapping, I have argued for metaphysical interculturality.

First, fore-structures of understanding are not fixed and immutable substances, but form the horizons of individuality beyond personnel experiences and expectations. Such collectiveness retains effective-historical consciousness that lays the foundations of intercultural interaction. As a set of values constitutes a particular cultural framework and formulates a belief system that guides our activities and judgement, values embedded in all participants' cultural fore-structures need to be explicit to commence intercultural interaction. Second, a fusion of horizons and paradigm shifts primarily focus on individual and collective pre-understandings of an event, respectively, and a precondition for both is intersubjectivity in which a collective consciousness has its own power over individuals. Furthermore, in multiple cultural realities, intersubjectivity becomes a collective pre-understanding and works as perspective-taking in intercultural interaction. Third, effective-historical consciousness as a result of a fusion of horizons connotes its collective understanding or intersubjectivity that is shared by a group of people and/or individuals. Intersubjective experiences create new meanings based on emergent values arising from intercultural interaction, and thus situated emergent values as a whole become interobjectivity that leads us to participate in an ongoing revelation of larger parts of the networked world. This is because interculturality

126 *Interculturality and its methodology*

is transcendental to our own cultural framework and at the same time it plays a part in the growth of our own culture. Fourth, the concept of interobjectivity is associated with the transcendence of emergent values that allows us to participate in larger parts of the networked world towards understanding interculturality and manifests culture-to-culture interaction beyond our cognition. In other words, interobjectivity (a) metaphysically supports the universal linguisticality of humane hermeneutic relations to the networked world and (b) methodologically articulates the ontological equality of value networks. Emergent values are neither extra nor contingent outcomes, but offer a holistic approach to the multilayered self and multiple cultural realities. In this sense, we are required to be aware that being-in-the-world and language are inseparable, and the interconnectedness can be observed through our speculative hermeneutics. Fifth, the rhizomatic theory proposes that interculturality can be a form of axiological mapping through an argumentation of ontological tensions and epistemological conflicts of intercultural interaction. The key argument is that value networks can legitimise the ontological equality at value-interaction and then axiological mapping can be implemented through symbolic-situated systems. This mapping process offers creative solutions to problems in a complicated situation of intercultural interaction by revealing larger parts of the networked world.

Consequently, intercultural hermeneutics aims to reveal values embedded in our cultural framework through our awareness of individual and collective pre-understandings of an event. To participate in discovering concealed parts of value networks and to identify a new ontic position of each culture in the networks, intercultural hermeneutics distinguishes intersubjective experiences and interobjective experiences of intercultural interaction, which forms hermeneutic duo circles. The former is viewed as a result of a fusion of horizons at an individual level, whereas the latter is viewed as a result of inherent intercultural interaction between cultures at an inter-collective level. Intersubjectivity produces interobjectivity, and in turn, the latter confines our historical consciousnesses to the former. In this way, intersubjectivity and interobjectivity are inherent in interculturality. The interaction between them allows our collective and individual participation in the networked world, and our identity as agents of the network change is legitimised not by that interaction per se, but emergent values arising from the interaction. The emergent values as newly situated in and transcendental to the interaction allow us to reshape the networked world as a whole in which we reveal larger parts of the networked world and engage in our multilayered self and multiple cultural realities. Such a holistic, interactive approach to the networked world lays the foundation for a new methodological approach to our participation in intercultural interaction, which is participants' ontological quality and meta-collaborative axiological mapping of value networks.

References

Chisholm, D. (2007, Winter). *Rhizome, ecology, geophilosophy* (A map to this issue). Rhizomes: Cultural Studies in Emerging Knowledge. Issue 15. Retrieved from http://www.rhizomes.net/issue15/chisholm.html

Intercultural hermeneutics 127

Cohen, L., Manion, L., & Morrison, K. (2005). *Research methods in education*. New York: Routledge Falmer.

Çüçen, A.K. (1998). Heidegger's reading of Descartes' dualism: The relation of subject and object. In S. Dawson (Ed.), *Twentieth World Congress of Philosophy*. Boston, MA: Karl Jaspers Society of North America. Retrieved from http://www.bu.edu/wcp/Papers/Cont/ContCuce.htm

Deleuze, G., & Guattari, F. (1987). *A thousand plateaus: Capitalism and schizophrenia*. (B. Massumi, Trans.). Minneapolis: University of Minnesota Press. (Original work published 1980)

Drenthen, M. (2011). Reading ourselves through the land: Landscape hermeneutics and ethics of place. In F. Clingerman & M. Dixon (Eds.), *Placing Nature on the Borders of Religion, Philosophy, and Ethics* (pp. 123–138). Farnham: Ashgate.

Duranti, A. (2010). Husserl, intersubjectivity and anthropology. *Anthropological Theory, 10*(1), 1–20.

Gadamer, H.G. (2004). *Truth and method* (2nd rev, ed.). (J. Weinsheimer & D.G. Marshall, Trans.). New York: Crossroad. (Original work published 1960)

Gracia, J.J.E. (1996). *Texts: Ontological status, identity, author, audience*. Albany, NY: SUNY Press.

Hainic, C. (2012). The Heideggerian roots of everyday aesthetics: A hermeneutical approach to art. In F. Dorsch & D.-E. Ratiu (Eds.), *Proceedings of the European Society for Aesthetics* (pp. 230–249). Amsterdam: The European Society for Aesthetics (vol. 4).

Hall, E.T. (1981). *Beyond culture*. New York: Random House.

Heidegger, M. (2009). *The Heidegger reader*. In G. Figal (Ed.). (J. Veith, Trans.). Bloomington: Indiana University Press. (Original work published 1962)

Heidegger, M. (2010). *Being and time* (J. Stambaugh, Trans.). Albany: State University of New York Press. (Original work published 1953)

Hoffmann, S.-J. (2003). Gadamer's philosophical hermeneutics and feminist projects. In L. Code (Ed.), *Feminist Interpretations of Hans-Georg Gadamer* (pp. 81–108). University Park: The Pennsylvania State University Press.

Horner, C., & Westacott, E. (2000). *Thinking through philosophy: An introduction*. Cambridge: Cambridge University Press.

Kuhn, T. (1996). *The structure of scientific revolutions* (3rd ed.). Chicago: University of Chicago Press.

Liu, C.H., & Matthews, R., (2005). Vygotsky's philosophy: Constructivism and its criticisms examined. *International Education Journal, 6*(3), 386–399.

Mills, J. (1997). The false dasein: From Heidegger to Sartre and Psychoanalysis. *Journal of Phenomenological Psychology, 28*(1), 42–65.

Mitscherling, J. (2009). Truth and method: Hermeneutics or history? *ARHE, 11*. Retrieved from http://www.arhe.rs/sh/arhe-11/truth-and-method-hermeneutics-or-history

Moghaddam, F.M. (2003). Interobjectivity and culture. *Culture & Psychology, 9*(3), 221–232.

Mootz, F.J. (2006). *Rhetorical knowledge in legal practice and critical legal theory*. Tuscaloosa, AL: University of Alabama Press.

Palmer, R.E. (1968). *Hermeneutics: Interpretation theory in Schleiermacher, Dilthey, Heidegger, and Gadamer*. Evanston: Northwestern University Press.

Rees, D.K. (2003). Gadamer's philosophical hermeneutics: The vantage points and the horizons in readers' responses to an American literature text. *The Reading Matrix, 3*(1), 1–17.

128 *Interculturality and its methodology*

Ricoeur, P. (1981). *Hermeneutics and the human sciences.* (B. Thompson, Trans.). Cambridge: Cambridge University Press. (Original work published 1973)

Sammel, A. (2003). An Invitation to dialogue: Gadamer, hermeneutic phenomenology, and critical environmental education. *Canadian Journal of Environmental Education, 8*(1), 155–168.

Sammut, G., Daanen, P., & Sartawi, M. (2010). Interobjectivity: Representations and artefacts in cultural psychology. *Culture and Psychology, 16*(4), 451–463.

Schein, E.H. (1985). *Organizational culture and leadership.* San Francisco: Jossey-Bass Publishers.

Selfridge, R., & Sokolik, S. (1975). A comprehensive view of organizational management. *MSU Business Topics, 23*(1), 46–61.

Part II Conclusion: New individuality

In Chapter 4, I have reviewed Nietzsche's dialectic relationship between the Dionysian and the Apollonian and a table of values in order to argue the essence of culture as the flow of values. Ontologically non-dualistic engagements in values are the way to revive the Dionysian world because the nature of the Dionysian world is the source of energy for the flow of values. Nietzsche's non-dualistic monism indicates that our will to power generated from the flow of values enables us to systematise values via the Apollonian world as a hierarchical structure of values in socio-cultural contexts. This raises a question: How are our minds structured to interact with values? By adopting cross-cultural psychologists' research, I have argued for the multilayered self: a personal, a relational, a collective, and a humane self. Cross-cultural psychologists demonstrate that individuals have a particular form of self-construal such as interdependence-primed and independence-primed. Significantly, they prove that a shift of self-construal is possible through priming techniques. They conclude that the relations between self-construal and cultural beliefs are dialectic, which facilitates value endorsement between those who have different cultural backgrounds. However, as I have critically stated, the independence-interdependence frame rejects the necessity of ontology and simplifies the diversity of ontological structures. This is because cross-cultural psychology focuses on a personal level of intercultural experience and regards the independence-interdependence frame as universal and both a personal self and a humane self as value-free. As a result, they cannot explain how multiple cultures can co-exist. Thus I have critically reviewed Popper's three worlds of knowledge and Habermas's theory of communicative action on the Lifeworld, which theorise the existence of multiple realities. Popper's World 3 indicates that the world is independent of individuals and exercises its own power over our minds. Intersubjectivity as World 3 objects allows us to observe our engagement in culture (values) and understand new meanings in intercultural interaction. Yet I have pointed out that Popper's intersubjectivity fails to explain why there are diverse cultural identities and formations. On the other hand, Habermas emphasises the intersubjective world by focusing on its emergent feature, which is the Lifeworld, and argues that people from a same culture share a same Lifeworld through communicative rational consensus. For Habermas, our approach to the whole world is subject to our understanding of relations between cultures/worlds. This legitimises the co-existence of multiple

130 *Interculturality and its methodology*

cultures and justifies the validity of intersubjectivity for the interaction between the worlds. Yet he absolutises rationalisation and substitutes the interaction between different intersubjective cultures for communicative rational consensus. I have concluded that Popper regards the structure of our engagement in the multiple worlds as universal and value-free, whereas Habermas views that rationality is culturally unbound. Consequently, the theory of self-construal, the three worlds of knowledge construction, the communicative action in the Lifeworld attempt to neutralise values embedded in their methodological approaches. This is the reason why I have argued for culturally bound methodologies – namely, methodological individualism, holism, and relationism – in the following chapter.

First, methodological individualism articulates synthetic expressions of individuals' activities in a subject-object relation and promotes abstractions for their actions. In methodological individualism, a whole is regarded as a pseudo-systemic or a reality that individuals experience. Hence it rejects that the substantiality of culture determines individuals' identities and thoughts. Second, methodological holism presupposes that we cannot understand a whole with its parts because a whole emerges from the relationship of or interaction between its parts. In methodological holism, however, the focus is not on how parts are interrelated and interdependent. As a result, individuals are required to accommodate themselves to a social whole without question: how their collective culture regulates their behaviour and minds. Third, methodological relationism presumes that what is real is relationships between individuals, groups, and society. Thus a socio-cultural world must be formulated based on the relationships. In methodological relationism, self-reflexivity and socio-cultural formation are equally emphasised as culturally unbound, which restricts intercultural interaction to an individual's epistemic process separating individuality from interculturality. In intercultural interaction, consequently, each methodology pursues a different image of an agent: methodological individualism, an independent being; methodological holism, an interdependent being; and methodological relationism, an agent of network change.

Interestingly, such images are needed in intercultural interaction. In this sense, I have proposed the five principles of *interactive methodology* (IM) for intercultural education by critically adopting the concept of nodes from the theory of distributed knowledge. IM addresses how (a) multiple (cultural) realities co-exist and are culturally mediated, and interculturality is one of them; (b) our mind structures are personally, relationally, collectively, and humanely shaped by a set of value networks (or an interstice of nodes) where our ontology is anchored; (c) emergent values arising from intercultural interaction are used to reveal a new cultural reality (i.e., interculturality) that is the foundation for social-cultural reformation because the values can initiate our self-transcendence through interpersonal and extrapersonal experiences and self-transformation through intrapersonal experiences; (d) as values articulate ontological tensions in and epistemological conflicts from intercultural interaction, we perceive value networks as a whole that connect between interculturality as an already interpreted world and interculturality as an emergent whole; and (e) such a holistic value connection allows us to initiate axiological mapping that reveals larger parts of the networked world and leads to the maturation of our minds, cultures, and interculturality.

A particular metaphysical framework has been predominant as a multicultural education model and enhanced through socio-cultural activities, institutions, and historical engagements. More importantly, *other cultures* have been subjugated to culturally unbound educational models and systems, which cause ontological inequality. In this sense, in Chapter 6, I argued for the five dimensions of the hermeneutical interculturality derived from critical understandings of philosophical hermeneutics: values, intersubjectivity, interobjectivity, emergent values, and axiological mapping. When we pay attention to our fore-structure of understanding of our own culture and other cultures in a situation, we can approach them as metaphysical frameworks and identify values embedded in our perception of an intercultural situation. Then we can be aware that values are intersubjectively formed and value shifts are interobjectively structured. Such a collective feature holds the epistemological foundation for individuals' fusions of horizons that creates intersubjective meaning, whereas such a relational feature confirms the axiological foundation for cultural shifts that creates interobjective values. In intercultural interaction, such hermeneutic duo circles imply that emergent values pre-exist as parts of intercultural reality. Thus intersubjective meaning emanates interobjective values of different collective consciousnesses, and, conversely, interobjective values constantly confine our historical consciousnesses to intersubjective meaning. Interobjective values affect a topological change of cultural networks, and, as a result, self-transformation and social transformation become non-dualistic.

Such metaphysical and hermeneutical understandings of interculturality lead us to pay attention to an emergent whole from value networks and allow us to reveal a new set of value networks or readjust an interstice of values (nodes). In this sense, intercultural interaction refers to axiological mapping (axiological interaction) that reveals new ontic positions of cultures in value networks (ontological expansion) and reveals larger parts of the networked world (epistemological reformation). In this way, intercultural hermeneutics criticises the concealment of assumptions and values for individuality by neutralising, or culturally unbinding, underlying concepts and methods, which radically articulates a new form of individuality construction for the interculturally networked world. The individuality is revealed as an ontologically collective, connected being, an epistemological co-participant of intercultural processes or interhistoricity, and axiologically interactive and creative in symbolic-situated systems. This can be shaped with three terms, intersubjectivity, interhistoricity, and interobjectivity. In short, the ultimate aim of intercultural education is to construct a new form of individuality in value networks by assuming ontological equality of all cultures, applying epistemological justification for culturally unbound values, and implementing axiological interaction between cultures whose major premise is that educational ideas and pedagogical values are culturally bound.

Part III
Intercultural valuism as emergent pedagogy

Part III Introduction:
Intercultural instruction

Constructivism as a theory of knowledge has mostly had wide-ranging impact on Western teacher education, although institutional systems, curricula, policies, and administration are composed of different '-isms' and values. While many constructivists rely on a relation of constructed reality and mind-independent reality, a variant of constructivism, cultural constructivists argue that a culture serves as a context for knowledge construction because "knowledge is positional" as it is "produced by human subjects located in the real world and contemplating real objects produce knowledge" (Webster, 1997, p. 114). For them, our knowledge construction is mediated by cultures, and cultural paradigms create multiple realities (Hutchison, 2006; Ogawa, 1989). In this way, the positionality of knowledge assumes that "the background, attributes, and *cultures* of subjects may be correlated with the knowledge they produce" (Webster, 1997, p. 114 [emphasis added]). In this context, multiple realities are created by positional knowledge, which justifies why different people have different understandings and expressions of the same ideas and objects (Hutchison, 2006). This means that cultural variations have a great impact on pedagogy and learning content and process. Cultural constructivists have developed their argument on the impact of culture by distinguishing between knowledge construction and cultural contexts. This is also consistent with Piaget's concept of *equilibration* – "an optimal state of equilibrium between people's cognitive structures and their environment" (Duncan cited in Bhattacharya & Han, 2001, para. 9).). "Human beings continually attempt to make sense of the world around them by assimilating new information into pre-existing mental schemes and accommodating thought processes as necessary" (Bhattacharya & Han, 2001, para. 9). It is well-known that constructivists, by focusing on social nature of cognition, suggest that learning occurs through our interaction with the environment and other people. In particular, Vygotsky (1929/1981) places more emphasis on the use of cultural tools affecting and shaping cognitive development.

However, such constructivists tend to disregard how multiple realities are culturally mediated and thus influence our multilayered self because their focus is on either our cognitive process or social/cultural impacts on cognition. Dewey, often cited as a philosophical founder among other constructivists (i.e., Piaget, Bruner, and Vygotsky), enunciates culture in constructivism. Dewey

136 *Intercultural valuism*

(1911/2009, 1911/1978) defines culture as "the habits of mind" that also indicate awareness of our interdependence, and he emphasises "plasticity, as openness to being shaped by experience" (Roth, 2012, para. 4). He believes that culture contributes to social order and progress and consequently there are no *cultures*, only *culture*. As Fallace (2010) points out, this means that Dewey and his followers advocate the view that minority ethnic groups such as African and Indigenous Americans and Aboriginal Australians do not contribute to the "social order and progress" of Western society. We can see the same issue addressed in Popper's three worlds of knowledge and Habermas's Lifeworld (Chapter 4). The concept of social order and progress as intersubjectivity remains unchangeable, and, as a result, there is no room for other cultures to make contributions to the world with their own cultural values. For them, intercultural interaction between cultures is only valid when their intersubjectivity attacks other cultural values and selectively absorbs them for their culture.

Furthermore, with terms such as *the modern mind* and *the primitive mind*, Dewey regards non-white people as socially deficient, while he argues that it is unfair for those people to be judged as the primitive mind in their social contexts (Fallace, 2010). Dewey also acknowledges that those people have the potential to develop the civilised mind through pragmatists' approach in education (Fallace, 2010). It is obvious that Dewey does not ignore cultural phenomenology and its interplay with its own habits and habitat. However, as Dewey understands culture as a functional concept, he pays little attention to its ontological nature and thus does not address metaphysical relations between our minds and cultures. This means that his ontological hierarchy places something or an ideal at a higher rank than culture and cultures. According to Garrison, Neubert, and Reich (2012), Dewey's primary concern is on pluralistic communicative democracy as the best form of shared experiences through the cycle of equilibrium and disequilibrium. As a result, Deweyans promote that developing habits of mind allows learners to keep learning and "cultivating the dispositions and habits of mind" to "prepare them to be effective employees, innovative workers, empathic family members, and successful citizens is the goal of education" (Edwards & Costa, 2012, para. 7–9). Like other constructivists, Dewey is also unintentionally ethno-centric in that he does not see non-white cultures beyond the modern-primitive minds relation (Fallace, 2010).

In modern individualism-based education, teachers tend to minimise social/cultural impacts on individual students because individual liberalism forms the backbone of the metaphysical foundations for liberal market economies. In this context, teachers are inclined to perceive the world as an absolute singular, and those who have the modern mind are supposed to hold the ontological primacy of independence with a recognition that individuals are free to act. As Duncan (1995) argues, such a framework is based on the premise that "the dualistic demarcation between the external world and internal psychological processes" only indirectly involves social and cultural influences and supports "a reliance on the individual (white) child as the primary analytical unit" (p. 465). This indicates that multiple realities remain as a conceptual model for analytic and atomistic thinking and as peripheral in the dualistic approach to other cultures. In value networks, however, cultural diversity refers to multiple realities that underlie our experiences of intercultural interaction. Multiple cultural realities are metaphysically formed with values that are interconnected, which indicates that our knowledge construction occurs in value networks. Knowledge refers to a new set of value networks that is revealed through intercultural value-interaction because our minds are entrenched in an interstice of particular values in value networks, and thus value-interaction should lead to a transformation of the interstice. An interstice transformation articulates a personal self in value networks, a new set of value networks expands a relational self (or individuality), and renewed value networks reshape a social or collective self (or social experience). Inversely, our minds have multiple sets of value networks as we engage in multiple realities and our minds can be formed with interculturality through intercultural value-interaction in value networks.

In the learning environment, then, teachers need to reconsider lesson components such as student activities, assessment, pedagogies, and resources in a way that addresses the issues of intercultural interaction noted in the previous chapters including the absence of the self in self-reflection (as a result, the absence of relations), the non-subject position of other cultures in intercultural interaction, and culture-unbound concepts and methods. In this sense, three chapters of this third part will deal with each issue in a practical way by using the principles of intercultural hermeneutics. First, to make an attempt to resolve the self-exclusiveness in self-reflection, a new model named *the intercultural valuism circle* was proposed in a teacher education program and its test results will be unfold in Chapter 7. Second, to articulate the subject position of other cultures in intercultural interaction, a few selected non-Western philosophical/cultural/religious concepts will be reviewed, and their metaphysical characteristics in value networks will be identified in Chapter 8. Third, and last, to understand how culturally different pedagogies can be reshaped in value networks, non-Western cultural/religious pedagogies will be introduced and compared with Western pedagogical theories in Chapter 9.

References

Bhattacharya, K., & Han, S. (2001). Piaget and cognitive development. In M. Orey (Ed.), *Emerging Perspectives on Learning, Teaching, and Technology*. Retrieved from http://epltt.coe.uga.edu/index.php?title=Piaget%27s_Constructivism

Dewey, J. (1978). Contributions to cyclopedia of education. In J.A. Boydston (Ed.), *The Collected Works of John Dewey: Vol. 6. The Middle Works* (pp. 357–467). Carbondale: Southern Illinois University Press. (Original work published 1911)

Dewey, J. (2009). *Democracy and education: An Introduction to the philosophy of education*. New York: Macmillan. (Original work published 1911)

Duncan, R.M. (1995). Piaget and Vygotsky revisited: Dialogue or assimilation? *Developmental Review, 15*, 458–472.

Edwards, J., & Costa, A.L. (2012). Habits of success. *Educational Leadership: College, Careers, Citizenship, 69*(7). Retrieved from http://www.ascd.org/publications/educational-leadership/apr12/vol69/num07/Habits-of-Success.aspx

Fallace, T.D. (2010). Was John Dewey ethnocentric? Reevaluating the philosopher's early views on culture and race. *Educational Researcher, 39*(6), 471–477.

138 *Intercultural valuism*

Garrison, J., Neubert, S., & Reich, K. (2012). *John Dewey's philosophy of education: An introduction and recontextualization for our times.* Vol 1st. New York: Palgrave Macmillan.

Hutchison, C.B. (2006). Cultural constructivism: The confluence of cognition, knowledge creation, multiculturalism, and teaching. *Intercultural Education, 17*(3), 301–310.

Ogawa, M. (1989). Beyond the tacit framework of 'science' and 'science education' among science educators. *Science Education, 80*(5), 579–610.

Roth, M.S. (2012, September 6). *Learning as Freedom.* Editorial. New York Times. A23. Retrieved from http://www.nytimes.com/2012/09/06/opinion/john-deweys-vision-of-learning-as-freedom.html

Vygotsky, L.S. (1981). The development of higher forms of attention in childhood. In J.V. Wertsch (Ed. & Trans.), *The Concept of Activity in Soviet Psychology* (pp. 189–240). Armonk, NY: Sharpe. (Original manuscripts 1929)

Webster, Y.O. (1997). *Against the multicultural agenda: A critical thinking alternative.* Westport, CT: Praeger.

7 Intercultural self-reflection

Teachers are asked to practise critical self-reflection in learning and practicum by using reflection models such as Bain, Ballantyne, Mills, and Lester's (2002) 5Rs framework for reflection; Gibbs's (1998) reflective cycle; Johns's (2000) model for structured reflection; Kolb's (1984) model of experiential learning; and Rolfe, Freshwater, and Jasper's (2001) *What* Model. By using a model, teachers are required to demonstrate their capacity to make effective use of knowledge and skills. A critical problem here is that the models incline towards self-exclusive and problem-focused strategies. In practicum, written outcomes of critical self-reflection on teaching practice are used as evidence to ensure teachers' acquisition of required skills and knowledge – that is, intellectuality-driven generalisation of individuals' experiences into other situations. In my professional experience of teacher education and professional development for teachers, I have also observed that teachers' reflections of themselves remain unknown or unexplored, and reflective processes undermine values and beliefs challenged by others. In other words, such self-exclusiveness in self-reflection involves the exclusion of interculturality and new individuality. A reflective process is used under a particular metaphysical assumption that can prevent teachers from shifting from one sense of self-construal to another. Nevertheless, I acknowledge the productivity of such self-reflection. For example, a problem-focused approach can turn our emotional and relational responses to a matter into motivational energy as a self-sufficiency guide towards a pre-set goal, which benefits us in terms of an expansion of knowledge about given educational systems. In intercultural contexts, however, such a reflective process can result in unintentional *othering* when teachers are unaware of how their selves and other selves are shaped by cultural frameworks, how the underlying values affect the quality of intercultural interaction, what outcomes the interaction brings about, and, practically, how they can equally participate in intercultural interaction.

Based on the five dimensions of metaphysical interculturality argued in Chapter 6, I proposed the *intercultural valuism circle*, proceeding with five stages that had been used in a cultural study subject in a teacher education program. The subject had been delivered for pre-service teachers' individual task of weekly self-reflection as part of the assessment for three semesters in 2013–2015. The pre-service teachers were required to conduct reflexive, reflective, and critical reflection on a chosen topic about Australian Indigenous cultural/pedagogical

140 *Intercultural valuism*

values and assumptions and to demonstrate how their pedagogical and/or professional ideas have been (re)shaped. I closely reviewed approximately 500 weekly reflection writings from 96 participants who received a grade six or higher on a seven-point scale and used either the intercultural valuism circle (IVC) or Bain *et al.*'s (2002) 5Rs framework for reflection (5Rs). As a result, I identified a few underlying values facilitating poor reflection and common mistakes in implementing intercultural reflection.

7.1 Intercultural valuism circle

Each reflection model was taught after an introduction of educational metaphysics, cultural assumptions, the multilayered self, and intercultural value networks. Then a rationale for each stage of the IVC and an example was presented.

7.1.1 Stage 1 intercultural introspection

The IVC is initiated with introspection rather than reflection and critical thinking. Reflection is an expansion of thinking to the point where we have different perspectives on a matter – outward thinking as an observer and activist, and, likewise, critical thinking is known as the ability to reason and analyse problem-solving environments and creative and complex approaches to an identified contradiction or problem. In Western education systems and culture, reflection and critical thinking have been used to facilitate disciplined self-directed independent thinking and action, self-reasoned judgement in problem solving, and self-efficacy for self-regulated learning (e.g., Brockbank & McGill, 2000; Epstein & Hundert, 2002; Gibbs, 1998; Hatton & Smith, 1995; Johns, 2000; Kolb, 1984; Rolfe, Freshwater & Jasper, 2001). This means that both are used to develop individuals' thinking skills rather than internal growth and sustainability of the selfhood. While a self-evaluation process of our own thoughts, feelings, and actions is required in any self-reflection, reflection, and critical thinking are used to encourage us to evaluate given information in a critical and comprehensive way and also to identify or reject non- or false-evidence-based information and unjustified or false beliefs. In particular, in education, reflection and critical thinking are used to encourage us to avoid our subjective and emotional views because it has been believed that those views could negatively influence rational economic decisions.

On the other hand, introspection for intercultural interaction is an examination process of our own subjective thoughts and emotional responses to a socio-cultural phenomenon by employing self-observation and self-awareness. It probes underlying values latent in our subconsciousness and unconsciousness that drive a particular pre-judgment and pre-decision. In this sense, it begins with two questions: Where does this feeling and/or thinking come from and how is it constructed? In an intercultural setting, we can implement introspection by distinguishing ourselves into two ontic cultural statuses: the *beinghood* for an independently identified being and the *selfhood* for an interdependently relational being. The former allows us to observe how *I* exist as an individual

Intercultural self-reflection 141

by holding what identity, whereas the latter helps us to detect *my* socially and culturally defined identity. In other words, both statuses help to reveal a complex and holistic individuality latent in the networked world that consists of two beings: a phenomenologically independent being and a noumenologically interdependent being. We also need to be aware that the beinghood and the selfhood are often hidden, as they are embedded in our unconscious minds, and we often treat them as separate. As both are ontologically inseparable, our introspection should be aimed at having access to our affective responses to a matter, which is supposed to determine our *lifehood* in the future. A note here is that we should not regard affection as a personal feeling. We need to distinguish that "feelings are personal and biographical" and "emotions are social and affects are prepersonal" (Shouse, 2005, para. 1). In this sense, we assess our feelings generated by a culturally sensitive matter/situation in order to identify underlying socio-cultural values that arouse such feelings. This is the reason why we participate in a cultural interface between an inner world (beinghood) and an outer world (selfhood), and at the same time that is the foundation for our holistic individuality (lifehood).

7.1.2 Stage 2 value-awareness

Intercultural introspection of our own emotional and cognitive responses to an intercultural matter/situation through the beinghood and the selfhood aspects results in value-awareness. We become conscious of values attached to our affection that arouse our reaction, judgment, and decision making. Value-awareness is different from self-awareness in which the latter is the ability to recognise our affective responses, which we completed in the first stage, whereas the former is a disclosure of value tensions or conflicts with other cultures. In other words, value-awareness is to be aware of our cognitive dissonance between our values and values in other cultures in our interpretation of a matter/situation. It is aimed at understanding that the cognitive dissonance is a by-product of our affective/reasoning responses to a different cultural value system and being aware that values have interconnected relationships in value networks. In this sense, value-awareness is neither egocentric nor allocentric because both are volitional processes that accompany our own affection and intention.

Metaphysically, value-awareness is both epistemological and meta-epistemological in that we seek answers to how value difference causes our cognitive dissonance. Value-awareness is primarily concerned with how our epistemology has shaped our response to an intercultural matter/situation. Two prerequisites of value-awareness are the concepts of decontextualisation and recontextualisation of our responses to a matter/situation. First, we objectify an epistemic distance between our understanding of a matter/situation and our understanding of ourselves that allows us to understand it. Second, we recognise that there is no ontological discrimination in value networks. Thus decontextualisation presumes that values can be interactive, as they are interconnected, whereas recontextualisation presumes that values can be rearranged to create a new value. Without accepting that our values are interconnected with values in other cultures, intercultural

142   *Intercultural valuism*

dialogue is impossible or performed at a superficial level. At this intercultural introspection stage, the concept of lifehood indicates an acknowledgement of the co-existence of other cultures in value networks and the relationships between values of both sides refer to multiple realities. Different forms of interculturality embedded in each side rise to the surface because of our awareness of value networks. In practice, it precipitates understanding others because both sides become not two, but a whole in value networks.

7.1.3 Stage 3 value-interaction

Such an ontological whole of value networks determines our epistemic engagement and cognitive presence in value networks to the extent that values interact with each other and current hierarchical value structure is changeable. At this point, value-interaction presupposes two facts: (a) the ontological wholeness discloses the flow of values and (b) the values of both sides can be compared to examine a matter/situation. With these presuppositions, we are able to articulate differences or similarities between values and then build a new perspective or a holistic view on a matter/situation. We may have new values/perspectives as a result. In this stage, we may experience emotional turmoil or cognitive reorganisation, probably temporarily, but value networks as a whole hold the continuation and cultivation of our thoughts because our counterparts have already been parts of our lifehood at our value-awareness of value networks as a whole. In practice, our individuality has detached from individual- "ism" and seeks emergent values by perceiving a larger part or new realm of value networks. Our epistemic engagement, knowing others, is changed from the object-to-be-known to an ontological axiological process of knowing equal agents. Such a process refers to a co-participatory revelation of values towards interculturality. Yet this process will be incomplete until we exercise substantial power over a matter/situation change by using emergent values.

   This value-interaction stage is a meta-ontological-driven or intersubjective process in which we are asked what to do with values rather than whether values exist or not. As the value-awareness stage proves the flexibility of value networks due to the flow of values, this value-interaction stage needs to be done through collaboration without having a tokenistic or tourist approach to values in other cultures. In practice, we need to be aware that we have already invited the counterparts in or they have existed in value networks at the previous stages. Our own value structure and hierarchical relationship with the counterpart have already been broken through decontextualisation and recontextualisation, which informs us that our value systems are sustained by our emotional attachments to socially and culturally beliefs. Thus, if we refuse the value-interaction, we expose our intention that we prefer to stay in our own culture, precisely an ideological realm, by ignoring the ontological wholeness of value networks. In other words, the value-interaction is not a negotiation process, but a (intra-, inter-, and extra-) collaborative process towards a topographic mapping of value networks. This mapping allows us to articulate emergent values that may help us to possibly resolve an intercultural matter/situation.

7.1.4 Stage 4 value-emergence

In the value-interaction stage, emergent values or new perspectives would not appear if we support egocentric-individualism and culturism because we tend to perceive that our values are superior to the counterpart or their values are insufficient to use in problem solving. Emergent values can be caught in the value-interaction when we view values of both sides in value networks. Emergent values are new properties of value networks that appear at a certain critical point because they manifest the intercultural wholeness by being transcendental from a specific intercultural matter/situation, or both sides. While the value-interaction is intersubjective, an emergent wholeness becomes interobjective because it is transcendental to the values of both sides and expands our understanding of value networks, as well as values to be inclusive of all cultures. This value-emergence stage is meta-ethical in that it is to reconsider a matter/situation and remaps our perception of value networks rather than judges values in an action. It can help to visualise ourselves making new engagement in a matter/situation. In practice, we are able to reason out a culturally inclusive answer to an intercultural matter/ situation when we reinterpret it with emergent values. As a result, we will be able to promote a new set of values towards a transformation of socio-cultural identity and socio-cultural formation. In this way, emergent values become a new whole that leads to an expansion of our own culture and our counterparts and fosters value networks in a more culturally inclusive way. This is the reason why intercultural interaction requires us to develop our whole individuality.

7.1.5 Stage 5 A set of value networks

An emergent whole appears from a topological change of value networks and motivates us to elaborate on new thoughts, emotions, and behaviours because a changed interstice of the value nodes loosens the interface between cultures and further facilitates the interaction between the beinghood and the life-hood. In this way, both sides become intercultural agents who have experienced self-transformation in intersubjectivity and self-transcendence in interobjectivity (or interhistoricity of culture). In value networks, self-transformation refers to the evolution of consciousness, whereas self-transcendence is the emergent, relational identity. Both have the potential to provide new directions and new maps for understanding and managing a group's transforming selves. Such co-participatory revelation of the networked values leads to new intercultural introspection, re-arouses value-awareness, re-initiates value-interaction, and reproduces emergent values. In this way, the IVC opens new horizons of the beinghood and the lifehood in an intercultural setting by reshaping our own cognitive limitations in the selfhood. In an interstice of value networks, the self-hood is neither independent nor a value, but manifests as co-revelation of values.

In addition, the IVC can be inversely used because value-interaction per se is the nature of interculturality, and the valuism is meta-cultural. In an intercultural situation, we can initiate value-interaction by asking the reverse questions: (a) what emergent values as a whole do we have to articulate in order to capacitate

144   *Intercultural valuism*

co-revelation of values, (b) what principles and/or conceptual framework of value-interaction do we need to use in order to reveal emergent values, (c) how can we facilitate ontologically equal interaction between values of both sides, (d) what value hierarchy do we have in correspondence to that of our counterpart, and (e) what values do we have in our understanding of a matter/situation? These reversed questions refer to meta-methodology that is a deliberate attempt to metaphysically reflect on our engagement in intercultural interaction and interculturality.

7.1.6 An example of the intercultural valuism circle

Table 7.1 is an example that was used as a practical guide of the IVC for preservice teachers. The left column shows instructional questions for each stage and the right column shows related reflection examples. The questions of each stage are formulated based on ontological, epistemological, and axiological aspects.

7.2 Analysis and discussion

First, I analyse the reflection writings of each stage of the IVC and the 5Rs in a comparative way that articulates understanding of a text (Bray, Adamson, & Mason, 2007). This comparison enables us to see (a) how each model works for participants by increasing sensitivity to differences and similarities (Crossley, 2003) and (b) how I as a comprehender engage in texts (Bray & Mason, 2007). Second, I use Fairclough's (2013) three stages of critical discourse analysis (CDA): description, interpretation, and explanation – as a scaffold for deep understanding and to identify the underlying values in poorly written reflection. This process leads to uncovering meaning, developing understanding, and discovering insights through examining reflection writings (Bowen, 2009) and the results add new values to a knowledge base that is a critical self-reflection (Cohen, Manion, & Morrison, 2005). Third, for further discussion, I present common mistakes identified from the CDA analysis and propose some recommendations for authentic intercultural self-reflection.

7.2.1 Comparative analysis

In Table 7.2, I present comparative analysis outcomes between the IVC and the 5Rs. To identify a typical pattern, each stage of both models was analysed by focusing on the following three questions: What things do they focus on? How are they represented? What factors influence their beliefs and reflection?

These findings from this comparative analysis can be summarised with a reflection pattern of each model. The IVC users tend to utilise four dimensions: value selection, value difference, solutions, and teachers' ability and role, whereas the 5Rs users incorporate three dimensions: a summary of reading material, emotional responses, and teachers' moral responsibility. It can be said that the IVC offers a more self-inclusive reflection in which the participants attempt to focus on a relational self and a professional identity. On the contrary, the 5Rs users tend

Table 7.1 An example of the intercultural valuism circle

Stages	*Chapter 3 Aboriginal early childhood: Past, present, and future (Martin, 2012)*
Intercultural introspection i) Summarise a concept(s), a theory, a story, an event, and/or a quote that I think is important or I am interested in. ii) While summarising it, observe my reaction such as a cognitive, an emotional, and a behavioural one. iii) Based on my observation, describe my reaction(s) by using the following questions: What value(s) do I have that supports my understanding? Is my value(s) compatible to my counterpart? Which values do I think important in education?	[**A concept**] *Relatedness* is "the ultimate premise of Aboriginal worldview and critical to the formation of identity" (Martin, 2012, p. 26). It is not limited to people, but extends to landscape features including animals, plants, rocks, and lands. In particular, this holistic view of human nature and the universe identifies and articulates a person's lifehood from birth to death. The lifehood transforms our egocentric minds into the selfhood in the connectedness to other people and natural environments. [**My reaction**] I believe that I am an independent person who holds a unique identity, although I don't deny that I belong to groups such as a family and a community. [**My judgement**] Relatedness is acceptable only when I try to establish a kind of contact with living beings. Am I really connected to landscape? I think independence is more important than or equally as important as relatedness in education.
Value-awareness i) Interpret my emotional/cognitive states concerning a chosen theme so as to identify the underlying values that caused my responses. Presume that my underlying values/beliefs are my pre-understanding of it. ii) Think about how I feel and what makes me feel that way. iii) Describe what happens if I place humanity, my professional identity, or my personal identity in my counterpart and if I still have the same reaction(s).	[**My values**] Relatedness asks how I define myself. I would define myself as fun-loving, outgoing, funny, caring, crazy, happy, and sometimes emotional! Theoretically, my personality, preferences, appearance, gender, and beliefs distinguish me from others. The underlying values that make me who I am would be *independence* and *uniqueness*. [**My values in the counterpart**] It seems that the Indigenous relatedness stresses their spiritual connectedness to the universe as well as human beings. It devalues my egoistic self and re-values the selfhood and lifehood that raise the question: what things are there to define who I am other than my own attributes? [**Teaching profession**] I have no problem with respecting Indigenous values in my teaching, and I as a teacher should encourage all individual students to respect each other and to be respected. But I am unsure of how to embed *relatedness* into my respect.

(*Continued*)

Table 7.1. Continued

Stages	Chapter 3 Aboriginal early childhood: Past, present, and future (Martin, 2012)

Value-interaction

i) From a perspective of a stakeholder (e.g., your Indigenous friend(s) or an Indigenous student(s) you teach) that may be contradictory to my value(s), describe underlying values/beliefs/assumptions by articulating similarities and differences between mines and theirs (or include references if necessary).

ii) What would I change about my learning environment and/or myself if I endorse a shift to values of the counterpart? (A note here is that you may experience that the interaction challenges or breaks your value system (morality) down. It is nothing but temporary emotion (hasn't happened yet).

iii) What would happen when my and their values are combined in a teaching and learning setting? Are there any new values that go beyond both sides?

[Similarities and differences] Connectedness indicates that my individual identity cannot exist without accepting the fact that I am a social being. I acknowledge that we cannot deny the fact that we are connected and interrelated with one another. However, I also believe that this acknowledgement may undermine self-independence and self-confidence. **[Impediments and mergence]** Conversely, it can be anticipated that a strong sense of individuality and independence may increase social isolation and loneliness that may contribute to a building of negative attitudes towards community. **[Emergent values]** The tension as a whole or in value networks implies that (a) both independence and self-esteem are still valid for the development of an individual's identity and competence and (b) the process should avoid engendering exclusion, isolation, and separation. In this sense, I agree with Martin's claim that *relatedness* facilitates individuals' engagement in and extension to the other, communities, and environments. Thus a new value of individuality that teachers can consider would be *an active contributor to community.*

Value-emergence

i) Apply identified values of both sides in a particular situation, system, or problem.

ii) Articulate the emergent value(s) in that application.

iii) Describe how my understandings of the situation/system/problem have been changed when applying the emergent value(s).

[A teaching perspective] How can we embed the value of relatedness in teaching without undermining "individuality" and vice versa? In a lesson design, for example, I might include more opportunity for individual students to think over community perspectives after or before they express their own interests. **[A learning perspective]** How can we ensure that our [Indigenous] students can practise both values equally in their learning? Like a skill mix analysis method, relational aspects need to be articulated in their learning processes. **[An emergent whole]** Thus *an active contributor to community* needs to be aware of both the needs of community and the impact of the needs of community on his/her life.

[Pedagogical/educational concerns] Individual freedom of choice should not undermine the identity of an active contributor to community. To achieve this, my teaching should aim to provide opportunities for students to develop the whole person. **[Emergent pedagogy]** Then my pedagogy needs to go beyond a frame of collective and individualistic person, but aims to provide students with multidimensional learning opportunities. This means teachers need to expand individuals' roles and responsibilities to themselves, people, community, and humanity. **[Whole person development]** Consequently, it is imperative for teachers to develop the whole person of themselves because teaching and learning are two sides of the same coin.

A set of value networks

i) Think of how to materialise the emergent values in the classroom and/or teaching. Are there any pedagogical or educational concerns?

ii) Do the emergent values encourage me to reconsider my initially identified values? Do they offer new perspectives on a teacher's professional identity?

iii) How does this new value/perspective (re)shape my personal, relational, and professional identities?

Table 7.2 The intercultural valuism circle versus the 5Rs framework for self-reflection

IVC stages	Analysis	5Rs levels	Analysis
Intercultural introspection	Express their initial emotional response to a chosen Indigenous value/perspective. They were either shocked by the massacres of Indigenous people in the past history, morally criticised cultural genocide of Indigenous Australians in the mainstream media, or expressed previously uninterested in Indigenous culture and history.	Reporting	Summarise what they have read. Some tend to focus on tragedies in the past and today's racism.
Value-awareness	Emphasise inclusive education and equity and focus on problems such as lack of education and opportunity for Indigenous people and stereotyping through media. Some attempt to identify the underlying values of both sides.	Responding	Stress that school and teachers should offer equal opportunities to all students. Some express their sympathy on historical tragedies caused by racial discrimination.
Value-interaction	Articulate differences rather than similarities/identities and claim that Western education system needs to be more inclusive of Indigenous culture and values. Some attempt to combine the values of both sides.	Relating	Try to include personal experiences of Indigenous people in their school days (most), English class, and grandparent's story. Some focus on academic deficiencies and issues of Indigenous students in school.

Value-mergence	Focus on what teachers can do and how a lesson can be designed in a more culturally sensitive and inclusive way, yet mostly emphasise that Indigenous students need extra support.	Reasoning	Focus on teachers' ethical principles such as fairness, respect, integrity, and responsibilities.
A set of value networks	Describe what they hope to do and what they will do in the future including utilising storytelling and inviting Indigenous people into class.	Reconstructing	Stress that they have treated or will treat Indigenous people in a fair and equal manner.

150 *Intercultural valuism*

to focus on a personal self and a professional practice. However, there were many cases of poor reflecting in both models in which (a) the multilayered self is not fully considered, (b) it is believed that all values are reducible to a particular value as a universal value, and (c) the reflection writings have tendencies to promote neither pedagogical actions nor in-depth engagement in Indigenous values. For example, many participants did not include a relational self and a humane self, they did regard individuals' equal learning as a key value with no room for any interaction with other values, they did misspell an Aboriginal pedagogy, *story-sharing* as storytelling, and they did literally understand *land-links* and *non-verbal*, but not as an interrelated whole and an expression of interconnection.

7.2.2 Underlying values of poor self-reflection

A further analysis was applied to identify underlying values of poorly written self-reflection. Interestingly, identified values are associated with the three metaphysical issues for intercultural interaction discussed in Parts I and II: the self-exclusiveness of self-reflection, the non-subject positions of others in intercultural interaction, and the myth of value-free methods. Each appears in the values – namely, *individualism, beneficiary,* and *equity*.

Individualism

The pre-service teachers tend to stress that they are non-Indigenous persons in their reflection writings. Although they often state their nationality and profession, their primary focus is on *I am an individual*. For example:

> *I would think that I am an individual that finds my identity in being "Australian". I value individualism, independence and am quite task driven. I certainly need community and family around me; however, I work best when I have individual goals in life.*
>
> *As a white Australian, I enjoy living a very individualistic life. I take pride in the ability to function and maintain, living predominately without the help from others, and my beliefs and morals rarely affect other people's actions. The principles I value, as a white Australian, are individualism and privacy.*
>
> *I believe that as a non-Indigenous person it is essential that I take this sentiment with me into my future teaching career in an effort to avoid being complicit in the oppression of Aboriginal and Torres Strait Islander people.*
>
> *My values are a reflection of the white middle-class Australian culture I grew up in. I value uniqueness and being an individual. I am aware that I (often unintentionally) put my needs above others, and I would describe myself as happy, accepting, caring, and a little reserved.*
>
> *I would define myself as a person who is interested in understanding individual's values and beliefs and reasoning in why they believe and follow those rules. The underlying values of my teaching will be to encourage all students to be individuals. The Indigenous students will become more engaged and will want to learn if all the students understand their meaning in life.*

Intercultural self-reflection 151

In intercultural introspection, their reflection writings appear to begin with recognition of their social identity as non-Indigenous individuals. This would be a typical dualistic approach to oneself and none of them begins their reflection with highlighting either *we are all human beings* or *we are all Australians*. In other words, a humane self and a collective self are not considered in self-reflection, and thus a relational self is rarely considered. This explains why a dualistic approach to an intercultural matter excludes *the self* in self-reflection. Furthermore, the dominant point of view was either the first-person singular (I, my, me, mine) or the third-person plural (they, their, them, theirs). None of them used the first-person plural (we, our, us, ours). This is also evidence that their fundamental approach to self-reflection is individualistic, deterministic, and dualistic, and their efforts to overcome *othering* remain superficial. This means that diverse narrative points of view are required to use in self-reflection.

Beneficiary

The pre-service teachers also stress roles and responsibilities of teachers in Indigenous education. In their reflection writings, teacher-Indigenous student relationships are defined as a benefactor-beneficiary relation. They tend to affirm that Indigenous people are eligible to receive extra support for their academic improvement and engagement, whereas a teacher is described as a person who can help them. The following statements are some examples:

> I hope as a future teacher I can encourage students to create their own perspective and opinions to develop their own sense of identity and culture. However, within this I will not pretend to understand an Aboriginal perspective because I am not Aboriginal and will never completely understand this; however, I will try my best to acknowledge this as a teacher and maintain an open mind.
>
> Becoming a teacher I will be a major influence in most children's lives and what I teach will give them the knowledge they need to know for and throughout their lives. As a teacher I often feel that it is our job to impart new knowledge into students and fill the "gaps" that they are missing.
>
> I can help turn the table in my profession; I can educate children with knowledge and respect of multiculturalism and draw upon Indigenous people to help me learn more about Aboriginal and Torres Strait Islander culture. I believe that education is a process of giving and assisting our students with the tools needed to develop into members of the society that surrounds them. I believe that students need to be given a solid foundation of knowledge to build upon even though these founding ideas are consistently changing.
>
> Indigenous children should be able to practise their values equally in their learning by the help of teachers encouraging and helping them through it. As a future teacher, I find it distressing to think that even today, we are still so narrow-minded to think that Indigenous children aren't succeeding in education because they can't conform to the dominant culture rather than the system not being able to accommodate them. I think the education system could help accommodate and support them.

152 *Intercultural valuism*

> *As a teacher who wants to support all of her students needs to include Aborigi-nal perspectives because after reflecting upon this chapter I have realized that Aboriginal voices and stories are ignored or omitted in order to continue a constructed view of history. Therefore, I need to develop a wider view of what it is to be an Australian and to make a change through my classroom so that the children are exposed to an inclusive vision of Australia.*

They tend to perceive teaching as value-free and culturally unbound, which is a barrier to intercultural interaction and self-reflection. In this circumstance, students' identity of equal participants cannot be promoted and retained by such a teacher. A person's membership in a social identity group is an important factor because social institutions influence social identity and the latter also supports the former. The concept of the multilayered self discussed in Chapter 4 needs to be utilised in self-reflection, particularly in a way that encourages teachers to consider their identity formation in personal and professional contexts in terms of their relational and collective selves.

Equity

Equity is emphasised as the most important value throughout the reflection writings. The pre-service teachers assert that students should be given equal opportunities in education programs regardless of their ability, race, ethnicity, culture, gender, and socio-economic class. In their reflections, equity is described as *equal opportunity* in the sense that all members of a society must have equal opportunities to learn. For example, they express

> *I believe as a teacher it is very important not to single out a student based on their background or cultural differences, whether of Indigenous or non-Indigenous background, but for children to understand and respect the history each one holds. As a teacher, I would want my students to feel as through they have an equal education and relationship with all around them. To do so, I would realise each child's full potential and talent in the classroom.*
>
> *I believe by understanding each person's history we can acknowledge and identify them as an individual yet equal and treat everyone with the same advantages and equal rights to education and learning. How can we ensure that our (Indigenous) students understand both values equally in their learning? It is creating the opportunities for the student to grow and learn to full potential and talents seen with equal advantage during their learning process.*
>
> *As a teacher, I will endeavour to make all students feel equal and encourage all cultures into the classroom. Teaching student's simple activities to make them understand the pressure and problems they face every day will help create awareness and fellow students will then have a little sense of how these students might feel sometimes throughout their schooling and in the education system. As a teacher, I'll endeavour to make all students feel equal and encourage all cultures into the classroom.*

Intercultural self-reflection   153

> *As a future professional teacher, I feel I'm accurate in predicting that the ethnic percentage of my future classes will only increase as multiculturalism increases in Australia. Then why are students from the various countries of the world assimilated into the mainstream education system while Indigenous students have access to politically funded programs and are held accountable to different outcomes? These actions scream lack of equity and equality and only widen the gap.*
>
> *I struggle within witnessing the "reverse marginalisation" of many white Australians through entitled political manoeuvres that benefit many Indigenous based on race and not merit. This only continues to widen the gap, not only on principle, but by action. This marginalisation is not just observed by teachers; students see it to and form their own conclusions.*

It seems that they tend to place equity at the highest level of their value hierarchy. This means that cultural values that they identified or perceived are consciously or unconsciously ranked based on equity. As I have argued in Chapter 1, promoting equity within the learning environment and inviting all students to bring their cultural heritages to the classroom discourse will cause two issues: first, the responsibility for inclusion will not be shifted from learners to educational institutions and second, more supportive values for equity within the dominant culture will be prioritised and the rest will be ignored. As a result, intercultural interaction will become an ideological apparatus to reconfirm the dominant value hierarchy. One action should be that we do not regard equity as value-free, but investigate how equity is understood in diverse cultural contexts. In essence, we need to understand concepts called value-free, such as equity and autonomy, as culturally bound.

7.2.3 Common mistakes and recommendations

Table 7.3 shows mistakes/misunderstandings that many pre-service teachers made because of dualism that is firmly anchored in their minds and relevant recommendations for their engagement in the IVC.

7.3 Conclusion: Towards whole individuality

Western education is based on hierarchical systems rather than human relations because of individualistic culture that needs to be systematically organised for a social function. The system here refers to a structuralised function and socialised scheme consisting of hardware (social-ethical) and software (cultural-moral) components that run an institution or institutions, determines roles and responsibilities, and freedom of individuals. Due to an atomistic and dualistic culture, Western education tends to maximise the liberty of an individual and the efficiency and effectiveness of social systems, while reducing individuals' collective will and morality, and relatively devaluing mutual interaction between individuals and cultures. In this context, Western pedagogical values pursue organised

Table 7.3 Common mistakes of and recommendations for the intercultural valuism circle

Common mistakes	Recommendations
Intercultural introspection	
• Teachers do not reflect an Indigenous value, perspective, and culture, but summarise a historical/social event that white individuals have involved. • Teachers do not focus on their affective and/or cognitive responses to a chosen theme, but attempt to judge it at a very superficial level, in particular with a binary opposition and self-exclusion.	• Ensure that teachers understand a self-inclusive sense of self-reflection or introspection and ultimate concerns of self-reflection. • From the readings, teachers must perform a deep understanding of a chosen Indigenous value/belief/perspective, NOT summarise what they have read. • Ensure that teachers observe their affective/cognitive involvement in a chosen theme from the perspectives of "we" and "I" rather than "you".
Value-awareness • Teachers make instant and unconscious judgements about a chosen theme or state a truism. • Teachers fail to identify underlying values being attached to their response to a chosen theme. • Teachers often focus on their own understanding of a chosen theme rather than Indigenous values of a chosen theme. • Teachers do not believe that their responses have significantly been affected and shaped by their social-cultural background (e.g., *White privilege*).	• Teachers are not familiar with observing themselves because of lack of practices of empathy and a third person's view. • Ensure that teachers understand their mind structure and cultural assumptions (i.e., about 90% of our brain is our unconsciousness, and the concept of multiple selves and cultural values are deeply embedded in the unconscious mind) • Teachers should be aware of the fact that their cognitive actions, including behaviours and thoughts, are initiated based on our subjective belief and experience – values. The latter does not occur without a priori condition that is significantly predetermined by their worldview. Most Westerners' worldview is dualistic, whereas that of Indigenous people is holistic.

Value-interaction

- Teachers implicitly address *white supremacy* and/or *white nationalism* because their unconscious judgement and responses convince them that their values are superior to those of Indigenous people.
- Teachers primarily focus on differences of underlying values of both sides and fail to identify any emergent values arising from value-interaction of both sides.
- Teachers are encouraged to view underlying values of both sides as a whole in association with their meaningful teaching and learning practices.
- Ensure that teachers understand the objectives of value-interaction, which is to find a way of self-cultivation for the development of the whole person rather than just acquire extra knowledge.

Value-emergence

- Teachers hold a strong belief that their understanding of a chosen theme is value-free. Hence their practical efforts come down to their own volition rather than structural (e.g., "I will respect . . .").
- Teachers' primary focus is on how to help or improve Indigenous students who are deficient in learning in the current school system and ethos. They seek additional supports for Indigenous students.
- Teachers need to be aware that whole person development and socio-cultural relation transformation can be achieved by applying emergent values.
- Teachers need to understand that emergent values are intrinsically ethical for collaborative value realisation.
- Teachers are encouraged to identify barriers to realisation/practice of emergent values in teaching and learning.

A set of value networks

- Teachers perceive that emergent values are a matter of personal refinement and/or individuals' intellectual capacity.
- Teachers tend to re-emphasise emotional and volitional words (e.g., respect, equity, fairness, community) rather than their behavioural and institutional transformation.
- Teachers are encouraged to develop an example reflecting emergent values in teaching and learning settings.
- Teachers are encouraged to create a new pedagogical or instructional value based on emergent values.
- Teachers are encouraged to materialise emergent values through cultural and institutional changes.

156 *Intercultural valuism*

behaviours of individuals in line with system maintenance and development and, as a result, moral systems are neither comprehensive nor inclusive, but localised and restricted for socially functional beings. In particular, reductionists recognise the concept of human rights as universal values by decontextualising cultural/religious values and restricting intercultural interaction to ideological commitments.

The intercultural valuism presumes that values embedded in cultures are ontological, epistemological, and axiological in which they are dynamically interdependent, interrelated, and interconnected and always form a specific value structure in our understanding of a situation. Intercultural interaction offers us a new pedagogical approach to interculturality, as it is meta-methodological and aimed at identifying new values from mutual value-interaction of cultures and redesigning the topography of value networks for culturally inclusive education. In this sense, intercultural valuism pedagogy fosters intersubjective competence of individual students and develops a mental model of new individuality. In particular, the latter facilitates intercultural interaction for self-, relational, and social transformation. Thus we experience new whole individuality, as boundaries between reality and individuals, between subject and object, and between cultural realms merge into emergent values. In turn, the whole individuality redefines the applied methodological approach to value networks by which emergent values disclose the fact that the relative importance of values is ideological and the values merge into the networked world. Such a circle is characterised as meta-cultural and axiological-ontological: the former examines one's cultural framework in a matter/situation and the latter discloses values that are predetermined by one's cultural framework. In practice, the whole individuality pursues a new methodological approach to value networks, which is meta-cultural, and the new methodology continues to enhance the whole individuality, which is axiological-ontological.

References

Bain, J.D., Ballantyne, R., Mills, C., & Lester, N.C. (2002). *Reflecting on practice: Student teachers' perspectives.* Flaxton, QLD: Post Pressed.

Bowen, G.A. (2009). Document analysis as a qualitative research method. *Qualitative Research Journal, 9*(2), 27–40.

Bray, M., Adamson, B., & Mason, M. (2007). *Comparative education research: Approaches and methods.* Hong Kong: Comparative Education Research Centre, University of Hong Kong.

Brockbank, A., & McGill, I. (2000). The requirements for reflection. In A. Brockbank & I. McGill (Eds.), *Facilitating Reflective Learning in Higher Education* (pp. 56–69). Buckingham, UK: Open University Press.

Cohen, L., Manion, L., & Morrison, K. (2005). *Research methods in education.* New York: Routledge Falmer.

Crossley, M., & Watson, K. (2003). *Comparative and international research in education: Globalisation, context and difference.* New York; London: Routledge/Falmer.

Epstein, R.M., & Hundert, E.M. (2002). Defining and assessing professional competence. *JAMA, 287*(2), 226–235.

Intercultural self-reflection 157

Fairclough, N. (2013). *Critical discourse analysis: The critical study of language*. Hoboken, NJ: Routledge.

Gibbs, G. (1998). *Learning by doing: A guide to teaching and learning*. London: Further Educational Unit.

Hatton. N., & Smith, D. (1995). Reflection in teacher education-towards definition and implementation. *Teaching and Teacher Education, 11*(1), 33–49.

Johns, C. (2000). *Becoming a reflective practitioner*. Oxford: Blackwell Science.

Kolb, D. (1984). *Experiential learning*. Englewood Cliffs, NJ: Prentice Hall.

Martin, K. (2012). Aboriginal early childhood: Past, present, and future. In J. Phillips & J. Lampert (Eds.), *Introductory Indigenous Studies in Education: Reflection and the Importance of Knowing* (2nd ed.) (pp. 26–39). Sydney, Australia: Pearson.

Rolfe, G., Freshwater, D., & Jasper, M. (2001). *Critical reflection for nursing and the helping professions: A user's guide*. London: Palgrave Macmillan.

Shouse, E. (2005, December). Feeling, emotion, affect. *M/C Journal, 8*(6). Retrieved from http://journal.media-culture.org.au/0512/03-shouse.php

8 Interculturality of non-Western cultures

In multicultural education, a common requirement for teachers is the "use of a range of resources appropriate to students' learning needs that should reflect students' identities" (Department of Education and Training, 2011, p. 29) and flexibility in and access to resources (McLoughlin & Oliver, 2000). As a practical approach to intercultural interaction, in this chapter, I will demonstrate how the three dimensions of educational metaphysics (ontology, epistemology, and axiology) can be used to be inclusive of diverse cultural/religious/philosophical concepts, narratives, and doctrines. In particular, an ultimate purpose of this demonstration is to articulate diverse perspectives on interculturality in value networks. Some may raise the question of whether these cultures/religions/philosophies can be precisely defined with any of the three metaphysical dimensions. Some may also argue whether sub-cultural variants of each can be encompassed by the three. As discussed in philosophical hermeneutics of Chapter 6, we always engage in prejudiced cultural horizons, and ontological hermeneutics is used to encourage us to face our own prejudiced fore-structure. This means that our understanding may produce an example of misinterpretation and misrepresentation of a chosen cultural concept, but it should be temporary because our prejudices are the hermeneutic foundations. The nature of such a metaphysical interpretation is not to set our minds on a particular doctrine, but to understand our own horizons (prejudices) and expand them further towards intercultural interaction. Also, I want to remind readers of the issue that pluralists' approach to cultural diversity could turn into culturalism unless one is able to understand the concept of pluralism from other cultural perspectives.

This chapter is a pedagogical demonstrative process and a form of communication towards intercultural interaction that are expected to help readers to participate in this metaphysical hermeneutic journey of interculturality. This metaphysical interpretation of each resource is not aimed at reducing an entire cultural/religious tradition to my interpretation, but aimed at demonstrating how we can expand our horizons through identifying metaphysical positions of cultural/religious/philosophical concepts, narratives, and doctrines in intercultural value networks. Again, my interpretation does not represent each culture/religion per se, which is also impossible, but probes into each culture/religion's metaphysical probability for interculturality. Following the review of diverse cultural/religious beliefs, I will argue different forms of interculturality embedded

Interculturality of non-Western cultures   159

in them, which enriches intercultural interaction and metaphysical approaches to cultural diversity.

8.1 Non-Western cultures/religions

In this section, I will review Aboriginal *Dreaming*, Hindu *Atman*, Buddhist *Sunyata*, Taoist *Yin and Yang*, Confucianist *Tao*, and Islamic *Tawhid*. Each one can be perceived as more religious, cultural, or philosophical than the others. Someone may raise a question regarding how these different domains can be treated equally. I would answer that the question itself reflects Western secularism. In Muslim, religion (دِين, dīn) means conformism and piousness, and in Chinese, religion (宗教) means the highest teaching. In effect, Muslim and Chinese people tend not to clearly distinguish between culture and religion. In both cultures, religion refers to cultural activities to unify cultivating spiritual stability, studying facts and principles, and selecting right conduct into their ultimate value, *the oneness*. This cultural characteristic also can be found in Hinduism and Buddhism, yet their predominant metaphysical understanding is *the-not-two-ness* rather than *the oneness*.

8.1.1 Aboriginal dreaming

Aboriginal and Torres Strait Islander people's worldview and understanding of the nature of the universe needs to be understood through holistic synthesis and spiritual perception (Hughes & More, 1997). Their worldview can be seen in the *Dreaming* that refers to *Creation period* when their totemic ancestors created mankind and the universe. Hughes and More (1997) state, "The Aboriginal universe is basically one in which physical, scientific qualities are irrelevant and the world takes on meaning through the qualities, relationships and laws laid down in the 'Dreaming'" (para. 13). It is the Aboriginal belief system that all sentient things in the universe are interconnected and interrelated and the networked relationships can be transcendental to spatiotemporality. Such Indigenous holism is "a philosophy that establishes the wholistic notion of the interconnectedness of the elements of the earth and the universe, animate and inanimate, whereby people, the plants and animals, landforms and celestial bodies are interrelated" (Grieves, 2009, p. 7). This means that there is an intrinsic and holistic link between spirituality and the relationship to land and landscape features since there is our tangible, eternal connectivity to sentient beings at the mental level, a non-verbal communication (Grieves, 2009). The following paragraph is one of the most-cited quotes to describe the Dreaming:

> Aborigines have a special connection with everything that is natural. Aboriginals see themselves as part of nature. We see all things natural as part of us. All the things on Earth we see as part human. This is told through the ideas of dreaming. By dreaming we mean the belief that long ago, these creatures started human society. These creatures, these great creatures are just as much alive today as they were in the beginning. They are everlasting and will never

160 *Intercultural valuism*

die. They are always part of the land and nature as we are. Our connection to all things natural is spiritual.

(Roberts as cited in Bourke, Bourke & Edwards, 1994, p. 77)

To deal with the metaphysics of the Dreaming, Dean (1996) argues that we should understand its ontological aspects, because the nature of reality is Aboriginal mythology that is expressed in an intuitive, visionary, and artistic way. In other words, the metaphysics appears logically contradictory and incomplete because of "the prelogical nature of Aboriginal thought" (pp. 55–56). In understanding Aboriginal culture, spirituality requires special care in comparison with religion. For Aboriginal people, "spirituality can be seen as an internal connection to the universe that includes a sense of meaning or purpose in life, a cosmology or way of explaining our personal universe and a personal moral code", whereas, religion is "the specific practice and ritual that is an external expression of some people's spirituality" (Wilson as cited in Grieves, 2009, p. 17). Grieves (2009) also argues that Indigenous spirituality is the driving force of resistance against Western colonialism because it is the essence of personhood and the seeds of Indigenous knowledge (p. 17). In this sense, Indigenous spirituality should not be understood as a sense of egoistic self or sense of personal identity, but existence as relational, collective, and transcendental, or an extended or a networked individuality. Such *interconnected* culture is characterised by a holistic link that "instinctively operates an immanentist sense of the metaphysical powers that hold together the universe, the profane and the holy are constantly commingled and interwoven" (Griffin, 2003, p. 69). The holistic link or *interrelatedness* is "the sets of protocols and practices" that "determine[s] the roles one has to the child, and this prescribes the levels of responsibility" (Martin, 2012, p. 28). For example, when a child is given an ancestral name at birth, the name reflects who he or she will become, which is based on interrelatedness to other people and other elements and, likewise, his/her roles and responsibilities of young adulthood, adulthood, and elderhood are articulated through interrelatedness (Martin, 2012). In this way, the interrelatedness integrates the living and the dead via land where the spirits of ancestral beings continue to reside, and the dead are allowed to enter the *Land of the Dead* (Monroe, 2013). The Land of the Dead is a place where a dead Aboriginal spirit resides or refers to a mergence with ancestral beings or returning to a totemic site (Monroe, 2013). Interrelatedness into the lifehood enables Indigenous people to approach the wholeness through collective-focused, holistic-driven, non-sequential thinking and behaviours.

8.1.2 *Hindu atman*

Hinduism conceives the universe as a single entity that accepts all forms of beliefs and rejects religious distinctive identities. Biswas (2007) argues that the whole emphasis of Indian philosophy is on the attainment of the supreme value – namely, the realisation of *Atman* through self-cultivation. Atman is the original identity of human beings that is identical to *Brahman*, the ultimate reality and the supreme essence of the universe whose qualities and forms are represented by the multitude of deities that emanate from it (Rukmani, 2008, p. 132). An enlightened person realises Brahman as his or her own Atman and the union of Atman and Brahman. Hindus believe that existence is governed by *karma*, which is "the substance of done deeds", a cause of samara, the cycle of successive lives – death and rebirth (Hacker, 2006, p. 490). As the next incarnation is dependent on a person's good deeds or bad deeds in this life, so this life has already been determined by karma that one has created in past lifetimes. The Atman passes through *samsara* (the cosmic life cycle). Attaining *moksha* (liberation from samsara) requires annihilation of all karmas, good and bad. When one gets into moksha, one will be liberated from samsara (Rukmani, 2008). Moksha is understood by people at the present time and concerned with the present world and everything related to human life (often used interchangeably with *nirvana* of Buddhism, but the latter is the ultimate outcome of moksha and the former is more relational and social). Mishra (2013) emphasises that the pursuit of moksha is helpful "not only in achieving success in personal and professional domains of life, but also in developing positive interpersonal and inter-group relationships" (p. 21). Mishra points out that people use collectivistic means (e.g., welfare activities) to achieve moksha which goes beyond their individualistic concern because a higher level of consciousness is transcendental to individualistic limitations. In other words, moksha is motivated by "love for and relatedness with others" and offers "solutions not only to individual problems, but also to familial, social, political, and professional problems", which represents the key concept of Indian philosophy and religion, co-existence, and holistic view (Mishra, 2013, p. 34).

In Hindu education, attainment of moksha is the main purpose of yogas (Biswas, 2007). Four yogas have been suggested: *karma yoga* (doing everything for the Supreme Lord), *jnana yoga* (realising the Supreme Lord everywhere), *raja yoga* (meditating on the Supreme Lord all the time) and *bhakti yoga* (serving the Supreme Lord in loving devotion) (Mishra, 2013, p. 27). Hindus do not think that one path is better than the others, although people can practise only one path. This is because *Dharma* (ethics/duties) is not the same for every person, and to the best of one's ability depends on one's class and social status (Penny, 1995; Siddhartha, 2008). In this sense, yogas can be personally understood as ways for purification of individuals' minds, but culturally and socially understood as a defence mechanism of Hindu metaphysical belief through individuals' internalisation of their holistic and collective ontological system. Like moksha, karma also sustains collective-holistic metaphysics that defines an individual as an integrated entity of the past, present, and future and puts a high value on spiritual individuality or networked individuality. At the same time, it defines this life as the result of previous lives and of actions in this life and as a seedbed of a moral imperative for the next life and some of this life. This collective and interconnected system not only justifies all kinds of sufferings of people who live very piously but also facilitates self-reliant spiritual life as networked rather than atomistic, materialistic life. The system also upholds their holistic culture that requires individuals to integrate all hierarchical values of this life into

162 *Intercultural valuism*

samsara by increasing individuals' awareness of intersubjectivity, in which desires, thoughts, and actions on relationships with all living beings are interrelated to form a whole system.

8.1.3 Buddhist sunyata

The Buddha taught that every sentient being has a combination of five psycho-physical aggregates of existence called the five *skandhas* (element): (a) the body or corporeality, (b) affect, (c) perception and cognition, (d) conditioning and volition, and (e) consciousness (MacKenzie, 2013). The five skandhas are inter-dependent components of a causally and functionally integrated psychophysical system or process (MacKenzie, 2013, p. 199) and are the foundations for the causality links (Khenchen, Rinpoche, & Lharampa, 2001). The human mind is made up of the five skandhas because of causes and conditions and their interplay (Khenchen *et al.*, 2001; Seiju, 2008). An essential component of the five skand-has is *change* (or interconnectedness) (Tomhave, 2010). Each of these skandhas is constantly changing, which denies the existence of *Atman* and thereby *Sunyata* (emptiness).

Nāgārjuna (circa 150–250 AD), the most important Buddhist philosopher and one of the most original and influential thinkers in the history of Indian philosophy, views that the core teaching of Buddha is causality (Westerhoff, 2010). Nāgārjuna states, "Something that is not dependently arisen, Such a thing does not exist. Therefore a nonempty thing Does not exist" (Chapter 24, Verse 19 as translated by Garfield, 1995, p. 304). This verse means that everything is totally interconnected with everything else, which means there is no separate existence. A thing can be perceived as independent of our perceiving minds, but its existence cannot be explained without relationships and interconnectedness to other things. Thus the nature of things is empty and void (*Sunyata*). Nāgārjuna states, "Whatever is dependently co-arisen, That is explained to be emptiness. That, being a dependent designation, Is itself the middle way." (Chapter 24, Verse 18 as translated by Garfield, 1995, p. 304). In the realm of absolute emptiness, it can be seen that there is interfusion and inter-penetration of ourselves and other selves, human beings, and the universe. The emptiness or the absolute void does not mean nothingness or non-existence, but something about the natural conditions of matters and the nature of matters that should be non-duality. Buddhist emptiness has multiple meanings: non-substantiality, the primal emptiness, birthlessness, and, specifically, the emptiness of absolute substance, truth, identity, reality, and ego (Gyatso, 2011). In a dualistic thinking framework or an egoistic approach, the emptiness can be interpreted in negating the activation of stereotypes, nullifying delusions of consciousness, and introspecting one's own thoughts and feelings. It is merely a name that refers to emancipation from delusions and suffering and indicates a guide to the achievement of *nirvana* – the highest state. It does not pursue the affirmation or the negation of existence, but is a metaphorical term that ontologically refers to the nature of matters and epistemologically points to the human mind where

Interculturality of non-Western cultures   **163**

the starting and ending place for enlightenment, emancipation, and nirvana should be. In short, "the emptiness is not nothingness but is the real nature of all phenomena" (Gyatso, 2011, p. 60).

There are the twelve nidāna (which means literally cause, foundation, and source or origin) in the chain of dependent origination that explain how ignorance develops *Dukkha* (often translated as suffering, pain, and misery, but the Buddha taught that it is life itself as all living beings are born and die). The direct order of the twelve links examines and explains the connections of all phenomena that manifest emptiness, egolessness, and impermanence. The causality links are more radical in that their focus is not on the truth, but on the conditions or status to be the truth. To overcome duality operative in the everyday standpoint, *the-not-two-ness* (non-duality) is most commonly used to point to the *Middle Way*. It means that two opposed concepts or two incompatible facts are regarded not as being separated from each other, but are derived from nothing – the nature of emptiness. For example, good and evil have a common root and everything has two sides. Zen Buddhists also support that an oppositional mode of thinking promotes "time-consciousness" and "space-consciousness", which sustains the epistemological structure of knower-known (Nagatomo, 2010). Its ontological foundation does not integrate a pair into one, but rejects its integration as well as distinction. In the *Heart Sutra*, known as the most popular Buddhist scripture, the Buddha taught that human cognitive processes tend to distinguish between ego and the rest of existence because of unawareness of the not-two-ness.

8.1.4 Taoist yin and yang

Tao means path, way, route, or channel in English, but it carries more philosophical and conceptual meanings to signify the fundamental nature of the world. To Confucius (*circa* 551–479 BC), Tao is the Way of man, of ancient sage-kings, and of virtue as he regarded it as *Ren* (仁, humanity) and *Yi* (義, righteousness). To Lao-tzu (*circa* 604–531 BC), who is known as the author of *Tao Te Ching*, Tao is fundamental to both philosophical and religious Taoism. Lao-tzu defines Tao as the *Natural Way* and *Truth of the Universe* and describes that all objects in the world have appearances and manifestations of Tao, and every object, as well as the entire universe, are operating within the doctrine of Tao, the flow of *Ch'i* (氣, energy) (or the interaction between *yin* and *yang*).

Yin and yang are the basic distinctions that are complementing and balancing each other in endless cycles. The cycles are the flow of yin and yang energies found everywhere in nature and this fundamental movement produces one from the other, thus being is fundamentally non-being.

> Know the male [yang], yet keep to the female [yin]: receive the world in your arms. If you receive the world, the Tao will never leave you and you will be like a little child.
>
> (*Tao Te Ching*: Chapter 28 as translated in Mitchell, 1995)

164 *Intercultural valuism*

Return is the movement of the Tao. Yielding is the way of the Tao. All things are born of being. Being is born of non-being.

(*Tao Te Ching*: Chapter 40 as translated in Mitchell, 1995)

The epistemological focus of Taoism is not on yin and yang, but the flow of yin-yang that keeps all things and the universe in balance and harmony. All things are interrelated and interconnected by the flow of yin-yang internally, externally, and inter-individually. Even a single object made by human also contains its own yin and yang (Park, 2009). The yin and yang symbol is known as the symbol of *Tai Chi*, the Chinese character (太極) that means literally the ultimate potentiality, the utmost extremes, and the Supreme Ultimate. The symbol illustrates a balanced state of yin-yang that can be found in all existence including natural phenomena, social order, and functions of our bodies. In the symbol there is a yin dot on the yang shape and a yang dot on the yin shape, which indicates that the yin-yang is not a dualistic system, but a dialectic monistic energy or principle. As a result, the rounded shape of the yin-yang symbol must be understood as a visualised form of continual movement and interaction of the two energies as one. The flow of yin-yang includes the four principles that explain why the yin-yang flows and each is not a conceptually distinct entity: mutual opposition, interdependence, counterbalance, and mutual convertibility (Park, 2009).

All things are interdependent and unique, but qualitatively interconnected within the flow of yin-yang energies (*Tao Te Ching* Chapter 22 as translated in Mitchell, 1995). In this way, Taoism emphasises the importance of interaction between self's inner voices and the voices of all things in a receptive manner, and the interaction will not be detected by rationality, but intuitions through the whole body. For Taoists, self-cultivation means taking responsibility for not only one's own actions but also social and environmental well-being. It is an everlasting challenge for any conscious being. Lao-tzu believes that Taoism does not attempt to obliterate ego, but to observe the self within the connectedness of all things and other selves in terms of the flow of Tao (*Tao Te Ching* Chapter 7 as translated in Mitchell, 1995). For him, attachment to rules or values is not giving freedom, but a certain limitation so that moderation between the upper bound and lower bound limitations will give the best status of freedom (*Tao Te Ching* Chapter 9 as translated in Mitchell, 1995). In this sense, life and death are the cycles of yin and yang, which liberates people from attachment to life and death. In this way, Lao-tzu argues that the goal of living things is to confirm to the cycle of life and death (*Tao Te Ching* Chapter 16 as translated in Mitchell, 1995). Attachment to life or fear of death causes people to have an unhealthy life and unrealistic fear. The flow of Tao helps people to pursue moderation and balance. It begins with having an empty mind, non-attachment (*Tao Te Ching* Chapter 30 as translated in Mitchell, 1995).

8.1.5 *Confucianist tao*

Confucianists understand the nature of Tao (Heavenly Tao, Heaven Way) through human nature and vice versa. For them, practicing or realising virtues

Interculturality of non-Western cultures 165

is the unity of one's entire life with Tao or Tian. Based on the categorisation of human nature with virtues (theses of human nature), Confucianists developed the ideally characterised models through history (e.g., Confucius's noble person, Mencius's great person, and Xunzi's capable person) based on a man of virtue and suggested how a virtuous man can be practised in their discourses of moral-practice and self-cultivation. Confucius (circa 551–479 BC) taught five virtues that a man of virtue should practise every day to live a healthy, harmonious life. The five virtues are *Ren* (仁, Humanity), *Yi* (義, Righteousness), *Zhi* (智, Knowledge), *Xin* (信, Integrity), and *Li* (禮, Ritual). Each virtue cannot be completely translated in English, but a thing we should remember is that the five virtues are fundamentally linked to Ren because it is the representation of Tao. To Confucius in the Analects, Ren denotes "a moral excellence that anyone has the potential to achieve" and it is related to "attitudes such as care and respect for others . . . in right or appropriate action according to the context" (Wong, 2013, para. 6). More fundamentally, it refers to a sense of a person together with others. The ideogram of Ren (仁) consists of two elements: the left element indicates a person or a human being, and the right element means the number two. Semantically, the latter indicates a human being together with other human beings – a human being in society (Riegel, 2013).

For Confucius, this is the Way of Heaven (Tao, 道 or Heavenly Tao, 天道) that refers to "both a purposeful Supreme Being as well as 'nature' and its fixed cycles and patterns" (Riegel, 2013, para. 21). This means that Confucianists presume that the social way and the natural world are designed according to the Way of Heaven and the natural course of events, whether related to society or nature, are due to the decree of heaven. In this sense, the Confucius concept of Heaven (Tian, 天) is different from the Christian concept of Heaven or God, Islam Paradise, and Buddhism Nirvana. Literally, it refers to the sky, but philosophically the permanent source of the universe and life (Huang, 2009). In particular, it refers to substance and activity that combines the principle of order (Li, 理) and the universal energy (Ch'i, 氣) (Huang, 2009) and "natural, Heaven-given principles" (Middendorf, 2008, p. 111). Virtues originate from natural human sentiments and extend to personal exemplification over explicit rules of behaviour (Riegel, 2013). Confucius virtue ethics rarely relies upon epistemic reasons and ethical methodologies, and individuals should understand and perform given roles (Wong, 2013). Virtues, innately embedded in human nature by Tian, are conceptualised and materialised through title normalisation (known as the *rectification of names*) in human and social relationships (Riegel, 2013, para. 30). Confucianists believe that a healthy and harmonised society can be achieved through individuals' performance of roles assigned by virtues.

The Confucianism tradition had further advanced during the neo-Confucian period (eleventh through early twentieth centuries) to find the metaphysical and epistemological foundations for the Way. While neo-Confucianists hold Confucius humanism (a man of virtue) as fundamental, they develop a metaphysical principle, *Li* (理, law or reason) that forms the universe (Wong, 2013). The most well-known neo-Confucianist, Zhuxi (1130–1200) developed a Confucianist metaphysics in which all things are representations of the union of two

166 *Intercultural valuism*

universal aspects of reality: *Ch'i* (or *Qi*, 氣) and *Li* (理) (Wong, 2013). The vital force, Ch'i, is the energy flow to form and sustain life and objects. The source and sum of Li is Tai Ch'i, the Supreme Ultimate (equivalent to Tian and Tao) – that is, the creation principles (like the continuous interactions between yin and yang). For example, a human being is a Ch'i composition, but one is distinguished from others and has one's own identity because of one's Li being assigned by Tai Ch'i. A human being consists of Ch'i and Li, but Li allows one to be a human being as a social being. Thus one should cultivate oneself to understand the Li of one's own mind and investigate it. Yet one should be aware that one's Li is not independent of and separate from other persons, texts (such as the Analects) and situations, so one needs the Li as "patterns of things" and "patterns in relationships between persons" (Wong, 2013, para. 65). In this sense, Li is the essence that makes things what they are supposed to be. It lays the axiological foundation for Confucianist morality that primarily focuses on virtue ethics by holding a monistic view of Li and Ch'i or the mind and nature. Confucianists do not view a human being as an independent entity, but an ontological extension of nature (as Tian or Tao) (Riegel, 2013). They do not clearly distinguish between human, society, and nature, but each is the same as its essence. This monistic cultural view upholds a moral imperative that everyone has the capability to realise human nature (virtues) that is intrinsically social or interdependent. The moral imperative is characterised by role virtues such as self-cultivation and rectification of names that sustain relational and collective discourses and culture.

8.1.6 *Islamic tawhid*

Islam pursues the unity of churches and states and Muslim-majority countries outline the role of Islam in their constitutions (Izutsu, 2007; Rizvim, 2006). Muslims believe that Islam is neither a religion nor a culture, but a theocracy subjugated to *Allah*, the complete version of a primordial faith, and the main focus of this life is preparing for the afterlife in accordance with the teachings of Allah (Izutsu, 2007; Rizvim, 2006). In an area of knowledge, the Islamic viewpoint is, "Being created in the image of God, man seeks to emulate the divine qualities of the Creator. To be objective is, in a sense, to emulate God. Man is capable of objectivity because of the endowment in his nature of the divine qualities of impartiality and justice" (Kamali, 2005, p. 2). While objective knowledge needs public verification, Islamic perception of objectivity is "measured by impartiality, universality and justice" (Kamali, 2005, p. 2). Internalisation of these qualities is the foundation for Islamic civilisation (Kamali, 2005). In everyday life, such Islamic civilisation is to realise the *Tawhidic* way of life (the doctrine of oneness [of God]). Its conceptual and practical form can be seen in the five pillars of Islam that are obligatory acts and the foundation of Muslim life. They make up faith (*Shahadah*), worship (*Salat*), Ramadan (*Sawm*), alms (*Zakah*), and the pilgrimage (*Hajj*) that are summarised in the Hadith of Gabriel. The practice of the five pillars is believed to sustain and enhance moral sensitivity of every human being and Muslim communities. This means that they do not distinguish

Interculturality of non-Western cultures 167

between moralities of individuals and societies, but view them as the whole universe that is functioning under Allah's command. In this sense, they diminish the gap between individuals and groups and minimise individuality by merging psychological and physical aspects of individuals under the will and plan of Allah. The Prophet Muhammad's nine commands for Muslim morality and the eight doors (good deeds) of *Jannah* (Paradise or Heaven) in Hadith are evidence that these moral virtues and norms confine Muslims to other and Muslim communities. The Prophet Muhammad states,

> My Sustainer has given me nine commands: to remain conscious of God, whether in private or in public; to speak justly, whether angry or pleased; to show moderation both when poor and when rich, to reunite friendship with those who have broken off with me; to give to him who refuses me; that my silence should be occupied with thought; that my looking should be an admonition; and that I should command what is right.
>
> (as cited in Akhter, 2009, p. 135)

Based on God-consciousness, including "humbleness, modesty, control of passions and hopes, truthfulness, wholeness, patience, staunchness, and carrying out one's promises are honourable values which are accentuated again and again in the Qur'ān", moral values in family and society are elucidated (Akhter, 2009, p. 135). For example, social obligations include benignity and thoughtfulness of others, and specific responsibilities based on lifehood are enumerated including parents, husbands, wives, children, neighbours, acquaintances, friends, orphans, widows, the destitute of the community, their associate Muslims, and all fellow humans and creatures (Akhter, 2009, p. 135). These social obligations are described as the eight doors of *Jannah* (Paradise or Heaven) that are for those who perfect their prayer, perform jihad, constantly give charity, constantly fast, perfect Hajj (pilgrimage), control their anger and forgave others, perfect their iman (faith) with sincerity and truthfulless, and remember and be aware of Allah (Rifai, 2015, p. 12). Rifai (2015) explains that the doors are opened for one "as a consequence of one's effort in life" and thus "people will only enter by one" and "others will be given a choice", "but perfecting wudu [the practice of ritual washing before daily prayer] and affirming the shahada (testimony of faith) will open all eight" (p. 12). This means that social obligations merge into religious obligations and the latter dominates this life. In this way, the moral system of Islam supports a theocrat society and upholds a monistic worldview that combines this life and the afterlife into oneness (being aware of Allah with predetermined values), neither life-centred nor afterlife-oriented, and promotes a totalistic approach to morality by diminishing egoistic individuality. A substantial form of the collectivistic culture appears in the concept of Muslim *Ummah* (literally nation or community) that refers to a connected and collective community of all Muslims. In the Qur'ān, *Ummah* refers to the unity of Muslims all over the world. It is believed that *Ummah* is responsible for upholding the religion and giving benefits to both Muslim and non-Muslim communities. As Bakar (2011) explains, this religious identity, as the destiny of Islam, is the role of synthesiser

168 *Intercultural valuism*

and is a synthesis of ideas in all sectors of human life and thought. Izutsu (2007) argues that the idea is based on the unity of existence and is the most influential philosophical concept among the majority of Muslim thinkers. He also argues that it can be experienced when "the empirical selfhood is annihilated" and "the ego-consciousness is completely dissolved" in the Tawhidic way of life (pp. 13–14). It can be simply understood that life is nothing more than a test of the faith of Islam, but strictly speaking, His Will is that Muslims as vicegerents or representatives of Allah fulfil their given positions in this life (Hussien, 2007). The role is morally grounded in their apocalyptic belief that, at the end of the day, Allah judges the living and the dead and admits those who have lived a proper life into *Jannah* and some people will be sent to Hell for all eternity or for a certain period of time for intense purification (Rizvim, 2006). This ascriptive dualistic monism sustains a collectivistic culture through a synchronic culture of moral intervention based on His Will.

8.2 Interculturality of value networks

In the concept of intercultural value networks, cultures as different entities are interconnected through pre-set values of each one. When values of one party are apparent, impermeable and incompatible with those of the other, this can cause indifference and alienation. A subordinate culture acculturates and readjusts itself to a dominant culture or it sustains a certain cultural and emotional distance. In other words, value incompatibility places both parties in a hierarchical distance that causes superior or inferior emotions. Thus harmony and solidarity are promoted by a dominant culture through acculturation of a subordinate one, but in essence, harmony and solidarity are valid only within a range of a dominant one's tolerance. In an intercultural situation/interaction, therefore, values of a dominant culture are ideologically anchored in notions of difference and diversity, whereas values of a subordinate culture are placed in notions of either similarity or severance, which indicates continuous oscillations between ontological and epistemological frames. In intercultural value-interaction, in this sense, impermeable values tend to conceal ontological dualism and hierarchical systems that control situations and facilitate non-reciprocal interaction. This dualism enhances ideological beliefs by drawing a sharp line of demarcation between system-friendly and -unfriendly values and focusing on enhanced institutional and individual capacities. It also isolates individuals from their human relationships unless the system prioritises building and sustaining relationships. Inversely, its potential productivity for interculturality appears when it merges into intersubjectivity. When those negative features are recognised by intercultural experience of members of society, predetermined institutional and individual roles can be further facilitated by ongoing development of sustainable community. It also enhances inclusiveness in pluralitarian systems even further by systematising and institutionalising predefined concepts and ideas that can lead to a change in social-cultural human relations. Therefore, values should not be left as individuals' accountability or universal or consensual things, but be examined and articulated through diverse metaphysical assumptions of cultures. As reviewed, the

Interculturality of non-Western cultures   169

concepts of non-Western cultures/religions imply that they demythicise dualistic thinking and accelerate such productivity.

8.2.1 Holistic interculturality

The key common mystical concept found in Aboriginality, Hinduism, and Buddhism is reincarnation/transmigration, which connects the present, past, and future and the previous life and afterlife beyond life and death. Aboriginal Dreaming interconnects all living beings, ancestral beings, land (the earth), and landscapes and determines Aboriginal lifehood and relevant social roles and responsibilities as part of an ecological system. Hindu's *Karma* integrates all hierarchical values of this life into *samsara* through intersubjectivity. Buddhist causal links also connect and integrate the self and the universe synchronically and diachronically. Aboriginal *Dreaming*, Hindu *Atman*, and Buddhists *Sunyata* have the following facts in common: (a) there is no substance, but human senses and consciousness manipulate our psychophysical responses, (b) the highest status can be gained through self-awareness and self-cultivation (Hindu *Moksha*, Buddhism enlightenment or *Nirvana*, and Aboriginal's *Land of the Dead*), (c) by concentrating on interconnected moments (right here and now), we can have a state of non-duality in which there is no cognition, only pure being, (d) a holistic approach promotes non-reductive individualism, and (e) individuals are interconnected and interrelated, which underlies the multiplicity and unity of the universe.

In intercultural value networks, such holistic cultural values promote networked individuality and non-dualistic thinking. Values are ontologically driven and become implicit in a networked form. Hence the primary path to values is experiential and affective, which has already been predefined in (the networked) individuals' minds. In this sense, those people who are driven by ontological dualism may not be able to grasp holistic cultural values because they are concealed and implicit in relational forms. Even those who are in a holistic culture may not be able to articulate values in a way that others who have non-holistic culture can understand because they practise and reproduce values through their intersubjectively spiritual experiences. In an intercultural situation, concealed values can intensify a tension or cause a conflict if both parties are not able to reach an agreed upon position or values of secularism and independent individualism achieves superiority over intrapersonal intersubjectivity. In other words, there is always a possibility that the conflict or superiority can provoke violence and/or turn into trauma unless either party is aware that an obsession with and adherence to their own value system can cause psychological distress and/or physical collision with the other. For example, Australian Indigenous children were forcibly removed from their families and raised in white families is evidence of a one-way dualistic approach to the other (or a fixed subject-object relation). In addition, ignoring concealed values also appears in a reversed binary opposition that is found in left-essentialist multiculturalism and critical multiculturalism. It is believed that intercultural interaction is reducible to social actions of individuals without presuming interculturality.

170 *Intercultural valuism*

Networked individuality of holistic cultures is consistent with the nature of value networks, which is the interrelated mind (or human co-existence). It is different from abstract individualism or virtue agents and attacks reified and dehumanised relationships. Aboriginal *Dreaming*, Hindu *Atman*, and Buddhists *Sunyata* have a common goal of promoting that the true self is the interrelated mind. In these holistic cultures, dualistic thinking has to be avoided because it facilitates an egocentric mind and an atomistic approach to the world. The inter-related mind sustains an irreducibly complex whole that, in turn, controls individuals' practices of cultural values. In consequence, an intercultural value of the holistic cultures is the ontologically networked individuality, which focuses on an axiological whole. Yet its epistemic structure easily becomes loose because holistic cultures tend to negate not only dualistic thinking but also systematic morality, as they are more concerned with a spiritual sense of mental processes.

8.2.2 Monistic interculturality

Metaphysics of Taoism, Confucianism, and Islamism is characterised by monistic metaphysics and role ethics (or virtues). Their monistic mode of thinking is characterised by the concept of oneness that should not be understood as a noun, but a verb. Tao, Tian, and Tawhid do not refer to a person or thing, but indicate what we are supposed to do and what happens to our minds. As seen earlier, Taoists teach the Way *we should follow*, Confucianists uphold the virtue(s) *we should practise*, and Muslims believe the given life that as God's vicegerents *we should perform*. In this sense, the oneness is axiologically driven as well as ontologically oriented, as we are supposed to be clear about values we have to pursue, practise, and realise. From this point of view, we can infer that people in these monistic cultures tend not to perceive cultural diversity or multiple-reality as a problem or difficulty unless it does challenge their collectivistic social/moral values and roles that are assigned by the oneness. This means that they tend to hold a strong sense of intersubjectivity (or more interobjectivity driven) that needs to be reviewed in various intercultural settings, otherwise their collectivistic values drive them to not confront those of other cultures or to dismiss them as trivial matters. Because of their oneness-driven approach to social and personal aspects that sustain collectivistic relationships, in practice, monistic cultures are to promote tolerance for contradiction in reality and intolerance for individuals' different understandings of given values. For example, people tend to tolerate and endure dualistic oppositions and contrasts because Taoist *Yin and Yang*, Confucianist *Way of Heaven*, and Islamic moral intervention of His Will are the nature of all things and the focus is on how individuals can merge into and participate in the oneness through moderation and balance. On the other hand, individual differences are acknowledged and acceptable when individuals contribute to the oneness and, in turn, this enhances their social (collectivistic) self. This understanding explains why happiness and freedom can be achieved when in search of balanced and harmonised moments. For example, the flow of yin-yang as the energy source of the oneness manifests the *Middle Way*, and Islamic *Ummah* cosmologically promotes an equally ineluctable fate ordained for every individual from one's birth. Both

Interculturality of non-Western cultures 171

explicitly and implicitly stress transcendence and reconciliation of the extremes in order to balance the contradiction.

In a monistic culture, intercultural value-interactions are mostly situational because of their relativistic and contextual thinking habits. There is nothing else that can be claimed as an absolute or pure thing because the oneness is manifested in diverse contexts of the rise and fall of yin-yang and Islamic moral intervention of human life. In this internally dynamic contexts, prescribed values of the oneness must be represented as and expressed through moral exemplars or agents. Tao is systematised through the role of ethics in Confucianism and throughout history (Confucius's noble person, Mencius's great person, and Xunzi's capable person). In line with God's consciousness, Muslims as vicegerents or representatives of Allah are supposed to fulfil given roles in this life. The Confucianism exemplars control cultural aspects of social structures and individuals, whereas Islamic vicegerents control socio-psychological aspects of individuals. Both represent predetermined moral values which individuals and community should pursue to maintain given value systems from/towards the oneness. For example, Confucius ritual principles (禮, Li) determine ritual processes of ancestor worship and virtues of social behaviours and attitudes, whereas Islamic moral intervention (i.e., Hadith) governs human birth and destiny and upholds Islamic social laws. In this sense, the best description of monistic ethics would be *role ethics/virtues*, which is different from Aristotelians' specific form of virtue ethics (Rosemont & Ames, 2009). Aristotelians' virtue ethics are based on rationality, individuality, and freedom, whereas monistic cultural ethics promote exemplar/ vicegerent individuals and roles in communities (e.g., as a father/mother/son/ daughter, a teacher, and a leader). In this sense, intercultural interaction would only be valid for their roles that have been and must be assigned by communities.

In intercultural value networks, monistic cultures can promote permeable and compatible value-interaction as long as values are aligned with role virtues and are shared by participants, although titles and names vary. In this sense, value convergence would be a matter of time not because of the belief that it will happen, but because of the virtuous person who perceives the right reason and performs the right judgement. Reason in monistic cultural contexts neither indicates Kant's *pure reason* as unaided ability to form concepts nor Hume's understanding of reason as a subjective faculty, but as *the will of historicity* that perpetuates the virtue(s) through generations. In other words, the ultimate concern is the historicity as a conceptualised unity and perpetuity sustaining the conviction that different values are supposed to converge on the virtue(s). In practice, one may think and behave as if a tension between values has already been resolved or one may try to dismiss it. This collective auto-suggestive thinking prevents one from being aware of how values are institutionalised and internalised through cultural activities and experiences. In intercultural value-interaction, in this sense, monistic cultures may not actively facilitate the perception of emergent values because the focus is on the individuals' intuitive capability to perceive the oneness in situations, not on a reformation of value networks. On the other hand, monistic cultures have a productive aspect for interculturality in which the agreed/shared virtues can facilitate individuals' moral values, such as tolerance and perseverance,

172 Intercultural valuism

and can be used as a barometer of participants' ethical engagement in intercultural interaction.

8.3 Conclusion: Metaphysics of interculturality

In intercultural value networks, emergent values develop from epistemic tensions of values, which is epistemological interculturality; intercultural interaction requires a clear description of roles and responsibilities of individual participants, which is axiological interculturality, and different cultural assumptions and values are interrelated and interconnected, which is ontological interculturality. Conversely, when a culture becomes dominant in intercultural interaction, it may negate interculturality. For example, if a dualistic culture or epistemological interculturality achieved a dominant position, value-interaction can isolate and reify human relationships because its demarcated and atomistic approach to interculturality promotes analytic and systemic development of intercultural interaction without considering morality. If a holistic culture or ontological interculturality holds hegemony over others, value-interaction can be either unstructured or malstructured because of its rejection of dualistic thinking and its devaluing of systematic morality, and if a monistic culture or axiological interculturality is more noticeable than others, value-interaction tends to ignore emergent values because its focus is on the individuals' intuitive capability to perceive and practise shared or given values of interculturality. Such limitations can be turned into positives when they are understood with value networks for interculturality.

First, axiological interculturality encourages us to think about participants' moral values or ethical engagement in intercultural interaction. This implies that interculturality is based on the premise of disclosing underlying values of a dominant culture towards an intercultural situation rather than uncritically accepting a proposed system or framework for intercultural interaction. If this approach is rejected, we can presume that there would be a danger in a proposed intercultural model that would systematically and implicitly promote a particular agent model (e.g., abstract individualism, a collective moral agent, and networked individuality) and as a result ideologically restrict other cultures.

Second, epistemological interculturality tends to systemise intercultural value-interaction through a dichotomised thinking towards a predefined concept of interculturality, which articulates interculturality on one side by eradicating, suppressing, or taking precautions against the other side. In other words, a dualistic and linear approach can be used to encourage us to develop a methodical system that facilitates participants' engagement in intercultural value-interactions and identifies emergent values as a result of its ongoing system development. If this process is rejected, we can presume that participants' self-reflection on intercultural interaction is improperly practised or attempt to protect or promote a particular value that cannot be negotiable.

Third, holistic interculturality can be used to expose the ontology of value networks that our minds are interrelated and interconnected, and this holistic individualism sublates egocentric and atomistic mindsets. In a holistic approach to value networks, things are understood within a whole-part relationship, not

Interculturality of non-Western cultures   173

a part-whole relationship, and there is no redundancy and no inconsistency between them. This implies that holistic interculturality focuses on how values are embedded to hold the mind in the networks, which protects individuals from wishful and delusional ideologies of atomism and dehumanisation. If this perspective is rejected, we can presume that we are trapped in either of the following: a dualistic approach drives us to keep pursuing its parts only by ignoring a whole or our monistic values motivate us to be virtuous men who have no interest in understanding interculturality. Such productivity indicates some methodological requirements for participants in intercultural interaction: (a) ontological approach: the revelation of networked individuality is to realise our individuality determined by our engagement in value networks through our multilayered self; (b) epistemological approach: the practice of open rationality is our awareness that our multilayered self is reproduced in accordance with our intended engagement in value networks, and emergent values arising from our participation in intercultural interaction help us see larger parts of value networks; and (c) axiological approach: our involvement in the multiple realities of value networks is required to develop and negotiate for sharable moral values or frameworks. Without presuming these approaches in Western education systems, for example, we may uncritically participate in ideological reproduction of the dominant culture and its value system.

References

Akhter, S. (2009). *Faith and philosophy of Islam*. New Delhi: Gyan Publishing House.
Bakar, O. (2011). Islamic science, modern science, and post-modernity: Towards a new synthesis through a Tawhidic epistemology. *Revelation and Science, 1*(3), 13–20.
Biswas, N.B. (2007). Knowledge and pedagogy: An essential proposition in response to teacher preparation. *US-China Education Review, 4*(7), 1–14.
Bourke, C., Bourke, E., & Edwards, B. (1994). *Aboriginal Australia: An introductory reader in Aboriginal studies*. Brisbane: University of Queensland Press.
Department of Education and Training. (2011). *Embedding Aboriginal and Torres Strait Islander perspectives in schools: A guide for school learning communities*. Queensland Government, Australia. Retrieved from http://indigenous.education.qld.gov.au/SiteCollectionDocuments/eatsips-docs/eatsips_2011.pdf
Garfield, J.L. (Trans. and comm.) (1995). *The fundamental wisdom of the Middle Way: Nāgārjuna's Mulamadhyamakakarika*. New York/Oxford: Oxford University Press.
Grieves, V. (2009). *Aboriginal spirituality: Aboriginal philosophy, the basis of Aboriginal social and emotional wellbeing*. Casuarina, NT: Cooperative Research Centre for Aboriginal Health. Retrieved from http://www.lowitja.org.au/sites/default/files/docs/DP9-Aboriginal-Spirituality.pdf
Griffin, R. (2003). Shattering crystals: The role of 'Dream Time' in extreme right-wing political violence. *Terrorism and Political Violence, 15*(1), 57–94.
Gyatso, G.K. (2011). *Modern Buddhism: The path of compassion and wisdom* (Volume 1: Sutra). New York: Tharpa Publications.
Hacker, P. (2006). Dharma in Hinduism. *Journal of Indian Philosophy, 34*(5), 479–496.

174 *Intercultural valuism*

Huang, P.Z. (2009). *Confronting Confucian understandings of the Christian doctrine of salvation: A systematic theological analysis of the basic problems in the confucian-christian dialogue.* Leiden, Netherlands: BRILL.

Hughes, P., & More, A.J. (1997). *Aboriginal ways of learning and learning styles.* In the Annual Conference of the Australian Association for Research in Education (AARE). Brisbane. Retrieved from http://publications.aare.edu.au/97pap/hughp518.htm

Hussien, S. (2007). Critical pedagogy, Islamisation of knowledge and Muslim education. *Intellectual Discourse, 15*(1), 85–104.

Izutsu, T. (2007). *The concept and reality of existence.* Kuala Lumpur: Islamic Book Trust.

Kamali, M.H. (2005). *A text of Hadith studies: Authenticity, compilation, classification and criticism of Hadith.* Wiltshire, UK: The Islamic Foundation.

Khenchen, V., Rinpoche, T., & Lharampa, G. (2001). *The twelve links of interdependent origination.* (G. Hollmann & K. Holmes, Trans.). Crestone, CO: Namo Buddha Publications.

MacKenzie, M. (2013). Enacting selves, enacting worlds: On the Buddhist theory of karma. *Philosophy East and West, 63*(2), 194–212.

Martin, K. (2012). Aboriginal early childhood: Past, present, and future. In J. Phillips & J. Lampert (Eds.), *Introductory Indigenous Studies in Education: Reflection and the Importance of Knowing* (2nd ed.) (pp. 26–39). Sydney, Australia: Pearson.

McLoughlin, C., & Oliver, R. (2000). Designing learning environments for cultural inclusivity: A case study of Indigenous online learning at tertiary level. *Australian Journal of Educational Technology, 16*(1), 58–72.

Middendorf, U. (2008). Again on Qing: With a translation of the Guodian Xing zi ming chu. *Oriens Extremus, 47*, 97–159.

Mishra, R.C. (2013). Moksha and the Hindu worldview. *Psychology and Developing Societies, 25*(1), 21–42.

Mitchell, S. (Trans.) (1995). *Tao Te Ching.* Retrieved from http://acc6.its.brooklyn.cuny.edu/~phalsall/texts/taote-v3.html

Monroe, M.H. (2013). *The afterlife in Aboriginal Australia.* Australia: The Land Where Time Began. Retrieved from http://austhrutime.com/afterlife.htm

Nagatomo, S. (2010). Japanese Zen Buddhist philosophy. In E.N. Zalta (Ed.), *The Stanford Encyclopedia of Philosophy* (Winter 2010 ed.). Retrieved from http://plato.stanford.edu/archives/win2010/entries/japanese-zen/

Park, J.Y. (2009). A conceptual framework for a systematic mapping of layout design principles by using Yin and Yang theory. *Design Principles and Practices: An International Journal, 3*(1), 369–382.

Penny, S. (1995). *Discovering religions – Hinduism.* Oxford: Heinemann.

Riegel, J. (2013). Confucius. In E.N. Zalta (Ed.), *The Stanford Encyclopedia of Philosophy* (Summer 2013 ed.). Retrieved from http://plato.stanford.edu/archives/sum2013/entries/confucius/

Rifai, S.R.A. (2015). *The Islamic Journal |04|: From Islamic Civilisation to the Heart of Islam, Ihsan, Human Perfection.* SunnahMuakada.wordpress.com Retrieved from https://sunnahmuakadasupplementary.files.wordpress.com/2015/08/the-islamic-jounral-04.pdf

Rizvim, S.M. (2006). *Islam: Faith, practice & history.* Qum, Iran: Ansariyan Publications.

Rosemont, H., & Ames, R.T. (2009). *The Chinese classic of family reverence: A philosophical translation of the Xiaojing.* Honolulu: University of Hawaii Press.

Rukmani, T.S. (2008). Philosophical hermeneutics within a darśana (philosophical school). *Journal of Hindu Studies, 1*(1–2), 120–137. doi:10.1093/jhs/hin003

Seiju. (2008). Looking and seeing. *Kai Han, 8*(2), 1 & 6. Retrieved from http://www.azc.org/wp-content/uploads/2013/08/2008July.pdf

Siddhartha. (2008). Open-source Hinduism. *Religion and the Arts, 12*(1–3), 34–34.

Tomhave, A. (2010). Cartesian intuitions, human puzzles, and the Buddhist conception of the self. *Philosophy East and West, 60*(4), 443–457.

Westerhoff, J.C. (2010). Nāgārjuna. In E.N. Zalta (Ed.), *The Stanford Encyclopedia of Philosophy* (Fall 2010 ed.). Retrieved from http://plato.stanford.edu/archives/fall2010/entries/nagarjuna/

Wong, D. (2013). Chinese Ethics. In E.N. Zalta (Ed.), *The Stanford Encyclopedia of Philosophy* (Spring 2013 ed.). Retrieved from http://plato.stanford.edu/archives/spr2013/entries/ethics-chinese/

9 Pedagogical interculturality

In contemporary Western education, dominant epistemologies are objectivism, pragmatism, and interpretivism and relevant learning theories are behaviourism, cognitivism, and constructivism, respectively. These have formed the basis of many of today's pedagogical branches. In other cultures, there are Confucian virtuological pedagogy, Islamic totalistic pedagogy, Aboriginal holistic pedagogy, Hindu spiritual pedagogy, and Buddhist mindful pedagogy. These are strategically and ideologically used to promote cultural/religious values and are practised in special/religious (ethnic) schools because the governments of most countries have adopted Western education models (e.g., Bhutanese *Gross National Happiness* and Thai *Green and Happy Society*). What we call *ethnic pedagogies* (like *cultures*, *pedagogies* and *knowledges* have become countable general nouns in cross-cultural contexts) is partly adopted for multicultural education or inclusion of indigenous people in postcolonial societies (i.e., Aboriginal holistic education). In this context, contemporary pedagogies refer to widely known educational theories based on modern Western education systems. In this chapter, I will argue for pedagogical understandings of intercultural value networks through reviewing objectivist, constructivist, and critical pedagogical theories, as well as ethnic pedagogies, and I will describe what pedagogical interculturality looks like.

9.1 Western pedagogies and interculturality

Jörga, Davisc, and Nickmansa (2007) argue that educational research has been in crisis partly because it is a victim of fundamentalism with "positivistic, objectivistic, deterministic, individualistic, dualistic, and reductionistic characteristics" (p. 147). They point out that educational research has adopted research frames of other fields such as psychology, sociology, literary criticism, and cultural studies, which are characterised by the "calculable and predictable" based on the age of Enlightenment. They also assert that this is "a wrong copy based on a wrong notion of the natural sciences itself" (p. 147). Kettley (2010) ascribes this to dualism that has been reproduced through epistemological parochialism (e.g., parsimonious approach to objectivism and constructivism) and lack of epistemological breaks in education studies (e.g., partial definitions, neglecting the history of ideas, and personal favouritism for a particular methodology). Kettley also points out that methodologies in social science tend to treat the meaning

Pedagogical interculturality 177

of objective knowledge by assuming that the existence of the real world can be analysed through empirical testing of a hypothesis, independent of researchers' subjective interpretation. To overcome dualism, Jörga *et al.* (2007) propose that researchers need to develop a theory of complexity based on a transphenomenal frame that goes beyond our old ideas and habits of thinking – dualism and reductionism. They argue that a transphenomenal frame should result in a transdisciplinary and interdiscursive approach. Jörga *et al.*'s and Kettley's arguments on the crisis of education studies are pointing out the absence of ontology that will be seen in various Western pedagogical theories.

9.1.1 Objectivist pedagogy and interculturality

Objectivism influenced by early behaviourism assumes an ontological belief that the world is relatively fixed and real and exists outside of an individual (Schuh & Barab, 2008). For objectivists knowing means that an individual engages in specific behaviours in contexts of particular stimuli (Schuh & Barab, 2008, p. 73). Skinner's behaviourism still widely impacts education today in line with reinforcement theories, behaviour modification theories, and social development theories. Skinner (1958) states, "behavior is shown to be shaped and maintained by its 'reinforcing' consequences rather than elicited as conditioned or unconditioned response to stimuli" (p. 972). In this sense, an instructional context can be planned and programmed towards predetermined outcomes or desired behaviour, and this can be conditioned by a reinforcer, which can increase frequency or probability for a specific defined outcome (Schuh & Barab, 2008). For behaviourists, learning is conceived as a process of changing or conditioning observable outcomes that are indicative of individuals' responses to instructions. In other words, the student mind is seen as *a tabula rasa* and a teacher's role is to transmit knowledge to the blank slate. Hence this highly teacher-directed instructional strategy defines teaching as transmitting interpreted knowledge from a teacher to students and learning as replicating it in students' minds (Jonassen, 1991). This process assumes that the real world consists of entities structured based on their properties and relations as abstract symbols (Schuh & Barab, 2008), and symbols are representations of reality so that the real world can be modelled (Jonassen, 1991). Such an objectivist approach to education as teacher-centred and knowledge transmission may possibly result in a stereotyped image of education.

Objectivism is typically associated with positivism, reductionism, and dualism. In research processes, positivists pursue objectivity in which they believe they can produce objective knowledge or discover an objective truth or reality (Taylor & Medina, 2011). This means that we must remain objective as an outsider, an independent observer, and a controller of research processes (Creswell, 2003). In research of social science, for example, our subjectivity should not be allowed to impact on research processes, as it would lead to an invalid picture of reality (Taylor & Medina, 2011). Post-positivists express their concern about interactions between researchers and participants by applying additional qualitative methods in social science and arguing that epistemology manifests through quasi-experimental research design that triangulates data, methods, and theories

178 *Intercultural valuism*

for objectivity, validity, and reliability (Taylor & Medina, 2011). This argument is consistent with reductionism in which they tend to describe social phenomena primarily in terms of psychological or individual properties. In this sense, they deny that social structures are deterministic factors and individuals' actions are associated with social structures. Their underlying epistemological assumptions are that individuals are the only driving power of history and society, and collective entities cannot exist as independent substances. As they do not accept a social structure as an object of study, they believe that teachers should follow correct sequences of learning designed by curricula and achieve pre-set learning objectives (Vrasidas, 2000). In this sense, learning is defined as development of students' cognition and behaviour through effective transfer of objective knowledge into their minds (Vrasidas, 2000).

Such a dualistic approach to the mind and the world and the known and the knower supports teacher-centred education. It assumes that there is only one true and correct reality that we can come to know only through objective methods and sequential processes. In this sense, a culture is only valid when it is suited for knowledge that a teacher predetermines. In intercultural value networks, then, objectivist pedagogy tends to facilitate practice of mono-culture or culturism. This means that objectivists (a) reject the existence of value networks and (b) perceive that a culture is merely a by-product of activities of individuals and has little or no impact on our minds. They also presume that (c) we cannot extract values from facts or there is no relationship between values and facts, and as a result, and (d) interculturality cannot develop from intercultural interaction. To convince objectivists of the existence of interculturality, hence, interculturality needs to be presented at least as a scientifically proven reality or a logical-metaphysical system that produces new pedagogical values for a culturally diverse environment.

9.1.2 Constructivist pedagogy and interculturality

Piaget's individual cognitive constructivism and Vygotsky's socio-cultural constructivism are often contrasted with each other.

Cognitive constructivists' fundamental tenet is that individual learners build knowledge from their own experiences using their cognitive mechanisms (Levy, 1997). Piaget (1953; 1970; 1980) argues that learners learn through *assimilation* and *accommodation* processes. The former refers to a process of adjustment to a new experience based on learners' existing mental schema, whereas the latter refers to revisions of existing schemas. These two complementary processes are regarded as evidence of learners' cognitive development. For cognitive constructivists, a critical point is that individuals learn at different rates and in different ways because they have different experiences (Cobb, 2005). This implies that personalised learning is one of the core pedagogical values in cognitive constructivism (Meyer, 2012). In this context, a teacher becomes a facilitator who is capable of providing "comprehensible input" and opportunities for learners to participate in "meaningful and communicative activities" (Lamy & Hampel, 2007, p. 20). However, this view is criticised to the extent that, as Barker (2008) argues, cognitive constructivists tend to ignore other significant

Pedagogical interculturality 179

factors influencing learning processes including individual learners' competence, classroom discourse, and institutional and social settings.

On the other hand, socio-cultural constructivists emphasise the significance of social and cultural contexts in learning processes. Vygotsky (1930–34/1978) argues that social aspects of learning are primary, whereas individual attributes are derivative and secondary. He insists that social interaction determines individuals' mental functioning and perceptual development and, hence, a specific learning structure and process can be traced. Three underlying concepts of socio-cultural constructivism are known as mediation, zone of proximal development (ZPD), and social learning (Berk, 2002; Palincsar, 1998). First, human action is mediated by tools and signs rather than directly interacting with the physical world. A post-Vygotskian, Lantolf (2000) divides tools into psychological tools (number, music, arts, and language) and physical tools (materials, labour, and tools) and argues that through these tools, learners can generate higher mental capacities including logical and critical thinking and problem solving. He also argues that a higher form of human mental activity is mediated by others, cultural artefacts, and the learner; therefore, collaboration and communication with others are considered key forms of mediated learning. Second, in this sense, it is assumed that relationships between learners and socio-cultural factors are captured in ZPD. Vygotsky (1930–34/1978) defines ZPD as follows: "[ZPD is] the distance between the actual development level as determined by independent problem solving and the level of potential development as determined through problem solving under adult guidance or in collaboration with more capable peers" (pp. 86–87). ZPD is often understood as a scaffolding teaching strategy that Berk defines as

> a changing quality of support over a teaching session in which adults adjust the assistance they provide to fit the child's current level of performance. Direct instruction is offered when a task is new; less help is provided as competence increases.
>
> (Berk, 2002, p. 261)

The presumption of ZPD is that people can co-construct meaning and knowledge when they work together, and they achieve more as a result of emerging expertise from their group work (Jonassen, Davidson, Collins, Campbell, & Haag, 1995). As Corden (1992) and Hammond and Gibbons (2001) stress, we should not regard ZPD as an attribute of learners but as an attribute of each learning interaction. This means that the essential feature of learning is to create a new ZPD based on quality of socio-cultural interaction with others by highlighting the fact that learning is situated. Third, social learning presumes that learning is regulated by social and cultural contexts in which knowledge is not seen as an independent reality (von Glasersfeld, 2005). Vygotsky (1930–34/1978) explains that learning occurs first through social interaction with others and social-cultural environments, and then learners internalise the learning process and outcome as knowledge. With their communities of practice theory, Lave and Wenger (1991) explain the process as situated learning and articulate it with three stages

180 *Intercultural valuism*

of enculturation from marginal participation, to peripheral participation, to full participation. They argue that learning is profoundly influenced by interpersonal, personal, and contextual factors that are embedded in a situated physical and socio-cultural context.

As seen in the two constructivism variants, constructivism assumes that (a) learners are active participants who apply new learning through active experimentation, (b) teachers are facilitators of learning experiences, and (c) knowledge is situated and a product of interaction with its context and culture. In this sense, the aim of education is to facilitate learners to investigate meanings and interpretations of social actors according to learners' understanding of and engagement in specific situations (Cordella & Shaikh, 2006; Freimuth, 2009). Hence the social world exists only inside the minds of learners, actors and reality are inseparable, and the world can be reconstructed through human interaction and meaningful action (Paul & Marfo, 2001). In this sense, a culture "is a system of shared beliefs, values, customs, behaviors, and artifacts that the members of society use to interact with their world and with one another" (Bates & Plog, 1990, p. 7). As Ernest (2004) describes, a deeper awareness and level of cultural understanding occurs in an interpreter's mind by which one interacts with cultural artefacts by distinguishing between oneself and a culture. Ernest (2004) further explains that constructivist approaches to cultures are determined by nominalism and conventionalism: for nominalists, understanding a culture refers to data collection from the object-to-be-known and a subjective data interpretation, whereas, for conventionalists, "all knowledge presuppositions are the results of different forms of accepted practices, agreement, or decision, and can all be questioned and reconsidered" (p. 27), which requires a more detailed and thorough analysis of a social situation. In this understanding, Ernest (2004) argues that for constructivists, learners and cultures are ontologically independent and there is little connection between them. Yet as the ontological connection is realised through knowledge manipulation and construction for an imaged world, *little connection* should be understood as *a different form of the connection*.

For interculturality, as Evanoff (2004) exemplifies, an educational approach is a dialogical process that encourages participants to criticise existing norms of their own culture and address common problems they face. Evanoff claims, as all norms are constructed and reconstructed in ways that we understand the world and interact with it, new norms and values can be constructed through intercultural interaction, and this may result in an entirely new perspective that is transcendental to us. Evanoff's study is a typical example of both nominalists and conventionalists being applied in social constructivism and legitimises emergent values developing from intercultural interaction. As Cordella and Shaikh (2006) point out, however, interpretivist aspects of constructivism restrict its further development. This is because constructivists consider reality as an outcome of an interpretation process and, as a result, they do not pay attention to the fact that the reality holds a reciprocal feedback and feedforward relationship between actors and reality. In practice, their pedagogical concern remains (a) committed to promoting categorical moral imperatives of individual learners towards cultural differences (b) without awareness that the imperatives have already been

Pedagogical interculturality 181

shaped by a dominant cultural framework. This is because their ontological belief, which is subjective social reality, advocates self-constructed reality and ignores that new values emerging from value-interaction affect our perception of social reality. In intercultural value networks, furthermore, constructivist pedagogy becomes relativistic and excludes learners from their engagement in interculturality because knowledge can be only valid in an individual learner's mentality. This means that constructivists tend to (a) emphasise fostering cognitive autonomy and self-evaluation skills and (b) devalue the fact that learners' cognition is structured by interacting with their own cultural values.

9.1.3 Critical pedagogy and interculturality

Early critical theorists are associated with the Frankfurt School that shares the "attempt to assess the newly emerging forms of capitalism along with the changing forms of domination that accompanied them" (Giroux, 1983, p. 50). Horkheimer (1982), who was a leader of the Frankfurt School, states the aim of critical theory is "to liberate human beings from the circumstances that enslave them" (p. 244) In education, it is used to practise critical pedagogy that emphasises the importance of questioning and challenging "the seeming obviousness, naturalness, immediacy, and simplicity of the world around us, and in particular, of what we are able to perceive through our senses and understand through the application of our powers of reason" (Nowlan, 2001, p. 2). The aim of critical pedagogy is to encourage learners "to question and challenge the social, racial and sexual oppression embedded in the education system and the very fibre of culture itself" (Bethel, 2006, p. 51). Giroux (1988) argues, "School practices need to be informed by a public philosophy that addresses how to construct ideological and institutional conditions in which the lived experience of empowerment for the vast majority of students becomes the defining feature of schooling" (p. 1). In this sense, critical pedagogy is about "how to provide a way of reading history as part of a larger project of reclaiming power and identity, particularly as these are shaped around the categories of race, gender, class, and ethnicity" (Giroux, 1988, p. 1).

Unlike objectivism and constructivism, critical theory and pedagogy draw on an ontological understanding of human beings in historically, socially, and culturally situated contexts. The Frankfurt School's view of human beings is as agents of history who can change themselves through critical self-reflection and thus formulate new conceptions of self and society (Fay, 1987). For example, Fay (1987) understands human beings as having four aspects: historical, social, rational, and active. As historical beings, individuals can change identity and society through self-reflection and self-interpretation. Historical beings are further divided into social, rational, and active beings: as social beings, individuals can change society through transformation of their social practices and relations; as rational beings, individuals have the ability to reflect on their social practices and relations; and as active beings, individuals can reconstruct their social practices and relations based on their own rational reflection. An underlying assumption of these aspects is that individual change is directly interrelated to social

182 *Intercultural valuism*

change. Thus, for critical theorists and educators, cultural change is not exceptional because historical beings shaped by social and cultural environments can change their culture through self-reflection and self-interpretation. This rationalistic perspective of human beings is supported by Habermas's (1968/1971) theory of knowledge constitutive interests. Habermas argues that human interest generates three primary generic cognitive areas of knowledge that determine categories related to what we interpret as knowledge. First, work knowledge refers to instrumental action that allows people to control and manipulate their environments. Its domain is created based primarily on empirical investigation and is also governed by technical rules. Its predominant methodology is empirical-analytic science using hypothetical-deductive theories. Second, practical knowledge refers to social interaction in that the knowledge is governed by social norms. Its practical domain is used to identify what is appropriate action based on communication and intersubjectivity of mutual understanding of intentions through empirical or analytical propositions. Third, emancipatory knowledge refers to emancipation through self-reflection and self-knowledge. "Emancipation is from libidinal, institutional or environmental forces which limit our options and rational control over our lives but have been taken for granted as beyond human control" (Mezirow, 1981, p. 5). Knowledge obtained through critical self-awareness is emancipatory, and, as a result, its process results in a transformation of consciousness. In the context that knowledge is historically, socially, culturally, politically, and economically constructed, critical pedagogy educators claim that Habermas's theory of knowledge constitutive interests makes human beings more conscious and aware of their own existing beliefs and views (e.g., Giroux, 1983; Mezirow, 1981; Murphy & Fleming, 2012; Torres & Morrow, 1998).

Critical theorists emphasise the role of education that liberates, enlightens, empowers, and emancipates individuals. Habermas's transformed consciousness can be found in Freire's (1970/2000) *Pedagogy of the Oppressed*. For Freire, self-directed, appropriate education through critical self-reflection (i.e., *become conscientisation* (Crotty, 1998)) as one of the methods to empower the oppressed should be aimed at educating both the oppressors and the oppressed in order for them to see how capitalism reification dehumanises them. Freire stress a cultural synthesis of the oppressors and the oppressed:

> Instead of following predetermined plans, leaders and people, mutually identified, together create the guidelines of their action. In this synthesis, leaders and people are somehow reborn in new knowledge and new action. Knowledge of the alienated culture leads to transforming action resulting in *a culture* which is being freed from alienation. The more sophisticated knowledge of the leaders is remade in the empirical knowledge of the people, while the latter is refined by the former.
>
> (Freire, 1970/2000, p. 181 [emphasis added])

In this context, a culture has two meanings: one is a collective identity of individuals that needs to be reflected in culturally sensitive inclusion – *cultural identity* – and the other is one of the key categories alongside race, gender, class, and ethnicity that needs to explore how it has been structured – *cultural formation*. The notions of cultural identity and cultural formation are consistent in Freire's codifications and decodifications of cultural action in line with Habermas's emancipatory knowledge. In literacy learning, which is the primary practice of emancipatory knowledge for him, codifications refer to representative images that the words students read represent problematic social conditions, whereas decodifications refer to "a reading of social dynamics and forces of reaction or change" (Burbules & Rupert, 1999, p. 45). For Freire, codification is "reflecting an existential situation must objectively constitute a totality. Its elements must interact in the makeup of the whole", whereas decodification is "externalize[ing] their thematics and thereby make explicit their *real consciousness* of the world" (1970/2000, p. 115 [emphasis in original]). In practice, decodifications raise the consciousness of people that tests mistaken beliefs and distorted perceptions against the truth and is the ground for "*structures of oppression* and *relations of domination*" (Burbules & Rupert, 1999, p. 53 [emphasis in original]). The assumption of Freire's emancipatory knowledge is to educate critical, reflexive individuals who are able to decodify texts and the world and have willpower to change education; otherwise, the structure for the oppressors will not be altered. In other words, it distinguishes between the world controlled by the oppressors and the oppressed and encourages individuals on both sides to be critical and active towards social injustices and ideological and institutionalised inequality.

For critical theorists, (the dominant ideology of a) culture is an important domain of oppression like race, class, and gender and thus it is their centrality in teaching and learning. They argue that students should be able to describe their own ethno-cultural backgrounds and stereotypes of other ethnic groups, and as activists, they should seek social and cultural transformation of schools for the oppressed. Based on cultural Marxism, a goal of critical pedagogy is social transformation that aims to construct social justice at a collective level. Like constructivism, critical theorists stress that cultures are socially constructed and relations must be interpreted, which challenges logical positivism. However, while constructivists are primarily interested in individual actions in light of genuine activists as agents, critical theorists are more interested in understanding relationships between societal structures and ideological patterns of thought, which confronts injustice and oppression and changes unjust social systems (Freire, 1970/2000). Such double standards for a culture are a result of the dichotomy of the preservation of (the oppressed) culture and the transformation of (the oppressors) culture. This dichotomy is problematic in that (a) it tends to regard intercultural interaction as a propaganda campaign and/or rejects interculturality as a new whole – in a response similar to that of interpretivism constructivists – and thus (b) an ontological presumption of critical theorists seeks to analyse possibilities and limits of (oppressed) individuals within (the oppressor) culture rather than to understand cultural identity and formation as a whole in value networks. Some arguments, including Fay's four aspects of human beings, Habermas's three knowledge categories, and Freire's codification and decodification, have the potential to approach value networks as they propose multilayered

184   *Intercultural valuism*

reality and individuals' diverse engagement. However, they believe that a culture is epistemologically conceptualised rather than ontologically understood and axiologically topographicalised in value networks because they do not distinguish between intersubjectivity and interobjectivity.

9.2 Monistic pedagogies and interculturality

As seen in the previous chapter, Confucian heritage culture (CHC) and Islam heritage culture (IHC) hold strong monistic or axiological metaphysics in which both reduce cultural activities to the third entity and substance – *oneness*. Epistemologically, they tend to understand cultural phenomena as outcomes of the dynamic interaction between humans and oneness (Nature or God). In this sense, both also highly emphasise axiological understanding of human nature, and moralism is an educational foundation. In this context, their pedagogical values are characterised by memorisation and recitation, autonomous interdependence, and lifehood.

First, an interpretation of personified sayings that appear in the classics and the holy books (In CHC, the classics are also called holy books, 聖經, 經典) requires study through memorisation and recitation. Otherwise, one's interpretation may rely too much on personal understandings, and one's situational application could be of no benefit to communities. In this sense, their dominant instructions are repetition, memorisation, and recitation (Biggs, 1998; Diallo, 2012). In CHC, repetition refers to deep-memorisation and repetitive learning, ensuring accurate recall of the classics (Biggs, 1998). In IHC, recitation, especially at the initial stages of learning, involves the "complete mastery of memorisation of the Qur'ān" (Diallo, 2012). Such learning styles are known as surface learning or rote learning in Western education because students are supposed to listen and memorise answers rather than to construct knowledge. Such a misunderstandings arise because of different teacher roles. In both CHC and IHC, teachers are expected to use various teaching methods to *push* students for high-cognitive-level thought processes by implementing provocative questions and reflections to suit individual students. For example, Islamic religious leaders, *Imams*, not only lead prayer and teach people, but also need to be role models in their communities and the sources of Islamic laws (Nigerian, 2004; Rosowsky, 2008). In the learning environment, teachers are expected to mutually participate in learning and provide personalised learning by having comprehensive considerations of individual learners' spiritual and socio-economic environments (Nigerian, 2004; Rosowsky, 2008). This is why reverence and authority are given to teachers/leaders for their status in social and moral hierarchy and students are to obey their teachers with little or no resistance (Biggs, 1998; Nigerian, 2004). In Western education systems, CHC and IHC pedagogies are also perceived as teacher-centred approaches and result-oriented learning because they promote learning with fixed and decontextualised knowledge (Biggs, 1998; Diallo, 2012). However, it is noted that those traditional pedagogies have been marginalised because Western knowledge became the only legitimate system of learning and schooling, and Western epistemology dominates most Eastern Asian academic systems (Wu, 2011). Hence we need to understand the contemporary pedagogy as "the result of a cultural interaction embedding modern Western epistemology into a traditional Eastern framework" (Wu, 2011, p. 571).

Second, autonomous interdependence is used to encourage learners to realise and practise collective values and beliefs with their own willpower. Autonomous interdependence is not a stand-alone value but a collective subjectivity in which both cultures encourage individuals to exercise the full range of subjectivity through collegial encouragement and mutual management. CHC and IHC encourage individuals to accept their spontaneous reduction of individual differences for their ultimate values (e.g., Taoist *WuWei*, Confucian *Virtues*, and Muslim *Tawhidic*). These monistic pedagogies place less emphasis on independent beings, but more emphasis on collective beings because the variety of existing things are to merge into a single reality or substance (e.g., *Nature, the Way*, and *Tawhid*). The ultimate goal is to attain external harmony with collective subjectivities, although practical methods of Confucianism, Taoism, and Islam differ: Taoism is all about humans' relationships with nature, Confucianism is about humans' relationships with others, and Islam is about humans' vicegerent roles of God and *Ummah* (brotherhood). In this monistic ontology, there is no such thing as outside of the universe. Hence Taoism extends its epistemic into the human body, precisely human biology and well-being. Confucianism develops social axiology and moralism, and Islamic education highlights both personal and social development and transformation towards the universal God's vicegerents (Berkey, 2007). As active meaning-makers, every Muslim needs to perform given duties as God's vicegerents according to one's situatedness (Hussien, 2007). A common focus of these monistic pedagogies is not on a degree of freedom for *individuals*, but on *conditions of life* to be naturally harmonised with the oneness.

Third, due to moral collectivism of lifehood, education of both cultures is aimed at filling the gaps between individuals through *interobjective* transformation of individuals – interobjectivity here means that cultural values per se educate individuals to follow social spirituality and roles assigned by the oneness, and values manifest through individuals' sharing processes (e.g., many Asian parents are more interested in ensuring that their children are ready to learn [rather than that schools are ready for children], although there is no mutual communication or social agreement between parents and teachers). Monistic cultures explicitly nominalise virtues in line with role ethics and specify practical values for human relationships and moral responsibilities at a subtle level. "Confucius applied the term 'ritual' to actions beyond formal sacrifices and religious ceremonies to include social rituals: courtesies and accepted standards of behaviour – what we today call social mores" (Shakir, 2008, n.p.). For example, Confucius's *The Great Learning* describes the following:

> The way of great learning lies in manifesting bright virtue, in regard for the people, and in walking the way of the highest good. . . .
> Those who desired to establish rulership over their own state first brought their family into harmony.

186 *Intercultural valuism*

Those who desired to bring their family into harmony first cultivated themselves.

Those who desired to cultivate themselves first rectified their minds.

Those who desired to rectify their minds first made their thought sincere.

Those who desired to make their thoughts sincere first increase their knowledge.

Increase one's knowledge is based on analysing the physical world.

When the physical world is analysed, supreme knowledge is gained.

When supreme knowledge is gained, ideas become sincere.

When ideas become sincere, the mind is rectified. . . .

When rulership over the state has been established, there will be peace among all things under heaven.

(Chapter 33, as translated in Richter, 2005)

In this sense, CHC education emphasises that ritual and moral duties in an individual, a family, and a state elevate all people to the highest level or a higher form of moralism. On the other hand, Muslims believe that "the destiny of the religion of Islam [is] to play the role of synthesiser in the last age of humanity", and "Islam is meant for the whole of mankind" (Bakar, 2011, pp. 14–15). Hence the principle of *Tawhid* is its synthesis agenda, and it is universal in nature and global in scope (Bakar, 2011, p. 15). In practice, Muslim *Ummah* transcends all these boundaries of socio-economic status, linguistic background, ethnicity, and nationality, and thus Muslims all around the world must face the same *Kaaba* (a cuboid building in *Mecca* considered by Muslims everywhere to be the most sacred spot on Earth) five times a day, which confirms their brotherhood. Muslims believe that God created Islamic brotherhood and fraternity and, thus, cultural and economic disparity must be resolved through collective charities. The six rights of Muslims as practical guides show how collectivistic culture of Muslim brotherhood has been practised in their moral systems. In the Qur'ān, the six rights Muslims have over each other are as follows:

11. Let not a group scoff at another group, it may be that the latter are better than the former; nor let (some) women scoff at other women, it may be that the latter are better than the former, nor defame one another, nor insult one another by nicknames. . . . How bad is it, to insult one's brother after having Faith . . . 12. Avoid much suspicions, indeed some suspicions are sins. And spy not, neither backbite one another. Would one of you like to eat the flesh of his dead brother? You would hate it (so hate backbiting).

(49: 11 and 12, as translated by Khan & Al-Hilali, 1999)

The first three rights indicate what mindset an individual Muslim must hold towards other Muslims. Verse 11 ends with the following statement, "And those who (commit such sins and) do not ask forgiveness, they are the unjust people." This verse emphasises that Muslims are spiritually connected with each other regardless of their physical appearance, and, as just people, they should bear brother-in-faith in mind. The last three rights indicate how individual Muslims behave towards other Muslims. Such a spiritually and morally connected collectivistic feature of brotherhood is further enhanced by avoiding the three sins – suspicion, spying, and backbiting. In CHC and IHC, interobjective transformation of brotherhood in line with their ultimate concerns involves stringing together individual differences and increasing individuals' morality and virtues to sustain unified, harmonised community.

Although researchers and educators of both pedagogies complain about negative impacts of Western culture and industrialisation on their beliefs and values, much of their cultural heritages are still retained in contemporary education and actively preserved by their cultural practices in their daily lives (Bakar, 2011; Wu, 2011). Regardless of ideological aspects of cultural preservations, most Chinese people are proud to be called descendants of Confucius, and Muslims practise their rigid religious/cultural mores in their daily lives. Although Western dualistic educational systems have permeated all levels of society, their cultural and pedagogical values continue to promote high moral expectations against secularism and emphasise collective selfhood and lifehood. Yet their metaphysical *oneness* may lead to further enhance interdependent individuality or promote insularly and locally collective selfishness to preserve their values against the permeation of Western values. In this sense, monistic pedagogies may be ineffective in improving individuals' independence and self-driven creative capability, which may result in high totalism when individuality is continually overwhelmed by highly structured and collective moralism.

The high morality of CHC and IHC has ideological and hegemonic functions to sustain their values such as rote learning, autonomous interdependence, and lifehood transformation. Hence individual learners' needs are subservient to those of community as a whole unless they enhance or merge into the *oneness*. In early childhood education, monistic pedagogies facilitate children to practise basic knowledge and build moral intelligence based on harmony with nature or human nature given by *Tao, Tian*, or *God*, which resultantly leads to a reduction of individual differences. In adulthood education, monistic pedagogies continue to facilitate individual autonomy to practise the highest status of moralism in one's family and communities. In particular, teachers are required to be role models of practicing humanness and righteousness in community and mentors of morality and ethics. In this way, teachers' social authority is formed and given by collective will that represents the *oneness* and the role of teachers is to realise an organic totality of human relations and its embedment in individual learners.

Such collectivistic moralism and totalism tend to prevent individuals from participating in interculturality by applying the ultimate concern into an interobjective process and axiological activism (i.e., the indefinable Tao, the flow of the universe energy, God's vicegerents) in the historic world. In intercultural value networks, on the other hand, monistic pedagogies can facilitate moral values of individuals when their moral/historic orientation reaches consensus towards intercultural interaction. In other words, interculturality has to be formed to provide an interobjective transformation of community. Monistic pedagogies also advocate co-creation of values when a goal in line with self-cultivation and community prosperity is shared and opens up their interobjective sphere for all people from culturally diverse backgrounds. This can be the axiological foundations for

188   *Intercultural valuism*

interculturality. Collective moral responsibilities can promote collective creativity and reduce totalism if intercultural interaction is facilitated by epistemological interculturality and is upheld by ontological interculturality.

9.3 Holistic pedagogies and interculturality

Holistic education and pedagogies are found in Hinduism, Buddhism, and indigenous education in Australia, Canada, New Zealand, and the U.S.A., and also in anti-racist and anti-oppressive education. Holistic education is known as an alternative educational system in which learners are encouraged to take intellectual, emotional, social, physical, and spiritual development into consideration as a whole (Behrendt, Larkin, Griew, & Kelly, 2012). Holistic educators ensure that each learner finds the meaning of life in connection with community, nature, and humanitarian values. Hence, the aim of holistic education is to nurture the development of the whole person by recognising the interconnectedness of body, mind, emotions, and spirit (Behrendt *et al.*, 2012). Metaphysically, holism is often regarded as a thesis that a whole is more than the sum of its parts and thus, methodologically, a whole can be sought by values or principles that govern and control such a complex system. In this sense, holism is often used to criticise a hierarchical model of the Western education system, particularly its dualism and reductionism (de Plevitz, 2007).

In education, a holistic mode of thinking is used to emphasise interconnectedness of all living things and to facilitate students' personal and collective engagement and responsibility in their selfhood and lifehood. To Australian Indigenous people, for example, the source of education is their collective lifehood stages: childhood, young adulthood, adulthood, and elderhood (Martin, 2012). Each stage entails gaining and living knowledge and skills, which allows individuals as parts of a whole to exist through their interconnected and interrelated identities (Dumont, 2005). Thus learning cannot occur in a binary system, as it engenders exclusion, isolation, and separation (Martin, 2012). The centeredness of Aboriginiety affirms that Australian Indigenous people are primarily motivated by their collectivistic consciousness; Aboriginal capacity to total responsiveness that they recognise their function from spirit, mind, and body as inseparable entities; and responsiveness and connectedness to a collective whole that is located at a high place in their value hierarchy (Park & Lee Hong, 2013, p. 40). In this sense, Aboriginal thinking and being are less effective for logical, linear, and analytic processes and in dualistic, individualistic systems (Sonn, Bishop, & Humphries, 2000). de Plevitz (2007) also argues that a hierarchical model of Western society is incompatible with Indigenous culture and "this mismatch produces feelings of alienation, which are manifested in students dropping out, poor attendance, low self-esteem and under-achieving" (p. 60). This indicates an epistemological limitation of Western education that tends to focus on Indigenous deficits in a dualistic system rather than their comparability with Western culture. Western schooling systems typically use instructional methods consistent with patterns that are only applicable to a dualistic culture (Rasmussen, Sherman, & Baydala, 2004). In practice, students are supposed to pay attention to structural distinctions between languages, communities, and cultures so that knowledge construction focuses on individuals' capabilities of critical, creative, and analytical thinking, and effective problem solving against the natural world. Christie (2005) argues that such learning styles do not properly work for Indigenous people because Aboriginal metaphysics has no such dualistic distinction and their knowledge construction is more social, negotiated work based on their collective memory practices and traditions. In this sense, Aboriginal education emphasises "interconnected pedagogies that see teaching and learning as fundamentally holistic, non-linear, visual, kinaesthetic, and contextualised" (Yunkaporta, 2009, p. 10). Interestingly, the same results can be found in transitional groups who had more contact with Western culture and education (Kleinfeld, 1971; Rasmussen *et al.*, 2004).

Indigenous holistic learning is aligned with observational and experiential learning that enables people to exercise a whole-community-focused approach (Yunkaporta, 2009). Thus visual-spatial ability is more demanded than verbal or auditory ability (Yunkaporta & McGinty, 2009). Visual discernment, visual memory, and spatial skills of Indigenous children substantially outperform Caucasian students (Rasmussen *et al.*, 2004; Yunkaporta, 2009). As Hughes, More, and Williams (2004) articulate in their model of pedagogy based on four sets of bipolar adjectives (Indigenous vs. non-Indigenous), there are clear differences such as *global-analytic, verbal-imaginal, concrete-abstract, and trial/feedback-reflective*. Yunkaporta and Kirby (2011) also assert that these pedagogies bring Indigenous ways of knowing and being "out of the dusty corners of anthropology and linguistics" and into the learning environment (p. 206). Aboriginal learning refers to how an individual's sense of worth fits in community life and values, and the reverse (self-driven or egoistic) is not acceptable (Hughes *et al.*, 2004). Consequently, it can be confirmed that Aboriginal culture places a greater emphasis on individuals' efforts for connectedness and relatedness to community.

Hindu regards a human being as an amalgam of all elements that cannot be kept apart: a physical, mental, and spiritual being, but predominantly as a spiritual being. Like Aboriginal's concept of lifehood, Hindu education conceives the entire course of human life that is composed of four successive stages: studentship, householders, hermits, and homeless wanderers. In this context, education aims at the emancipation of individual students through *sarvana, manana,* and *nididhyasana*: "Sarvana means listening to the words or texts from the teacher or Guru; manana means deliberation or reflection on the topic and nididhyasana means meditation through which truth is to be realized" (Sharma, 2013a, p. 83). Hindu emphasises that "there is a greater life beyond this life", which presumes "there is a larger world enveloping this apparent world" (Swarup, 2015, p. 8). The mind is only a segment of a greater life of the spirit and forms the true purpose of human life (Swarup, 2015). Hence the ultimate goal of Hindu education ensures that learners are aware of the true life and teaches how to reach the spirit of the eternal and infinite life. To do so, its fundamental aims are to give up egoistic life and individual's physical and mental desires and to develop empathy and sympathy for human life through revealing the true self through *yogas* and *mantra* (Swarup, 2015). Yogas offer various paths such as the path of knowledge

190 *Intercultural valuism*

(jnana yoga), the path of meditation (dhyana-yoga), the path of devotion (bhakti yoga), and the path of good works (karma yoga) (Mishra, 2013; Scheifinger, 2008). A mantra is a word or phrase repeated by Hindus (Buddhists as well) when they meditate, or to help them feel calm. In this context, Hindu education has two learning objectives that are interconnected: (a) one is to strengthen the mind-body because they believe the mind and senses are the power of spirit that allows the self to control this life – desires and impulses – and to increase the power of will and concentration and (b) the other aim of education is to understand full knowledge rather than general knowledge. In this sense, Hindu people tend to believe that general knowledge is subject-based and fragmented because it does not enhance the power of mind to understand full knowledge.

Like Indigenous holistic education, modern Hindu education primarily focuses on mind cultivation and criticises intelligence-driven Western education, which causes the infirmity of minds (Biswas, 2012). Western education celebrates personal and professional success and social achievement so that the modern mind is sick and restless and in conflict with itself, whereas Hindu education has followed the "monastic, scholastic, realistic, idealistic and pragmatic trends" (Biswas, 2012, p. 1). In fact, ancient Hindu education's purpose is to discover "the spiritual at the heart of life" and "to alert the student to the hidden realm of the spirit and instruct them in the appropriate rituals and ceremonies" (McCann, 2007, p. 919). Yet since the nineteenth century, Hindu education has been reformed "in direct competition with secular and missionary schools" (McCann, 2007, p. 919). For example, Gandhian education follows Hindu metaphysics in that it views a human being as a united being of three parts, intellectual, physical, and spiritual, which makes "the whole man" and "constitutes the true economics of education" (Biswas, 2012, p. 6). This naturalism in education can be described as "naturalistic in setting, idealistic in aims and pragmatic in methods" (Patel cited in Biswas, 2012, p. 6). Biswas (2012) summarises the modern Indian education as follows: "Gandhi's experimentation resulted in a service to man; Tagore's experimentation resulted to a unity in humanity and Aurobindo's experimentation effected to develop an integral man" (p. 6). Those three aspects indicate that Hindu education should sustain connectedness with others and nature and facilitate harmony with ourselves, others, and environments. Furthermore, it is also believed that values of modern education systems, such as competition, consumption, and exploitation, are totally opposite to Hindu values because the former engenders conflict with itself, others, and environments. In this sense, Hindu education prioritises the importance of a certain collective atmosphere (rather than individuals' attitudes) including a strong rapport between teachers and students based on the pursuit of truth, respect, and deference. Like monistic pedagogies, Hindu teachers are supposed to be "role models in their virtues and morality, live exemplary lives and change human society toward wellbeing" (Sharma, 2013b, para. 11). Hence Hindu education is not teacher-centred, but "teacher-fronted", with "students engaged in a process of collective learning in a shared domain of human endeavor" (Sharma, 2013b, para. 6).

The characteristics of Indigenous holistic education and Hindu spiritual education can be found in Buddhists mindful education. The locus of Buddhist

Pedagogical interculturality   191

pedagogy is an ideal model, *bodhisattva*, an enlightened being, who defers entering *nirvana* until after all other sentient beings have learned to do so. Labbé (2010) interprets bodhisattva's role in "service in the form of education", and bodhisattva "delays his or her own arrival at nirvana for the benefit of the student" (para. 3). Labbé asserts that this philosophy recalls womanist, or black feminist, bell hooks's (1989) (she prefers to spell her name in all lowercase letters to focus attention on her message rather than herself) *engaged pedagogy* in a sense that Buddhist pedagogy is to being *engaged* in Buddhist practice by being *engaged* with the world. Thus hooks emphasises "the intellectual and spiritual growth" of students, and she argues that teachers should care about the souls of students and provide engaged pedagogy with "progressive, holistic education" (1994, p. 14). To do this, a teacher needs to be a "being wholly present in mind, body, and spirit" (hooks, 1994, p. 21). She also asserts that holistic learning is "a place where teachers grow, and are empowered by the process" (hooks, 1994, p. 21). Like Hindu education, engaged pedagogy does not highlight distinctions between teachers, students, knowledge, and life, but enhances interconnected, interdependent, and interrelated chains, groups, and systems. Indeed, the aims of yogic meditation practices in Hindu and Buddhist traditions are to "loosen attachment to dualistic and essentialized thinking and consequently to the destructive ways of living that all *cultures* produce in their members" (Orr, 2002, p. 486 [emphasis added]). Hindu and Buddhist holism encompasses the wholeness of one's experiences that can be achieved through an experiential awareness of that (Orr, 2002) Such an experiential awareness gives rise to a moment-focused and non-judgemental status, which is free from preconceptions and biases.

By adapting Buddhist *emptiness*, Orr (2002) suggests *without-thinking* pedagogy that "takes no intentional attitude; it neither reifies nor rejects concepts, nor does it involve an identification of the self with them" (p. 491), which is non-dualistic thinking. In doing so, anti-oppressive teachers need to be aware of binaristically constructed concepts of self, gender, and race that are deeply entrenched in our unconsciousness. In overcoming binaristic concepts, mindful meditation traditions (contemplative practices) have shown that one can focus on the mind changes and observe them without engaging with rising ideas, emotions, and sensations. Another modern application of Buddhist mindful is *contemplative pedagogy* that criticises "a deep sense of ontological disconnect and axiological crisis in all dimensions of human life" and "manifests the arts of physical, relational, and contextual awareness through holistic, experiential approaches to learning" (Bai, Scott, & Donald, 2009, p. 319). It is not grounded on any religious belief, but students are given their own choice of contemplative practice and it is about cultivating less belief (leads to no proselytisation), but more direct experience on attentiveness and awareness for the critical first-person approach (Coburn *et al.*, 2011). "Meditation is universal. It does not belong to the East or to the West, nor does it belong to Hinduism, Buddhism, or Sufism. Meditation is everyone's property, just as sleep is everyone's property; it belongs to humanity" (Siddha Yoga Foundation as cited in Coburn *et al.*, 2011, p. 171). Such holistic pedagogy does not focus on a part of anything nor a whole made up of parts because both are concepts, but not real. The only thing real is the status of

192 *Intercultural valuism*

interconnectedness, interdependence, and interrelatedness. Then students, as well as teachers who practise self-awareness, are able to empower themselves to make choices about their attitudes towards oppressive and discriminatory positions as they become conscious of their relatedness and connectedness to others and the environment.

Buddhist mindfulness was chosen as a core philosophy for national education reform in Thailand and Bhutan. First, *Green and Happy Society* representing the Thai social and economic reformation is aimed at creating community values based on Buddhism (Hewison, 1999). In education, the national strategy places special emphasis on morality and personal development through Buddhist mindfulness meditation (Morrison, 2009). Likewise, second, the role of Buddhism in Bhutan is critical in achieving their *Gross National Happiness*, which shows that true happiness can be obtained only through "cultivating inner contentment" (Tashi, 2004, p. 484). The cultivation is to "analyse our thoughts and actions in everyday life as well as those causes and conditions that are deeply inter-related" (Tashi, 2004, p. 483). Thai and Bhutanese national strategies share the following underlying views: (a) they reject the negative aspects of consumerism, industrialism, globalisation, and media technology and (b) they facilitate moral and psychological strength based on Buddhist mindfulness philosophy. It is believed that their holistic approach widens their scope of learning, significantly enhances self-concept and self-esteem, and, as a result, reduces alienation that discriminatory attitudes are rooted in (Orr, 2002, p. 493).

In an intercultural perspective, holistic pedagogies tend to stress transculturation that cares less about cultural uniqueness and identity, but focuses more on seeking transcendental values to encompass all cultures. In essence, holistic pedagogies understand cultural phenomena as a whole rather than analyse cultural features. A whole does not refer to a whole in opposition to its parts, but an emergent whole from interrelatedness and interconnectedness that cannot be found in parts. In education, hence, the primary concern is the ontology of learners that is characterised by three premises: relatedness, collectiveness, and circularity. First, the ultimate premise of holistic education is on *relatedness* that emphasises the connectedness of individuals to inner properties such as thoughts, beliefs, and behaviours in the outer world (Martin, 2012). The ontology of holistic frameworks presumes that individuals cannot be understood by being separated from community and nature. Thus, second, relatedness is understood as *collectiveness* to the extent that lifehood stages are collectively formed and the aim of education is to facilitate individuals to be harmonised with the stages. This is the reason why educational goals of Hinduism, Buddhism, and Aboriginal Dreaming are to conceive the entire course of human life. They emphasise lifehood as a set of experiences and realities from the womb to the tomb. Third, relatedness and collectiveness are not only valid in this life but also extend to the previous and the next lives – *circularity*. In this way, human life is fully integrated with the circle of nature or the universe. Interestingly, the three cultures believe in reincarnation, which refers to a cyclic rebirth of souls and supports a pantheistic view of reality.

The epistemology of holistic pedagogies seeks a wholeness that is emerging from the relatedness and connectedness of individuals and the circularity of their ontic status transcendental to spatiotemporality. In dualistic pedagogies, a culture is a fixation of content with a particular epistemic process, whereas in monistic pedagogies, a culture is regarded as a completely interobjective sphere where self-cultivation occurs and community prosperity is projected. In holistic pedagogies, on the other hand, cultural phenomena are considered products of desire and attachment when it comes to signs of egocentric attachment and products of desire. As holistic pedagogies pursue the practise of *the-not-two-ness* of learning and teaching, we can deduce that they would be highly critical, often radical, to dualistic cultural phenomena. On the contrary, they would also be very tolerant and flexible to different cultures when they perceive the co-existence based on respectedness rather than having controlling. Due to their high mindful individuality (low individualism) and high interrelatedness and connectedness, interculturality is perceived as immanent. As mental and spiritual aspects of individuality merge into a transcultural approach to wholeness, people of holistic culture have lower individualism and higher intersubjectivity than those of monistic and dualistic cultures. An epistemological question then arises is who determines the representation of wholeness, and how, with the exception of individuals' personal experience? The lifehoods of the three holistic cultures are sustained by community/religious leaders (Hindu *gurus*, Buddhist *bodhisattvas*, and Aboriginal *Elders*) who are enlightened figures and embodiments of spiritual interconnectedness, and values are reproduced and preserved by their moral intervention in daily life. Such cohesive and transcultural systems of life are enhanced by reincarnation culture – spatiotemporally transcendental, but spiritually (conceptually) connected. A holistic thought of human life is very open and free to cultural differences and offers the ultimate concern of individuality – the *subjecthood*. This is ontological interculturality because wholeness reduces conflicts and tensions between dualistic relations of things and local collectivism and facilitates long-term interactions between cultures. However, low individuality and high interrelatedness would result in less systematic axiology and low objective epistemology of interculturality. A radical fusion of horizon is unexpected and its progress is steady. In addition, there is a tendency to deify their teachers/leaders. In dualistic society, wholeness as emergent does not appear, but is determined by ideological and political reasons. In this sense, people with low individuality could be easily used for political gain. Yet their ultimate concern of individuality supports the ontology of interculturality in which intercultural value-interaction can occur by sharing ontic aspects of reality and ontically anchored cultural structures.

9.4 Conclusion: Towards an intercultural pedagogy

First, a dominant culture of Western education theories focuses on cognition and behaviour changes. Although there is a clear contrast between behaviourism and constructivism in terms of methodology, their ontological approach is based on a dualistic relation between individuals (or mind) and the world. Critical theory is also fundamentally based on two distinctive worlds: the oppressed and the oppressor. In education, as a result, they seek changes in

194 *Intercultural valuism*

individual minds or behaviour by assuming that (a) individuals are significantly influenced by external environments and (b) an individual change leads to a social change. On the other hand, social-cultural constructivists and critical theorists emphasise social and environmental changes for individuals' liberation and a just society, yet the primary concerns of education are self-awareness and self-transformation. In this way, regardless of their ideological pursuits, they tend to reproduce dualistic frameworks in their practice. In intercultural value networks, the intrinsic nature of tensions and conflicts between individuals (or mind) and the world offers ontological discourses on emergent values arising from intercultural interaction. In intercultural interaction, epistemological dualism allows participants to identify the fact that two different cultures are historically progressing as a whole.

Second, CHC and IHC have a strong monistic culture in education in which cultural phenomena are outcomes of the dynamic relationships between human and nature (or the Divine). Both cultures highly emphasise moralism in line with their cultural and religious beliefs and values. The role of education is to transform individuals so that they can practise values given by nature or the Divine, and pedagogical processes are very collectivistic and totalistic, as they share the same ultimate values. There is no clear distinction between culture and ethics; everyone must co-participate in the world through collective will. To do so, rote learning, autonomous interdependence, and lifehood transformation are facilitated throughout their cultural and educational systems. Such a co-participatory approach towards an ultimate thing/being is critical to interculturality in which intercultural interaction can be facilitated with shared collective morality and individual responsibilities.

Third, holistic pedagogies are concerned with interrelatedness and interconnectedness that form a whole in which there is no epistemic distinction between the world and individuals and the past, present, and future. Hence individuals are spiritually connected to collectively formed lifehood stages, which are very ontological beyond spatiotemporality. Reincarnation culture actively resists dualistic thinking and egocentric desire and promotes the-not-two-ness that sustains their holistic understanding of the co-existence of all things. A culture is perceived as transcultural, but people may be less tolerant if local collectivism is promoted by a particular group of people or when any hierarchical demarcation between nature (and the world) and human beings is observed. In intercultural contexts, holistic frameworks provide ontological discourses for the ultimate concern of individuality that cares about the status of relatedness of parts to understand a whole.

In this chapter, I have attempted to identify interculturality of cultural pedagogies and tried to demonstrate how each pedagogy metaphysically appears in value networks. Synthetically, Western pedagogies have the potential to reveal values embedded in each culture and emergent values arising from intercultural interaction (epistemological dualism) if participants of different cultures perceive conflicts and tensions between cultures in terms of intersubjectivity of interculturality (ontological holism) and attempt to interpret it for moral transformation of situated beings (axiological monism). Monistic pedagogies suggest collective moral responsibilities through interobjectivity of interculturality (monistic axiology)

Pedagogical interculturality 195

when participants attempt to respond to emergent values arising from intercultural interaction (dualistic epistemology) and practise self-awareness of the interobjective (or networked) individuality in intercultural interaction (holistic ontology). Holistic pedagogies extend the concept of transcultural and transcendental individuality to the not-two-ness by substituting one's perceptions of reality for the status of interrelatedness and interconnectedness (holistic ontology) in which multi-reality becomes an emergent whole (holistic epistemology), and interobjectivity of interculturality is instantiated in value networks (holistic axiology). In value networks, various cultural/religious frameworks are characterised by mutual feedback and feedforward relationships that support intercultural interaction and, in turn, facilitate a topographic transformation of the networks that results in a transformation of the mind.

References

Bai, H., Scott, C., & Donald, B. (2009). Contemplative pedagogy and revitalization of teacher education. *Alberta Journal of Educational Research, 55*(3), 319–334.

Bakar, O. (2011). Islamic science, modern science, and post-modernity: Towards a new synthesis through a Tawhidic epistemology. *Revelation and Science, 1*(3), 13–20.

Barker, C. (2008). *Cultural studies: Theory and practice* (3rd ed.). London: Sage.

Bates, D.G., & Plog, F. (1990). *Cultural anthropology* (3rd ed.). New York: McGraw-Hill.

Behrendt, L., Larkin, S., Griew, R., & Kelly, P. (2012). *Review of higher education access and outcomes for Aboriginal and Torres Strait Islander people: Final report.* Canberra: Department of Industry, Innovation, Science, Research and Tertiary Education.

Berk, L. (2002). *Child development* (5th ed.) Boston: Allyn and Bacon.

Berkey, J.P. (2007). Madrasa medieval and modern: Politics, education, and the problem of Muslim identity. In R.W. Hefner & M.Q. Zaman (Eds.), *Schooling Islam: The Culture and Politics of Modern Muslim Education* (pp. 40–60).Princeton, NJ: Princeton University Press.

Bethel, B. (2006). Critical approaches to inclusion in Indigenous teacher education in Queensland: The case of RATEP. *International Journal of Pedagogies and Learning, 2*(3), 30–41.

Biggs, J. (1998). Learning from the Confucian heritage: So size doesn't matter? *International Journal of Educational Research, 29*(8), 723–738.

Biswas, N.B. (2012). *Indian philosophy of education and pedagogy: An essential proposition.* Regional Seminar on Philosophy of Education. Retrieved from http://www.azimpremjiuniversity.edu.in/sites/default/files/userfiles/files/Prof_Nikunj_Biswas.pdf

Burbules, N.C., & Rupert, B. (1999). Critical thinking and critical pedagogy – Relations, differences and limits. In T.S. Popkewitz & L. Fendler (Eds.), *Critical Theories in Education* (pp. 45–66). New York: Routledge.

Christie, M. (2005). Words, ontologies & Aboriginal databases. *Multimedia International. Australia, 116,* 52–63.

Cobb, P. (2005). Where is the Mind? A coordination of socialcultural and cognitive constructivist perspective. In C. Fosnot (Ed.), *Constructivism. Theory, Perspectives, and Practice* (2nd ed.) (pp. 39–57). New York,: Teachers Collage Press.

196 *Intercultural valuism*

Coburn, T., Grace, F., Klein, A.C., Komjathy, L., Roth, H., & Simmer-Brown, J. (2011). Contemplative pedagogy: Frequently asked questions. *Teaching Theology & Religion, 14*(2), 167–174.

Cordella, A., & Shaikh, M. (2006). From epistemology to ontology: Challenging the constructed "truth" of ANT. *Information Technology and People*. Retrieved from http://is2.lse.ac.uk/WP/PDF/wp143.pdf

Corden, R. (1992). The role of the teacher. In K. Norman (Ed.), *Thinking voices, the work of the National Oracy Project* (pp. 186–195). London: Hodder and Stoughton.

Creswell, J.W. (2003). *Research design: Qualitative, quantitative and mixed methods approaches* (2nd ed.). Thousand Oaks, CA: Sage publications.

Crotty, M. (1998). *The foundations of social research: Meaning and perspective in the research process*. London: Sage.

de Plevitz, L. (2007). Systemic racism: The hidden barrier to educational success for Indigenous school students. *Australian Journal of Education, 51*(1), Article 5.

Diallo, I. (2012). The interface between Islamic and western pedagogies and epistemologies: Features and divergences. *International Journal of Pedagogies and Learning, 7*(3), 175–179.

Dumont, J. (2005). Cultural Framework (RHS). First nations regional longitudinal health survey (RHS). Retrieved from http://www.rhs-ers.ca/english/cultural-framework.asp

Ernest, P. (2004). Nominalism and conventionalism in social constructivism. *Philosophica, 74*, 7–35. Retrieved from http://logica.ugent.be/philosophica/fulltexts/74-2.pdf

Evanoff, R.J. (2004). Universalist, relativist, and constructivist approaches to intercultural ethics. *International Journal of Intercultural Relations, 28*(5), 439–458.

Fay, B. (1987). *Critical social science: Liberation and its limits*. Cambridge: Polity Press.

Freimuth, H. (2009). Educational research: An introduction to basic concepts and terminology. *University General Requirements Unit (UGRU) Journal, 8*, 1–9.

Freire, P. (2000). *Pedagogy of the oppressed*. (M.B. Ramos, Trans.). New York: Continuum. (Original work published 1970)

Giroux, H.A. (1983). *Critical theory and educational practice*. Victoria: Deakin University.

Giroux, H.A. (1988). *Teachers as intellectuals: Toward a critical pedagogy of learning*. Granby, MA: Bergin and Garvey. Retrieved from http://teacherrenewal.wiki.westga.edu/file/view/Rethinking+the+Language+of+Schooling.html

Habermas, J. (1971). *Knowledge and human interests*. (J.J. Shapiro, Trans.). Boston: Beacon Press. (Original work published 1968)

Hammond, J., & Gibbons, P. (2001). What is scaffolding? In J. Hammon (Ed.), *Scaffolding: Teaching and Learning in Language and Literacy Education* (pp. 1–14). Newton, NSW, Australia: Primary English Teaching Association.

Hewison, K. (1999). Thailand's capitalism before and after the economic crisis. In M. Beeson, K. Jayasuriya, R. Robison & H-R. Kim (Eds.), *Politics and Markets in the Wake of the Asian Crisis* (pp. 192–211). New York: Routledge.

hooks, b. (1989). *Talking back: Thinking feminist, thinking black*. Boston, MA: South End Press.

hooks, b. (1994). *Teaching to transgress: Education as the practice of freedom*. New York: Routledge.

Horkheimer, M., (1982). *Critical theory*. New York: Seabury Press.

Pedagogical interculturality 197

Hughes, P., More, A.T., & Williams, M. (2004). *Aboriginal ways of learning*. AbWol Project. Enfield, SA: Aboriginal Education Unit.

Hussien, S. (2007). Critical pedagogy, Islamisation of knowledge and Muslim education. *Intellectual Discourse, 15*(1), 85–104.

Jonassen, D.H. (1991). Evaluating constructivist learning. *Educational Technology, 36*(9), 28–33.

Jonassen, D.H., Davidson, M., Collins, C., Campbell, J., & Haag, B.B. (1995). Constructivism and computer-mediated communication in distance education. *The American Journal of Distance Education, 9*(2), 7–26.Jörga, T., Davisc, B., & Nickmansa, G. (2007). Towards a new, complexity science of learning and education. *Educational Research Review, 2*(2), 145–156.

Kettley, N.C. (2010). *Theory building in educational research*. New York, NY: Continuum International Pub.

Khan, M.M., & Al-Hilali, M.T-.U-.D. (Trans.). (1999). *Interpretation of the meanings of the Noble Quran in the English language with transliteration (Part 3)*. New York: Darussalam. Retrieved from http://www.noblequran.com/translation/

Kleinfeld, J.S. (1971). Visual memory in village Eskimo and urban Caucasian children. *Arctic, 12*, 132–138.

Labbé, J. (2010). Attraversiamo! Engaging Metta through Buddhist pedagogy and eat, pray, love. *Prapañca, 1*(2). Retrieved from http://www.prapancajournal. com/v1i2/labbe.php

Lamy, M.N., & Hampel, R. (2007). *Online communication in language learning and teaching*. Basingstoke: Palgrave Macmillan.

Lantolf, J.P. (2000). Introducing socio-cultural theory. In J.P. Lantolf (Ed.), *Socio-cultural Theory and Second Language Learning* (pp. 1–26). Oxford: Oxford University Press.

Lave, J., & Wenger, E. (1991). *Situated learning: Legitimate peripheral participation*. Cambridge: Cambridge University Press.

Levy, M. (1997). *Computer-assisted language learning: Context and conceptualization*. Oxford, UK: Clarendon.

Martin, K. (2012). Aboriginal early childhood: Past, present, and future. In J. Phillips & J. Lampert (Eds.), *Introductory Indigenous Studies in Education: Reflection and the Importance of Knowing* (2nd ed.) (pp. 26–39). Sydney, Australia: Pearson.

McCann, J. (2007). Religious education: An analysis of the perspectives of world religions. In M. de Souza, G. Durka, K. Engebretson, R. Jackson, & A. McGrady (Eds.), *International Handbook of the Religious, Moral and Spiritual Dimensions in Education* (pp. 917–936). Dordrecht, Netherlands: Springer.

Meyer, K.A. (2012). The influence of online teaching on faculty productivity. *Innovative Higher Education, 37*(1), 37–52.

Mezirow, J. (1981). A critical theory of adult learning and education. *Adult Education, 32*(1), 3–24.

Mishra, R.C. (2013). Moksha and the Hindu worldview. *Psychology and Developing Societies, 25*(1), 21–42.

Morrison, K. (2009). Educational innovation in Thailand: A case study. *International Education, 38*(2), 29–55.

Murphy, M., & Fleming, T. (2012). *Out now in paperback: Habermas, critical theory and education*. New York: Routledge.

Nigerian, S.A. (2004). *Islam: Its history, teaching, and practices*. Bloomington: Indiana University Press.

198 Intercultural valuism

Nowlan, B. (2001, September). *Introduction: What is critical theory and why study it?* Eau Claire, WI: University of Wisconsin-Eau Claire.

Orr, D. (2002). The uses of mindfulness in anti-oppressive pedagogies: Philosophy and praxis. *Canadian Journal of Education, 4,* 477–490.

Palincsar, A.S. (1998). Keeping the metaphor of scaffolding fresh – A response to C. Addison Stone's "The metaphor of scaffolding: It's utility for the field of learning disabilities." *Journal of Learning Disabilities, 31*(4), 370–373.

Park, J.Y., & Lee Hong, A. (2013). Cross-cultural web user interface design for Indigenous Internet users. In KODDCO (Ed.), *KODDCO 2013 International Design Conference: Cross Point of 'E to W'* (pp. 39–42). New York: KODDCO.

Paul, J., & Marfo, K. (2001). Preparation of educational researchers in philosophical foundations of inquiry. *Review of Educations Research, 71*(4), 525–547.

Piaget, J. (1953). *The origins of intelligence in children.* London: Routledge & Kegan Paul.

Piaget, J. (1970). *Biology and knowledge: An essay on the relations between organic regulations and cognitive process.* Chicago: University of Chicago Press.

Piaget, J. (1980). The psychogenesis of knowledge and its epistemological significance. In M. Piattelli-Palmarini (Ed.), *Language and Learning: The Debate between Jean Piaget and Noam Chomsky* (pp. 23–34). Cambridge, MA: Harvard University Press.

Rasmussen, C., Sherman, J., & Baydala, L. (2004). Learning patterns and education of Aboriginal children: A review of the literature. *The Canadian Journal of Native Studies, 24*(2), 317–342.

Richter, G.C. (Trans.). (2005). *Confucius: The great learning.* Truman State University. Retrieved from http://grichter.sites.truman.edu/files/2012/01/kongznew3.pdf

Rosowsky, A. (2008). *Heavenly readings: Liturgical literacy in a multilingual context.* Bristol, Buffalo, Toronto: Multilingual Matters.

Scheifinger, H. (2008). Hinduism and cyberspace. *Religion, 38*(3), 233–249.

Schuh, K.L., & Barab, S.A. (2008). Part 1. Foundations 7 philosophical perspectives. In J.M. Spector, M.D. Merrill, J. van Merriënboer & M.P. Driscoll (Eds.), *Handbook of Research on Educational Communications and Technology* (3rd ed.) (pp. 67–82). New York Taylor & Francis Group

Shakir, S. (2008). Confucianism and the Macartney mission: Dispelling the myth of Chinese arrogance. In L. Spees & P. Goo (Eds.), *Endeavours in Chinese History (Volume 2: China in World History)* (n.p.), Department of History, Emory University. Retrieved from http://history.emory.edu/home/documents/endeavors/volume2/SanaShakir.pdf

Sharma, B.K. (2013a). Hinduism and TESOL: Learning, teaching and student-teacher relationships revisited. *Language and Linguistics Compass, 7*(2), 79–90. doi:10.1111/lnc3.12013

Sharma, B.K. (2013b). *Hindu educational ethos and practices as a possible source for local pedagogy.* Retrieved from http://neltachoutari.wordpress.com/category/miscellaneous/page/3/

Skinner, B.F. (1958). Teaching machines. *Science, 128*(3330), 969–977.

Sonn, C., Bishop B., & Humphries, R. (2000). Encounters with the dominant culture: Voices of Indigenous students in mainstream higher education. *Australian Psychologist, 35*(2), 128–135.

Swarup, R. (2015). *The Hindu view of education.* New Delhi: Voice of India. Retrieved from http://www.voiceofin.com/pic/pdf/53.pdf

Tashi, K.P. (2004). The role of Buddhism in achieving Gross National Happiness. In K. Ura & K. Galay (Eds.), *Gross National Happiness and Development – Proceedings of the First International Conference on Operationalization of Gross National Happiness* (pp. 483–495). Thimphu: Centre for Bhutan Studies.

Taylor, P.C., & Medina, M.N.D. (2011). Educational research paradigms: From positivism to pluralism. *College Research Journal, 1*(1), 9–23.

Torres, C.A., & Morrow, R.A. (1998). Paulo Freire, Jürgen Habermas, and critical pedagogy: Implications for comparative education. *Melbourne Studies in Education, 39*(2), 1–20.

von Glasersfeld, E. (2005). Thirty years constructivism. *Constructivist Foundations, 1*(1), 9–12.

Vrasidas, C. (2000). Constructivism versus objectivism: Implications for interaction, course design, and evaluation in distance education. *International Journal of Educational Telecommunications, 6*(4), 339–362.

Vygotsky, L.S. (1978). *Mind and society: The development of higher mental processes.* (M. Cole, V. John-Steiner, S. Scribner & E. Souberman, Eds.) (A.R. Luria, M. Lopez-Morillas & M. Cole [with J.V. Wertsch], Trans.) Cambridge, MA: Harvard University Press. (Original manuscripts [ca. 1930–1934])

Wu, Z. (2011). Interpretation, autonomy, and transformation: Chinese pedagogic discourse in a cross-cultural perspective. *Journal of Curriculum Studies, 43*(5), 569–590.

Yunkaporta, T. (2009). *Aboriginal pedagogies at the cultural interface* [Doctoral thesis]. James Cook University. Retrieved from http://eprints.jcu.edu.au/10974/

Yunkaporta, T., & Kirby, M. (2011). Yarning up Indigenous pedagogies: A dialogue about eight Aboriginal ways of learning. In N. Purdie, G. Milgate, & H.R. Bell (Eds.) *Two Way Teaching and Learning: Toward Culturally Reflective and Relevant Education* (pp. 205–213). Melbourne, VIC: ACER Press.

Yunkaporta, T., & McGinty, S. (2009). Reclaiming Aboriginal knowledge at the cultural interface. *Australian Educational Researcher, 36*(2), 55–72.

Part III Conclusion: Intercultural valuism

In Chapter 7, I have presented a comparative empirical study by using two self-reflection models, the intercultural valuism circle and the 5Rs framework in order to identify underlying values that prevent self-inclusive intercultural reflection. The analysis results indicate that the three metaphysical issues of intercultural interaction – namely, the absence of the self, the non-subject positions of others, and the myth of value-free methods – appear as individualism, beneficiary, and equity. The proposed solutions are (a) to adopt diverse narrative points of view in self-reflection writing by using the multilayered self in personal and professional contexts, (b) the multilayered self needs to be used to encourage teachers to consider their relational and collective selves in personal and professional contexts, and (c) to understand concepts, such as equity and autonomy, as culture bound. Also, the chapter showed that a metaphysical approach to intercultural interaction has the potential to benefit teaching and learning by addressing the three metaphysics issues.

In Chapter 8, I have identified the three dimensions of metaphysical interculturality from the review of various concepts, narratives, and doctrines of non-Western cultures/religions. Each concept represents its own cultural identity and holds a metaphysical position in intercultural value networks, which is a major premise of intercultural interaction in the learning environment. Each cultural concept appears unique and incommensurate with other cultures, but it becomes commensurate when its metaphysical characteristics are understood and that each holds ontological, epistemological, or axiological interculturality. In sum, (a) axiological interculturality is found in monistic cultural concepts, which encourages us to think about participants' moral values for and ethical engagement in intercultural interaction; (b) epistemological interculturality from dualistic cultural concepts tends to systemise value-interaction through dichotomous thinking towards a predefined interculturality; and (c) ontological interculturality characterised by holistic cultural concepts can be used to disclose ontological value networks, as holistic individuality underlines our interrelated and interconnected minds and its networked nature sublates egocentric and atomistic mindsets. This is consistent with cultural pedagogies in the following chapter.

In Chapter 9, dualistic, monistic, and holistic pedagogies are characterised by their own metaphysical approach to interculturality: Holistic pedagogies emphasise ontological aspects of intercultural interaction. Dualistic Western pedagogies facilitate epistemological aspects of intercultural interaction, and monistic pedagogies articulate collective moral responsibilities of individuals by attenuating axiological limitations of dualism and holism in value networks. In intercultural interaction, for example, a dualistic culture may be less interested in coping with individual selfishness because of its high atomistic individuality (or less relationism and less collectivism). A holistic culture may be less interested in developing systematic moral reasoning because of its high intersubjective spirituality (or less individualism and less collectivism), and a monistic culture may be less interested in managing conflicts of group interest because of its high interobjective morality (or less individualism and relationism)

My intercultural valusim assumes that values embedded in cultures are interconnected and intercultural interaction aims to reveal larger parts of value networks. Our participation in intercultural realities allows us to observe our multilayered self, to cultivate our own cultural identity, and to enrich our shared interculturality formation. For intercultural interaction, in practice, we approach each culture in terms of metaphysical aspects of its values in order to identify its own interculturality, as it has already been connected to other cultures in value networks. We also realise our understandings of each culture being placed in value networks, which provokes our intersubjective understanding of interculturality. In this sense, value networks allow us to expand our understandings of interobjective interculturality that redefine our own cultural boundaries and self-construal in terms of new interculturality and emergent (inter)cultural values, and, as a result, we face a new form of individuality. If we approach a different culture without being aware of our own (Western) cultural framework and the three metaphysical dimensions of interculturality, we tend to pay attention only to its differences and unconsciously judge them based on our own value hierarchy. Inversely, by being aware of our own interconnectedness and interrelatedness in intercultural value networks, we will understand interculturality from multiple perspectives, and we will perceive the fact that intercultural values always reside in value networks. Thus, pedagogically, intercultural interaction aims to build a new model of individuality by exploring larger parts of value networks through ontological, epistemological, and axiological interculturality.

Conclusion
Intercultural valuism pedagogy

Interculturality value networks indicate (a) we can approach a culture or cultural phenomenon as a networked whole of cultures, (b) we can facilitate intercultural interaction by understanding underlying values of each culture in a situation, and (c) we can reveal new values from intercultural interaction that can reshape interculturality. Such ontological, epistemological, and axiological interculturality allows individuals of each culture to identify their own interculturality and participate in mutual feedback and feedforward relations between the multilayered self and multiple cultural realities. As argued in Chapters 8 and 9, for example, epistemological interculturality can be seen as crucial to revealing values embedded in each culture and identifying emergent values arising from intercultural interaction. This interculturality is yet to be a whole because its dualistic approach tends to conceal ontological assumptions and axiological interaction of values. In intercultural interaction, ontological interculturality articulates the subject-subject relationship and promotes a new form of transcultural and networked individuality in intercultural interaction, whereas axiological interculturality engenders collective and situated moral values that further facilitate transformative participation. However, low individuality of ontological interculturality and high totalism of axiological interculturality may restrict individual participants to verbalising and hypostatising intercultural values, which can be prevented by the constant tensions of value-interaction of epistemological interculturality. This metaphysically interrelated and interconnected interculturality justifies that intercultural education should aim to facilitate intercultural interaction by assuming intercultural value networks and to seek intercultural pedagogies by pursing new individuality. The three metaphysical dimensions of interculturality are meaningful and helpful in addressing metaphysical issues in today's multicultural education including the absence of the self in self-reflection, the non-subject position of non-Western cultures in intercultural interaction, and the culture-unbound methods and concepts. In the conclusion of this study, in this sense, I will further articulate my intercultural valuism as an alternative pedagogy for intercultural education through its integration into the key concepts of intercultural value networks addressed in Chapter 6.

In value networks, intercultural interaction is expected to capacitate us to develop meaningful cross-cultural relationships and to contribute to develop a socially and culturally inclusive community. This is because each culture has its own metaphysical questions on interculturality. For example, in a dualistic relationship between *I* and networks (or knowledge), *I* am in a node and looking for another node based on *my* interests. *I* in a node refers to a mode of *egocentric* thinking that cares about boundary points by questioning *who I am* and *what I want to do*, which is an interpersonal inclination; in a monistic understanding, on the contrary, *we* are interconnected by particular values in networks and *I* and *you* need to cultivate *myself* and *yourself* to preserve the values by practising *our* collective cultural identity rather than seek other values in different parts of value networks, although other values reveal a larger part of the networks. A collective cultural identity in value networks cares about *how we are interconnected* and *what we are supposed to do*, which is an extrapersonal inclination, and furthermore, in a holistic understanding, interconnectedness of value networks emphasises the significance of ontological foundations for knowledge and ethics. As a result, understanding a node (nodes) itself is out of interest, but instead the interconnectedness raises questions, *where we come from* and *where I am heading in life*, which is an interpersonal inclination. These metaphysical approaches of the three cultural frameworks to value networks show their potential intercultural tendencies towards interculturality and imply that a new form of intercultural pedagogy can be articulated for intercultural interaction in intrapersonal, extrapersonal, and interpersonal ways.

Such intercultural valuism pedagogy is aimed at providing a hermeneutic key to intercultural interaction that encompasses ontological, epistemological, and axiological aspects of interculturality for intercultural education. In practice, it is aimed at facilitating individual participants to understand how their cultural values are interconnected and interrelated in intercultural value networks. In intercultural interaction, participants are not encouraged regarding what they must learn, but they are encouraged to be aware of where their values are and how they affect them. In this sense, logical assumptions of intercultural interaction are (a) a culture as a set of value networks determines participants' ontological, epistemological, and axiological practices and (b) participants exercise their causal power in value networks where multiple cultural realities are metaphysically layered and the multilayered self is reticulated. Consequently, participants can reveal a new set of value networks through values reticulating for self-, relational, and social transformation. In this sense, learning is not *connecting activities*, but *revealing new values*, which shows larger parts of value networks, by *readjusting interstices* where they are ontologically anchored surrounding value nodes. As a pedagogical model of intercultural interaction, eventually, I will articulate five concepts that are consistent with the principles of intercultural value networks (addressed in Chapter 6) for individual students' intercultural introspection (its practical details were presented in Chapter 7): *value nodes, metaphysical realities, the multilayered self, interstice adjustments*, and *whole individuality*.

In intercultural value networks, first, a node is known as a connection point: either a redistribution point or a communication end point can be connected to other nodes such as organisations, information, data, feelings, and images. Its extended meaning is a learning community that is always part of a larger network. In value networks, we engage in values embedded in our own culture that are composed of a cluster of nodes (a set of value networks) and determine our thinking and behaviour. In this sense, values on nodes are neither neutral nor universal. Regardless of whether consciously or unconsciously, our thinking and behaviour are always triggered by particular values. In other words, a value in itself is implicit and has no effect on reality unless value-interaction occurs. As illustrated in Figure 1, a value is valueless and a value becomes a particular value only when it is interacting with a different value(s). In general, upholding a value means that we place it on top of other values in a situation. This practice of epistemological dualism tends to ignore value ontology that states values are *relational* and *interactive*.

The concept of value nodes indicates that we can investigate underlying meaning of values in an intercultural situation. This needs to be done by assuming that diverse values are revealed at different metaphysical domains. Metaphysically, value nodes allow us to recognise our ontic structure. As Figure 2 shows, we need to focus on an interstice of values rather than a value itself. A value per se is valueless, but its meanings occur in our mind via a set of values where we are situated.

Second, as I argued for a metaphysical understanding of cultural/religious concepts, narratives, and doctrines in Chapter 8, cultures form or are formed by multiple metaphysical realities: ontological, epistemological, and axiological driven or mixed. A metaphysical form can be visually understood in intercultural value networks as shown in Figures, 3, 4, and 5.

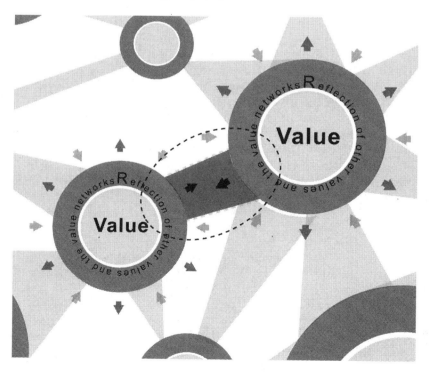

Figure 1 A value is valueless unless it works with other values

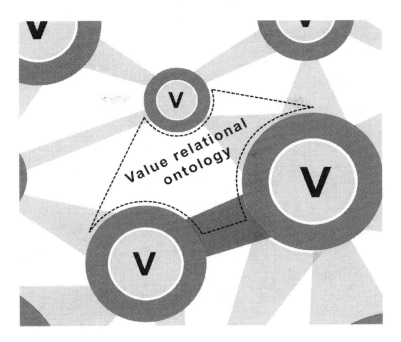

Figure 2 Value relational ontology

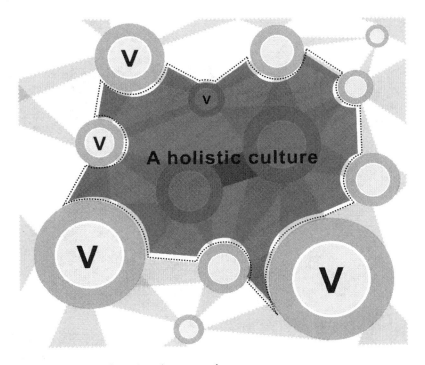

Figure 3 A holistic culture in value networks

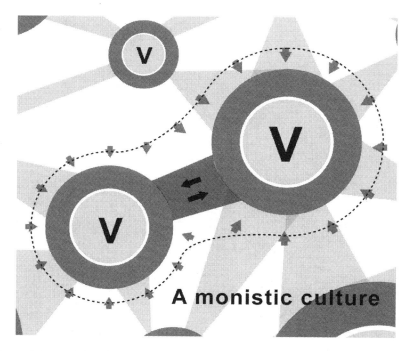

Figure 4 A monistic culture in value networks

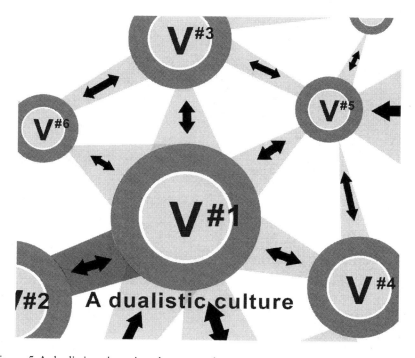

Figure 5 A dualistic culture in value networks

These figures indicate that a cultural framework has a particular set of value networks. When we see all three sets of cultural values as a whole, intercultural value networks looks like an image presented in Figure 6.

Such multilayered metaphysical interculturality prevents us from being trapped in *othering* processes in an intercultural situation because it enables us to see larger parts of value networks and to be aware that our values are interconnected and interrelated with other values. In this context, learning means a process of revealing hidden values on nodes and diverse ontic structures. Value nodes are also inclusive of concepts, principles, theories, frameworks, and methods, as they refer to particular ways of thinking that determine people's ontic structures.

Third, as intercultural value networks sustain multiple cultural realities, self-construal is also multilayered through a personal, a relational, a collective, and a humane self. While a humane self sustains intercultural value networks as a whole, a personal, a relational, and a collective self are defined as epistemological, ontological, and axiological. This implies that our engagement in value networks brings us down to a situational understanding and interaction-focused approach. Such a rhizomatic system rejects the view that self, culture, and humanity are seen as unique, fixed, and unchangeable entities and initiates intercultural interaction by disclosing emotional responses to and/or initial judgement on an intercultural situation/matter and articulating conflicts of interest including *potential* for financial,

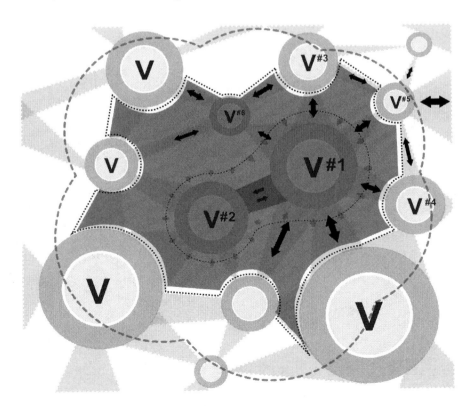

Figure 6 Intercultural value networks

208 *Conclusion: Intercultural valuism pedagogy*

professional, or other personal gain. In this sense, the intercultural valuism pedagogy relies on individuals' introspective capability-based interaction in which one is able to examine and consider one's own ideas, thoughts, feelings, and sensations.

Fourth, intercultural interaction can result in a change in our ontic structure because an interstice adjustment occurs as a corollary of extensions of our cultural horizons. When we are aware of interstices of values that we have engaged in, we are also aware that we are required to change our value structures by accepting or rejecting values and/or seeking new values. In this way, we can conceive of self-cultivation through pursuing new horizons of interculturality. In practice, intercultural interaction is aimed at rationalising and actualising an already interrelated and interconnected relationship in value networks. If a workshop or training, in the name of approaching cultural diversity, cultural competence, or cultural awareness, offers sharing personal or professional stories in cultural differences or focuses on sharing data and information about others' cultures, it is possibly or potentially ideological rather than intercultural because it neither facilitates a change in thinking or beliefs nor pursues relationship building.

Fifth, and last, the intercultural valuism pedagogy pursues whole individuality development, which is its ultimate pedagogical goal. Our participation in interaction between the multilayered self and metaphysical multiple realities sublates both egocentric and allocentric perspectives and posits de-centric principles. As emergent values arising from intercultural interaction reveal larger parts of value networks and require ontological adjustments, individuality is constantly challenged by a new form of individuality for a topological change of value networks. In value networks, individuals are required to introspect and transcend their own perspectives at the same time by (a) being aware of (provisional) current positions of their multilayered self in dynamic metaphysical realities, (b) disconnecting their multilayered self from current values and reconnecting it in unexplored areas of networks, and (c) expanding/overturning the boundaries of a dominant worldview/a theoretical tradition/a habitual practice. The critical self-inclusion, disconnection, and reconnection of the multilayered self and deboundarisation of metaphysical realms are the de-centric principles for whole individuality development. In this way, the de-centric principles allow us to experience new individuality that is not extra or additional, but a part of whole individuality, as we allow ourselves to grow and participate in the prosperity of our culture and interculturality.

Index

*Note: page numbers in **bold** type refers to Tables.*

Aboriginal: Aboriginal and Torres
  Strait Islander 15, 150, 151, 159;
  Aboriginal Dreaming 8, 159, 169,
  170, 192; Aboriginality 9, 169;
  Aboriginal mythology 160; Aboriginal
  pedagogy 150; Aboriginal people 58;
  Aboriginal worldview/perspective
  145, 151, 152
absence of relation, the 8, 84, 94, 137
absolute void, the 162; *see also*
  emptiness
abstract individualism 67, 71, 74, 117,
  170, 172
Afrocentrism 69
Agape (or unconditional love) 50
agonism 23
allocentric 92, 141
alms 166
already interpreted world, an 125, 130
altruism 48
ambivalence 6, 23, 28, 34; *see also*
  hybridity
Americanisation 58
Amin, A. 6, 29, 32–4
Ang, I. 1, 28–9, 57–9, 78; *see also* being
  together of strangers
anti-dualism 62
anti-realism 50–1
Apollonian worlds 87–94, 99, 119, 129;
  see also Nietzsche, F.
Aristotle 49; Aristotelians 171
asignifying rupture 124
assimilation 40, 53, 59, 67, 71,
  106, 178
Atman 8, 159–62, 169–70
atomistic 2, 121, 153, 161, 200–1;
  atomistic approach 121, 170, 172;
  atomistic individualism/individuality

2, 201; atomistic mindsets 172, 200;
  atomistic thinking 136
auto-suggestive thinking 171
axiological 9, 27, 30, 35, 37–9,
  46, 47, 50, 52, 53, 61, 79, 115,
  122, 131, 142, 144, 156, 166,
  170, 173, 184, 187, 191, 201,
  203–4, 207; axiological activism
  187; axiological assumption 37;
  axiological connectivism 107;
  axiological interaction 6–7, 30, 46,
  53, 73, 77–8, 83, 99, 107, 109,
  121, 123, 131, 202; axiological
  interculturality 8, 172, 200–2;
  axiological mapping 7–8, 111, 122,
  125–6, 131; axiological monism 194;
  axiological-ontological 156
axiology 2, 4, 34–5, 37–8, 47–8, 52,
  59, 71, 79, 99, 158, 185, 193–5

Banks, J.A. 1, 6, 16–17, 59–61, 78–9
behaviourism 8, 43, 176–7, 193
beinghood 140–1, 143; *see also*
  lifehood; personhood; selfhood;
  subjecthood
being-in-the-world 7, 109–12,
  120–1, 126
being together of strangers 28
beneficiary 150–1
Bhabha, H.K. 1, 6, 21–4, 29, 34, 57,
  77–8; *see also* cultural hybridity;
  Third Space
binary oppositions 5–6, 22, 25–8, 33–5,
  40, 60, 65, 72, 77–8, 83–4; *see also*
  dualism
Bodhisattva 191, 193
Bourdieu, P. 104–5
Brahman 160–1

210 *Index*

Brotherhood 185–7; *see also* Ummah
Bruner, J. 105–6, 135
Buddhist/Buddhism 8–9, 159, 161–3,
 165, 169–70, 176, 188, 190–3;
 see also bodhisattva; causal links;
 contemplative pedagogy; emptiness;
 engaged pedagogy; mindful
 pedagogy; nirvana; not-two-ness,
 the; Sunyata; without-thinking
 pedagogy

Cartesian/s 3, 43, 45, 95, 111, 112–13,
 122–3; Cartesian dualism 95;
 Cartesian subject-object dualism 112
causality/causal links, the 162–3, 169;
 causal power 203
centrism 69; ethno-centrism 21, 58, 118
Ch'i 163, 165–6
Chinese 28, 33, 159, 164, 187; *see also*
 Confucianism, Confucian heritage
 culture (CHC)
Chineseness, a global 28
Circularity 192
civilised/uncivilised mind 2, 62, 136
co-creation 187
codification/decodification 183
co-existence 32, 34, 98, 107, 116, 122,
 124, 129, 142, 161, 170, 193–4
cognitivism/cognitivist 8, 43, 50, 176
coherentism/coherentists 44–5
collaboration 6, 32, 44, 60, 64, 74, 79,
 104, 142, 179
collectiveness 118, 125, 192
collectivism 67, 185, 193–4, 201;
 collectivistic consciousness 188;
 collectivistic culture/s 35, 94, 167–8,
 186; collectivistic moralism 187;
 collectivistic selfishness 35
colonial/colonialism 21–5, 58, 83, 160
commensurability/incommensurability
 28–9, 34, 77, 119
communication: extrapersonal 119,
 130, 203; intrapersonal 21, 25,
 103, 113–14, 116, 130, 169, 203;
 interpersonal 21, 33, 93, 97, 113–14,
 121–2, 130, 161, 180, 203
communicative action, theory of
 7, 87, 94, 96–9, 101, 129–30;
 communicative competence 97–8;
 social actions, strategic actions,
 concealed strategic actions and open
 strategic actions, and communicative
 actions 96–7
communitarianism 80, 103 ; abstract
 communitarianism 103

community 2, 29, 30, 32, 35, 38, 40,
 45, 53, 60–1, 63, 65, 68, 70, 73, 80,
 90, 103–6, 121, 124, **145–7**, 150,
 155, 167–8, 171, 187–9, 192–3,
 202–3
Confucianism 9, 73, 165, 170–1, 185;
 Confucian heritage culture (CHC)
 184–7, 194
connectivism 104–7; *see also* Downes, S.;
 Siemens, G.
connectivity 64, 105, 123, 159
consequentialism/consequentialists
 48–9
constructivism/constructivist 8, 17,
 43–4, 51, 106, 135–6, 176, 178–81,
 183, 193–4
contemplative pedagogy 191
convivial/conviviality/convivium 6,
 32–3, 62, 77
co-participatory 142–3, 194
co-revelation 143–4
cosmopolitanism 31, 63–4, 78, 82;
 see also creolisaiton; heterogeneity;
 hybridity; multiplicity
cosmopolitan learning 6, 62, 79; *see also*
 Rizvi, F.
creolisaiton 29, 31–2, 34, 77
critical discourse analysis 144
critical pedagogy 69–70, 72, 79, 181–3;
 critical rationalist 94; critical theory 1,
 52, 181, 193
cross-cultural psychology 7, 44, 87, 92,
 94, 98, 129
cultivating humanity 6, 62–4, 79 ;
 see also Nussbaum, M.C.
cultural hybridity 6, 21–2, 24, 29, 34,
 77; *see also* hybridity
culturally bound 17, 42, 64–5, 70, 72,
 80, 83, 97–8, 101, 103, 130–1, 153;
 culturally unbound 6, 8, 17, 63–5,
 72, 84, 97, 130–1, 152
culturally inclusive learning 15–17
cultural phenomena: cultural awareness
 1, 208; cultural conflict 1, 47, 51;
 cultural differences 2, 24, 28, 34,
 40, 48, 57, 66–9, 71, 152, 180, 193,
 208; cultural diversity 2–6, 15–18,
 21–3, 29, 31–5, 37, 40, 42, 47, 53,
 57, 59, 61, 64–8, 70–4, 77–8, 80,
 90, 102, 109, 118, 137, 158–9,
 170, 208; cultural formation 1, 92,
 96, 99, 103, 106, 108, 130, 143,
 183; cultural identity 1, 3–6, 8, 17,
 21–4, 26, 28, 30, 34–5, 53, 67, 72,
 77, 80, 83–4, 92–3, 96, 118, 143,

183, 200–1, 203; cultural inclusivity 15–17, 40

cultural philosophy: cultural emotionalism 107; cultural hegemony 24, 58, 108; cultural intellectualism 107; cultural paradigms 135; cultural pluralism 28, 68, 70–1; cultural realism 90, 101; cultural voluntarism 107; culturism 118, 143, 178

curriculum/curricula 2, 15, 17, 48, 50, 57, 59–61, 63–4, 66–9, 72, 80, 105, 135, 178

Dasein 111–12, 121; *see also* Heidegger, M.; Sein

decalcomania 124

de-centric principles 208

Deleuze, G. and Guattari, F. 7, 30, 109–10, 123–4; *see also* rhizome

democracy 2, 62, 136

deontology 48–9; *see also* normative ethics

descriptive ethics 48–50, 52, 78; *see also* ethics

Dewey, J. 2, 62, 105, 135–6

Dharma 161

diaspora, diasporic 6, 28–30, 32, 34

Dionysian worlds 7, 87–9, 91, 94, 98, 112, 129; *see also* Apollonian worlds; Nietzsche, F.

discourse ethics 97

distributed knowledge, the theory 7, 101, 104–5, 124, 130; *see also* connectivism; Downes, S.; Siemens, G.

double consciousness 6, 29–30, 34, 77; *see also* Gilroy, P.

Downes, S. 104; *see also* connectivism; Siemens, G.

Dreaming *see* Aboriginal, Aboriginal Dreaming

dualism 2, 6, 25–6, 29–30, 32, 34–5, 59, 61–2, 65, 79–80, 87, 91, 93, 95, 98–9, 112, 117, 120–1, 123, 153, 168–9, 176–7, 188, 194, 201, 204; conservative dualism, liberal dualism, moderate dualism 79–80; *see also* binary oppositions

dualistic culture(s), dualistic worldview 153, 172, 188, 201, 206

Dukkha 163

ecological fantasy 6, 58–9, 78–9; *see also* Hage, G.

educational metaphysics 4, 6, 53, 80, 84, 103, 140, 158

egalitarianism 68, 73, 80, 103

egocentric 94, 114, 120, 141, 143, 170, 172, 193–4, 200, 203, 208; egocentric-individualism 143

Elders 193; *see also* Aboriginal

emergent whole 122–3, 125, 130–1, 143, **147**, 192, 195

empiricism 43

emptiness 120, 162–3, 191

encoding-decoding model of communication 27–8, 77; *see also* Hall, S.

engaged pedagogy 191

epistemic: epistemic assumption 64; epistemic dualism 65; epistemic extension 110; epistemic fracture 25, 29; epistemic horizon(s) 4; epistemic justification 6, 40–2, 78; epistemic relationship 7; epistemic tension 172; epistemic violence 6, 25–6, 34, 59, 77–8; epistemic virtues 64–5, 79; frame(work) 40, 78, 101; knowledge 99; process 38, 73, 103, 107, 130, 193

epistemological 2–3, 9, 23, 26, 35, 37–9, 42–4, 47, 52–3, 63, 78, 80, 83, 94, 102, 106, 122, 131, 141, 144, 156, 163–5, 168, 173, 176, 188, 193, 201, 204, 207; epistemological assumptions 2, 6–7, 27, 40, 46, 52–3, 72, 77–8, 101, 107, 178; epistemological conflict 126, 130; epistemological dualism 34–5, 194, 204; epistemological duplicity 26; epistemological interaction 121; epistemological interculturality 8, 172, 188, 200, 202–3; epistemological justification 52, 107, 131; epistemological parochialism 176; epistemological process 47, 73, 80, 94, 122; epistemological relationism 103, 107; epistemological relativism 114–15; epistemological world 115

epistemology 4, 25, 35, 37–8, 40–6, 50, 52–3, 71, 78–9, 106–8, 122, 141, 158, 177, 184–5, 192–3, 195

equality 17, 21, 39, 67, 70, 83, 87, 126, 131, 153

equilibration 135; equilibrium/ disequilibrium 136; *see also* Piaget, J.

equity 8, 16, 30, 40, 51, 74, 79–80, **148**, 150, 152–3, **155**, 200

equity pedagogy 16, 79

essential categories 26, 28

212 Index

ethics *see* descriptive ethics; meta-ethics; normative ethics
ethnic identities 21, 26, 27, 29, 32, 34
ethnicity (emergent ethnicity) 1, 5–6, 21–2, 24, 26–34, 60, 68–9, 102, 152, 181, 183, 186
ethnic pedagogies 176
ethno-centrism *see* centrism
eudaemonia (happiness) 49; *see also* Aristotle
Eurocentric, Eurocentrism *see* centrism
examined/unexamined life 62
exotic objects 58
externalism 42; *see also* internalism
extrapersonal 119, 130, 203
extremism 51

fantasy *see* ecological fantasy
Fletcher, J.F. 49–50
foundationalism/ foundationalists 44–5
Freire, P. 1, 182–3
functionalist 59
fusions of Horizons (A fusion of horizon) 7, 109, 114, 116, 122, 131, 193; *see also* Gadamer, H.G.

Gadamer, H.G. 1, 3, 110–13, 116–22, 125
Gandhian education 190
Gettir *see* justified true belief
Gilroy, P. 4, 29–32, 64
Giroux, H.A. 2, 57, 70, 181–2
global citizenship 61–2, 79; *see also* Nussbaum, M.C.
globalisation 61
Great Learning, The 185
Green and Happy Society 192
Gross National Happiness 192
Guru(s) 189, 193

Habermas, J. 7, 87, 94, 96–9, 114, 129–30, 136, 182–3
habitat 32–3, 136
habits of mind 105, 136
Hadith 166–7, 171; *see also* Islam
Hage, G. 6, 58, 78–9
Hajj 166
Hall, E.T. 1, 112
Hall, S. 26–9, 34
Heart Sutra 163
Heaven 90, 164–5, 167, 170, 186
Hedonists 48
hegemonic 16, 25–7, 187
hegemony *see* cultural philosophy, cultural hegemony

Heidegger, M. 7, 92, 109, 111–12, 119–20, 122–3; *see also* Dasein; Sein
hermeneutic duo circles 110, 122, 126, 131; *see also* intercultural hermeneutics
hermeneutics 3–5, 7, 84, 91, 97, 109–11, 114, 119–22, 125–6, 131, 137, 158; *see also* philosophical hermeneutics
heterogeneity 24, 28, 32, 34, 58, 77, 124
hierarchical 2, 29–30, 32, 79, 89, 93, 124, 129, 142, 153, 161, 168–9, 188, 194
highest teaching, the 159
high modernity 101
high moralism 187; *see also* moralism
high totalism 187; *see also* totalism
Hindu (Hinduism) 8–9, 25, 33, 159–61, 169–70, 176, 188–93
Hindu emancipation: sarvana, manana, and nididhyasana 189
historically effective consciousness (effective-historical consciousness) 7, 109, 116–17, 119, 125; *see also* Gadamer, H.G.
holism 7, 84, 101–4, 106–7, 130, 159, 188, 191, 194, 201
holistic: holistic axiology 195; holistic education 176, 188, 190–2; holistic epistemology 195; holistic interculturality 169, 172–3; holistic ontology 195
holistic culture(s), holistic worldview 161, 169, 172, 193, 201, 205
holistic pedagogy 8, 176, 191
homogeneous 23, 70
homogenization 68
hooks, b. 190
Horkheimer, M. 181
hybridity 6, 21–4, 28–9, 32, 34, 77
hypostatization 58
hypothetical-deductive theories 182

Iceberg model of culture 112–13
idealism 42–4, 95
ideology 22, 67, 70, 84, 97, 183
imaginative understanding 62
Imams 184
Iman 167
in-betweenness 28
inclusivity (Inclusive learning) 17; different cultural and linguistic backgrounds; diverse learning styles and cognitive preferences 17; inclusive

of all types of diversity 17; inclusivity and different orientations to learning 17; the variety of participants' cultural backgrounds 17
indefeasibilism 41
independence 9, 34–5, 47, 50, 61–2, 92–4, 99, 106, 129, 136, **145, 146,** 150, 187
Indigenous-centrism 68
Individualism *see* methodologies, methodological individualism
individualistic 35, 94, 118, 121, **147,** 150–1, 153, 161, 176, 188
individuality 2, 9, 35, 64, 68, 72–4, 79, 83, 98, 103–5, 117, 125, 130–1, 137, 142, **146,** 156, 167, 171, 173, 187, 193–4, 201, 208; atomistic individuality 201; culturally bound individuality 64–5, 72; egoistic individuality 167; high individuality; holistic individuality 8, 141, 200; interdependent individuality 187; intersubjective individuality 195; low individuality 193; mindful individuality 193; networked individuality 160–1, 169–70, 172–3, 202; new individuality 139, 156, 202, 208; rational individuality 6; spiritual individuality 161; transcendental individuality 195; whole individuality 9, 143, 156, 203, 208
infallibilism 41
infinite regress, an 44–6
infinitism/infinitists 44–5
instructional 5–6, 16–18, 37–8, 60, 64–5, 72, 79, 84, 93, 99, 104–5, 144, **155,** 177, 188; *see also* pedagogical
instrumentalism 44, 80
interactive methodology (IM) 101, 105, 107, 130; *see also* methodologies
interconnectedness 3, 62, 105–6, 126, 153, 159, 162, 188, 192–5, 201, 203; *see also* interrelatedness
intercultural hermeneutics 7, 114, 122, 125–6, 131, 137
interculturalism 22, 66
interculturality *see* axiological, axiological interculturality; epistemological, epistemological interculturality; holistic, holistic interculturality; monistic, monistic interculturality; ontological, ontological interculturality
intercultural value networks *see* value networks

intercultural valuism 5, 156, 202
intercultural valuism circle 8, 137, 139–40, **145, 148, 154,** 200; intercultural introspection 140–1; a set of value networks 143; value-awareness 141–2; value-emergence 143; value-interaction 142
intercultural valuism pedagogy 9, 156, 203, 208
interdependence 9, 34–5, 47, 50, 61–2, 64, 92–4, 99, 105–6, 129, 136, **145, 146,** 150, 164, 184–5, 187, 192, 194
interhistoricity 131, 143; *see also* interobjectivity
inter-intersubjectivity 8, 98–9, 110, 116, 118; *see also* interobjectivity
interlocutor 24, 34; *see also* speaker
internalism 42, 46; *see also* externalism
interobjectivity 7–9, 110–11, 116, 118–20, 122–3, 125–6, 131, 143, 170, 184–5, 194–5; *see also* interhistoricity
interrelatedness 3, 35, 62, 106, 153, 160, 192–5, 201; *see also* interconnectedness
interrogation 6, 28, 64, 79
interstices 9, 130–1, 137, 143, 203, 204, 208; *see also* nodes
intersubjectivity 7–8, 87, 95–6, 98–9, 110–11, 114, 116–20, 122–3, 125–6, 129–31, 136, 143, 162, 168–70, 182, 184, 193–4; *see also* inter-intersubjectivity; interobjectivity
Islam (Islamic) 8, 9, 73, 159, 165–8, 170–1, 176, 184–6; Islam heritage culture (IHC) 184–5, 187, 194

Jannah 167
Jihad 167
justified true belief, a (JTB) 41–2

Kaaba 186
Kagan, M. 1, 83
Kant/Kantianists 48, 171
Karmas 161
Kincheloe, J.L. and Steinberg, S.R. 66–70
knowledge constitutive interests, the theory of 182
Kuhn, T. 7, 92, 109–10, 114–15

Lacan, J/Lacanian 23, 58–9
land-links 150
Land of the Dead, the 160, 169

214 *Index*

Lao-tzu 163–4
Lave, J. and Wenger, E. 43, 179, 181
Li 165–6, 171
liberal dualism *see* dualism
liberal education 62–3
lifehood 141–3, **145**, 160, 167, 169, 184–5, 187–9, 192, 194; *see also* beinghood; personhood; selfhood; subjecthood
Lifeworld, the 7, 87, 94, 97–9, 101, 114, 129–30, 136
linguisticality 119–20, 122, 126
living with difference 32, 62; *see also* Amin, A.

manageable objects 58
Mantra 189–90
mapping 7–8, 111, 122–3, 125–6, 131, 142
Mecca 186
memorisation 184
meta-cultural 119, 143
meta-ethical images 51, 78
meta-ethics 48, 50–3; *see also* ethics
meta-methodology, methodological 37, 80, 144, 156
meta-ontology,-ontological 39, 78, 142
metaphor 30, 32, 110, 112–13, 162
metaphysical: metaphysical assumptions 33, 38, 61, 72, 139, 168; metaphysical conflicts 18, 26–7, 35, 80; metaphysical idealism 95; metaphysical interaction 53, 110; metaphysical interculturality 125, 139, 200, 207; metaphysical myths 7, 87; metaphysical realism 95; metaphysical tensions 6, 18, 35, 37, 51, 80
metaphysical dimensions *see* axiology; epistemology; ontology
metaphysics *see* educational metaphysics
methodologies: methodological holism 7, 101–4, 107, 130; methodological individualism 7, 84, 101–4, 106–7, 130; methodological relationism 7, 101–3, 107, 130
methodologism 42, 112, 123
Middle Way, the 162–3, 170
mindful pedagogy (Buddhist mindful pedagogy) 8, 176
moderate dualism *see* dualism
modern mind, the 136, 190
Moksha 161, 169
monism: axiological monism 194; dialectic monistic 164, 166;

dualistic monism 168; non-dualistic monism 129
monistic: monistic axiology 194; monistic culture(s); monistic interculturality 170, 190; monistic ontology 185; monistic pedagogies 9, 185, 187, 190, 193–4, 201; monistic worldview 72, 167, 170–2, 185, 194, 201, 205
mono-culturalism,-cultural 35, 66, 68, 73, 116, 118, 178
moral: moral anti-realism 50–1; moral judgement 48, 50, 96; moral nihilism 51; moral realism 50–1
moralism 184–7, 194
morally responsible individuals 74
multicultural education 1–6, 16–18, 21, 38, 40, 52–3, 57, 59–63, 64–7, 69–73, 78–80, 109, 131, 158, 176, 202
multicultural education models: conservative multiculturalism 7, 65–6, 68, 71–3, 102; critical multiculturalism 7, 65, 69–70, 72, 102, 118, 169; intercultural dialogue 7, 65, 70–1, 73–4; left-essentialist multiculturalism 7, 65, 69, 72–4, 102, 118, 169; liberal multiculturalism 7, 65, 67–8, 71–4, 102; pluralist multiculturalism 7, 65, 68, 71, 73–4, 103
multiculturalism 2, 6, 21–2, 28, 30, 32–3, 53, 57–8, 64, 151, 153, 169
multilayered self, multilayered mind 7–9, 91, 94, 96, 99, 110, 118, 123–4, 126, 129, 135, 140, 150, 152, 173, 200–3, 208
multiplicity 28, 32, 34, 77, 113, 124, 169
mutual interaction 74, 83, 93

naming 38, 88–9, 91, 112–13, 120
neo-Confucianists 165
Nieto, S. 1, 60–1, 79
Nietzsche, F. 7, 52, 87–91, 93, 110; *see also* Apollonian worlds; Dionysian worlds; table of values, a; will to power, the; Zarathustra
nihilism *see* moral
Nirvana 161–3, 165, 169, 191
nodes 7, 9, 101, 104–7, 124, 130–1, 143, 203–4, 207; *see also* interstices
non-attachment 164
non-dualistic 6, 29–30, 34, 60, 77–9, 107, 129, 131, 169, 191

non-linear 88, 189
normative ethics 48–50, 52, 78; *see also* consequentialism; deontology; ethics; virtue ethics
not-two-ness, the 159, 163, 193–5
Nussbaum, M.C. 6, 62–5, 79; *see also* cultivating humanity

objectivism 43, 104, 113, 116, 123, 176–7, 181, 187
oneness, the 111, 159, 166–7, 170–1, 184–5, 187
ontological: ontological complexity 7, 104; ontological connectivism 106; ontological contour 53, 78; ontological dualism 34, 74, 93, 98–9; ontological equality 39, 83, 87, 126, 131; ontological equity 30, 51; ontological hermeneutic 117, 125; ontological holism 107, 194; ontological interculturality 8, 172, 188, 193, 200, 202; ontological justification 6, 16, 35, 39–40, 42, 44, 47, 53, 65, 71, 77–8, 84, 87, 109; ontological layer 1; ontological pluralism 95; ontological reductionism 6, 40, 59, 78–9; ontological relationism 103, 107; ontological tensions 27; ontological world 115
ontology 2, 4, 34–5, 37–9, 52, 59, 71, 93, 102, 129–30, 158, 172, 177, 185, 192–3, 195, 204, 205
orientalism 6, 22–4, 94; latent orientalism 22, 24, 29, 34, 77; manifest orientalism 22, 25
othering 2, 6, 17, 24–5, 34, 40, 57, 77, 139, 151, 207

Palmer, R.E. 111–12, 120–1
pantheistic, pantheism 192
paradigm shift(s), a 7, 109–10, 113–16, 125
Paradise 165, 167; *see also* Jannah
pedagogical 1–2, 4–6, 8–9, 15, 18, 34, 37–8, 40, 44, 48, 50, 52, 60, 63–5, 70–2, 79–80, 84–5, 92, 101, 131, 137, 139–40, **147**, 150, 153, **155**–6, 158, 175, 177–8, 180, 184, 187, 194, 203, 208; *see also* instructional
peripheral 21, 59, 66–7, 120, 136, 180
personhood 68, 160; *see also* beinghood; lifehood; selfhood; subjecthood
perspective-taking 8, 116, 125; *see also* pre-understanding

philosophical (ontological) hermeneutics 3–5, 84, 109–11, 120, 122, 125, 131, 158
Piaget, J. 43, 106, 135, 178
pilgrimage *see* Hajj
Plato 41, 51, 95
pluralism 28, 32–4, 68, 70–1, 95, 158
plurality of audience 119
plural worlds 42
Popper, K.R. 7, 87, 94–9, 114, 129–30, 136
positivism 95, 177; empirical-analytic science and hypothetical-deductive theories 182; logical positivism 96, 183
postcolonialism 22, 25; *see also* cosmopolitanism; creolisaiton; heterogeneity; hybridity; multiplicity
postmodern 61, 63, 87, 110
pragmatism 43–4, 104, 176
praxis (cultural praxis of the praxis) 18
pre-understanding 3, 8, 111–12, 115, 125–6, **145**; *see also* perspective-taking
priming techniques 93–4, 99; *see also* cross-cultural psychology
primitive mind, the 136; *see also* modern mind
probabilification 42
proneness 27; *see also* encoding-decoding model of communication

racism, racists 15, 26, 59, 61, 69, **148**
Ramadan 166
rationalism 43–4, 88, 96
realism 43, 50–1, 90, 95, 98, 101–2; *see also* anti-realism; cultural, cultural realism; moral, moral realism
recitation 184
reconnection 107, 208
reductionism 117, 177–8, 188; dualistic reductionism 72, 102; moralistic reductionism 69; *see also* ontological, ontological reductionism
reflexivity 65, 104, 106, 130; *see also* relationality
reincarnation 161, 169, 192–4
relationality 65, 79; *see also* reflexivity
relationism 84, 107, 130, 201; *see also* methodologies, methodological relationism and ontological, ontological relationism
reliabilism 41
Ren 163, 165
repetition 184

216   *Index*

rhizomatic networks 30, 32, 34, 77, 207; *see also* Gilroy, P.
rhizome (rhizomatic theory) 7, 30, 64, 109–11, 122–4, 126
Ricoeur, P. 3, 113–14
Rizvi, F. 6, 64–5, 79; *see also* cosmopolitan learning
rupture *see* asignifying rupture

Said, E. 22–4, 47, 106, 114, 117, 144
Salat 166
Samsara 161–2, 169
Sawm 166
scepticism, skepticism 42, 47–8, 50, 63
Sein 111; *see also* Dasein; Heidegger, M.
self *see* self-construal
self-construal 7–8, 87, 92–6, 98–9, 101, 118, 123, 129–30, 139, 201, 207; collective self 4, 93–4, 96, 137, 151, 207; humane self 93–4, 96, 118, 129, 150–1, 207; personal self 93–4, 129, 137, 150; relational self 93–4, 96, 137, 144, 150–1; *see also* multilayered self
self-cultivation 160, 193
selfhood 140; *see also* beinghood; lifehood; personhood; subjecthood
self-inclusion 208
self-in-social-relations 102
self-in-social-vacuum 102
self-observation 140
self-transcendence 130, 143
self-transformation 60, 72, 79, 107, 130–1, 143, 194; *see also* social transformation
Shahadah 166
Siemens, G. 104; *see also* connectivism; Downes S.
situated beings 194
situated ethics (or situational ethics) 49–50
situated surplus 33
situated view of mind 105
situative theory 43
skandhas 162
Skinner, B.F. 177
social field 105
social genes 83
social transformation 9, 60, 65, 70, 72–4, 79–80, 103, 107, 131, 156, 183, 203; *see also* self-transformation
society-independent-of-self 102
socio-cultural constructivism *see* constructivism
spatiotemporality 159, 193

speaker 23–4, 34, 120; *see also* interlocutor
speculative awareness 120–1; speculative hermeneutics 121, 126; speculative mode 121; speculative philosophy 84
spirituality 159–60, 185, 201
spiritual pedagogy (Hindu spiritual pedagogy) 8, 176
Spivak, G. C. 22, 24–5, 27
story sharing 150
strangers *see* being together of strangers
Stratton, J. 57–9, 64, 78–9
subaltern 24–6
subjecthood 193; *see also* beinghood; lifehood; personhood; and selfhood
subjectivity 30, 50, 69, 111, 177, 185; transcendental subjectivity 111
subject-object 4, 103–4, 112, 120–1, 130, 169; subject-subject 4, 6, 8, 34, 40, 202
Sunyata 8, 159, 162, 169, 170
super-diversity 6, 29, 31–4, 62, 77
Supreme Ultimate 164, 166
symbolic-situated systems 125; ill-structured situations 125; well-structured situations 125
synthetic expressions 102

table of values, a 7, 87, 90, 98, 112, 120; *see also* Nietzsche, F.
tabula rasa, a 177
Tai Chi 164
Tao, Heavenly Tao 8, 159, 163–6, 170–1, 187
Taoism/Taoist 163–4, 170, 185; *see also* yin and yang
Tao Te Ching 163–4
Tawhid 8, 159, 166, 170, 185–6; *see also* Islam
temporality 111–12
territorialisation 124
theocracy 166
Third Space, a 6, 22–4, 34, 77; *see also* Bhabha, H.K.
Third World 21, 23–5
three-isms *see* cultural philosophy, cultural emotionalism, cultural intellectualism, cultural voluntarism
three worlds (Popper's) 7, 87, 94–5, 99, 101, 129–30, 136
Tian 165–6, 170, 187
togetherness-in-difference 6, 28
topographic 8, 142, 156, 195; *see also* axiological, axiological mapping; mapping

totalism 187–8, 202
totalistic pedagogy (Islamic totalistic pedagogy) 8, 176
totemic 159–60
transcendence 121, 126, 171
transcultural, transculturality 1, 4, 6, 8, 64, 34, 77, 79, 84, 119, 193–5, 202
transformative, transformational learning 64, 72, 92
transnational, -ism 28–9, 31, 34, 64
transphenomenal frame, a 177
transposing 117

Ummah 167, 170, 185–6; *see also* brotherhood
UNESCO 1, 3, 61, 71
universality 68, 71, 94, 117, 119–22, 166
utilitarian 49

validity (Habermas') 96–8
value networks, intercultural 7, 9, 87, 111, 140, 158, 168–9, 17–2, 176, 178, 181, 187, 194, 200–4, 207
valuism *see* intercultural valuism
Vertovec, S. 29, 31–3
vicegerents 168, 170–1, 185, 187
virtue(s) 163, 165–6, 170–1, 185; *see also* Li; Ren; Xin; Yi; Zhi
virtue ethics 48–9, 165–6, 171
virtuological pedagogy 8, 176
Vygotsky, L. S. 135, 179; *see also* ZPD

white: Anglo white 58; white culture 58, 59, 74; white knowledge 69, 71; white multiculturalism 6; white nationalism 58, **155**; whiteness 40, 46, 58, 66–7, 71–3, 80; white privilege 57, 78; white superiority 80; white supremacy 6, 58, 59, **155**
whole individuality 9, 143, 153, 156, 203, 208
whole person (development) **147**, **155**, 188
wholistic 159
willpower 123, 183, 185
will to power, the 88–90, 98, 129; *see also* Nietzsche, F.
without-thinking pedagogy 191
worldview 3, 70, 79, 83, **145**, **154**, 159, 167, 208
Wu Wei 185; *see also* Taoism/Taoist

Xin 165; *see also* virtue(s)

Yi 163
yin and yang (yin-yang) 8, 159, 163, 166, 170–1; *see also* Taoism/Taoist
yoga(s) 161, 189–91

Zakah 166; *see also* alms
Zarathustra 90; *see also* Nietzsche, F.
Zen Buddhists 163
Zhi 165; *see also* virtue(s)
Zhuxi 165; *see also* Confucianism
ZPD (zone of proximal development) 179; *see also* Vygotsky, L.S.